Designing Organizations

Designing Organizations

Designing Organizations

Strategy, Structure, and Process at the Business Unit and Enterprise Levels

Third Edition

Jay R. Galbraith

JB JOSSEY-BASS™
A Wiley Brand

Published by Jossey-Bass
A Wiley Imprint
One Montgomery Street, Suite 1200, San Francisco, CA 94104-4594
www.josseybass.com

Jossey-Bass books and products are available through most bookstores. To contact Jossey-Bass directly call our Customer Care Department within the U.S. at 800-956-7739, outside the U.S. at 317-572-3986, or fax 317-572-4002.

Wiley publishes in a variety of print and electronic formats and by print-on-demand. Some material included with standard print versions of this book may not be included in e-books or in print-on-demand. If this book refers to media such as a CD or DVD that is not included in the version you purchased, you may download this material at http://booksupport.wiley.com. For more information about Wiley products, visit www.wiley.com.

Library of Congress Cataloging-in-Publication Data
Galbraith, Jay R.
  Designing organizations : strategy, structure, and process at the business unit and enterprise levels / Jay R. Galbraith.—3rd Edition.
     pages cm
     Includes bibliographical references and index.
  ISBN 978-1-118-40995-4 (hardback); ISBN 978-1-118-41729-4 (pdf);
ISBN 978-1-118-46382-6 (epub)
  1. Organizational effectiveness. 2. Strategic planning. I. Title.
   HD58.9.G35 2014
   658.4'012—dc23

                                                                    2013040235

Printed in the United States of America
THIRD EDITION
HB Printing   V10007887_012519

The Jossey-Bass

Business & Management Series

Contents

List of Figures and Tables

Figures

Tables

Preface

The last revision I did for this book was standard. I updated the examples and references, modified some ideas based on new research, and added a new chapter or two. For this revision, I took more time and substantially rewrote the book. The basics, like the Star Model and lateral forms of organization, remain the same. But the organization design thinking throughout the book is much more driven by strategy. It follows the research and theory that started with Alfred Chandler's *Strategy and Structure* (1962).

The first couple of chapters explain the approach of strategic organization design. It is a top-down approach as opposed to a sociotechnical systems approach, which is bottom up. Sociotech is much more influenced by the actual work of the first level of the organization. The strategic approach to design is based on the Star Model, a holistic framework for combining strategy, structure, processes, rewards, and people. (I am the holder of the copyright and trademark on the Star Model.) In addition to discussing the Star Model, the first chapters set the methodology of growth leading to strategic transformation. I assume that companies pursue growth to attract capital and talent and, for those that are publicly traded, to drive their stock price. However, a company can grow only so far in its core business and home country. As a result, growth drives a diversification strategy from a single business into a multiple business portfolio. These two stages of growth—a single core business strategy and a multiple business portfolio strategy—are covered in this book. Growth also drives companies to expand outside their home country into host countries. These companies take on three-dimensional structures where functions, businesses, and geographies all report to the CEO. I have described these organizations in more detail in *Designing the Global Corporation* (2000).

A fourth-stage organization arises when companies focus on a customer dimension. I discussed these organizations in *Designing the Customer-Centric Organization* (2005). In chapter 13 of this book, I speculate about a fifth dimension that could result from the impacts of analytics and big data. Throughout the book, I refer to "big data," which denotes the greater volume, variety, and velocity of data that are available today.

In chapters 3 through 7, I describe the different types of single-business functional organizations. Chapters 3 and 4 focus on the functional structure and the cross-functional lateral processes that characterize most single-business organizations. In this edition, I highlight the growing interest in social technologies to coordinate work flows, products, and services across the company. I also distinguish between the different types of business strategies and organizations. I follow Treacy and Wiersema's (1997) three organizational types: cost-centric, product-centric, and customer-centric. In chapter 5, I discuss the organizations for each of these strategies along with several case studies to bring them alive. In that same chapter, I present some ideas about the real-time decision processes that are enabled by big data.

Chapter 6 is devoted to the reconfigurable organization. When competitive advantages do not last long, neither do the organizations that implement them. So today we design organizations to be easily and quickly changeable. This capability requires us to become even more adept at lateral forms of organization. The final chapter in this group, chapter 7, focuses on the network organization. Rather than vertical integration, many companies are using virtual integration. That is, companies are using partnerships rather than ownership to coordinate the components of their businesses. This is particularly true for companies using embedded microchips in their products. Such companies are building networked ecosystems of app developers to write applications for their software platforms.

Chapters 8 through 12 examine the variations on the enterprise strategies and organizations. In chapter 8, I review what we know about portfolio strategy and the continuum spanning from related portfolios to unrelated or conglomerate portfolios. Historically, the literature has focused on either pure types of strategies in the related portfolio with its multidivisional structure or on conglomerates with their holding company structures. Chapter 9 elaborates on the mixed model. Chapters 10 and 11 treat the subject of how corporate centers add value to their portfolios. That is, these companies create portfolios that are more valuable than the sum of their stand-alone businesses. I focus on three conglomerates: General Electric, Danaher, and Illinois Tool Works. Finally, chapter 12 examines two different approaches to creating value through synergy. One type leverages intellectual property across business units. Disney and Armani are examples I use to show how companies leverage characters, brands, and fashion designs across diverse portfolios. The other model is the solutions strategy. IBM and medical products companies combine products, software, and services from diverse business units into smart solutions for their customers.

In chapter 13, I speculate about the effects of big data on organization design and whether they will result in a new dimension of organizational structure. Disney and Nike are already creating digital divisions that are generating new sources of revenue.

Therefore, this edition is both an update of the basic content of organizational design and a presentation of a lot of new material. As social networking and big data work their ways through organizations, there will be much more to uncover and analyze in the years to come.

Breckenridge, Colorado   Jay R. Galbraith
December 2013

Designing Organizations

Designing Organizations

1

INTRODUCTION

Organization design, as opposed to organization theory, is a prescriptive body of knowledge. It is intended to inform the choices of how to organize and manage institutions and serve the leaders who have been entrusted with the stewardship of these institutions. These organizations are purposeful: they have been created to accomplish specific goals and objectives. Organization design is therefore focused on creating organizations through which these goals and objectives can be accomplished.

The knowledge base underlying the choice of organization designs has its roots in scientific management and classical management principles. The practitioners and scholars who developed the knowledge in these areas were searching for the one best way to organize. Those early thinkers created many of the principles, like span of control, and much of the useful language, like centralization, that we still use today. However, it was not difficult to find effective organizations that violated many of the principles of classical management. As a result, modern organization design grew out of efforts to explain these exceptional observations.

Modern organization design came out of a variety of work in the 1950s and 1960s. One stream, developed in the United States, is best illustrated by the work of Alfred Chandler in *Strategy and Structure* (1962). He found that the different organizational structures we had observed could be explained by differences in companies' strategies. Therefore, different strategies lead to different organizations. This stream, referred to as strategic organization design, is a top-down design process that begins with the entity's strategy and can be applied at the enterprise, business unit, geographical, and functional levels.

A second stream of thought developed in Europe around the work of Eric Trist and his followers (Trist and Murray, 1993). It was referred to as the sociotechnical systems approach. It was bottom up. It focused on the alignment of the technology involved in doing the work and the social system that could be created to perform that work. Sociotechnical systems' thinking and tools are best at designing organizations at the bottom levels of the structure. The strategic design thinking and tools are best used for designing organizations' top levels. The strategic organization design approach is the one that I follow in this book.

Today's Organization Design

The interest in organization design has been increasing over the past couple of decades. One of the reasons is that our organizations have been increasing in complexity over that time. "Doing what comes naturally" is not a sufficient guide to organizing today's institutions. Most leaders today rose up through a far simpler structure. Nor are the old dismissives relevant: "All you need are good people. They'll make any organization work." And people do make a misaligned organization work, but at a price. The people in an organization that is misaligned with its strategy and stakeholder environment cannot serve its customers and work around the system at the same time. They can perform much more effectively when the system supports them in doing their work. Besides, high-performing companies do not want organizations that just work; they want organizations that excel. The discipline of organization design has evolved along with the increasing organizational complexity and the desire to create high-performing organizations.

In the following chapters, I trace the organizational stages through which companies have progressed from the simple, single-business strategy to the complex multibusiness, multicountry, multicustomer segment strategy. The first organizational stage is the single-business strategy, sometimes called the U form, or unitary form of organizations. Almost all companies start as a single business that is organized around functions, like sales, marketing, operations, product development, finance, and human resources. It is a unitary or one-dimensional form because it is structured only around functions. All people reporting to the CEO are functional leaders. Chapter 3 is devoted to the design of the single business or business unit, I introduce the concept of the lateral or horizontal organization. In order to get anything done, companies have to work across functions to deliver customer orders, new products, and projects. These processes are executed through lateral forms of cross-functional coordination. The functional structure or hierarchy is the vertical form, and the processes are the lateral forms, which vary from informal and self-organizing processes, to formal teams, to the matrix form. Lateral forms are present in all types of organizations, but I present them in a discussion about business units in chapter 3 since they are the principal design challenge facing business unit leaders.

The second stage arrives when a single business diversifies into new business areas. The company then creates a business unit and a profit and loss center for each new business area. Each business unit is another functional organization. The organization design challenge is thus to create a corporate center to govern the various business units. This center typically contains functional staffs to coordinate the functions across business units. The role and size of the center vary with the diversity of the businesses in the corporate portfolio. Since the CEO of the enterprise has both functions and businesses reporting to the center, the company has a two-dimensional organization structure.

The third stage develops when a company expands out of its home market into new host countries. This strategy adds a third dimension—a geographical dimension—to the organization. Initially companies simply add a geographical division to their multiple business unit divisions. But when international sales reach around 30 to 40 percent of total sales, the international division disappears. In consumer goods companies, the division is replaced by regional profit centers, one of which is the home country. In the business-to-business (B2B) world, the international division is split and the parts are added to their respective business units, creating global business unit profit and loss centers. However, in the global business unit structure, there is still an international or regional overlay on the global business units. And in the regional structure, there are global business units that are overlaid across the regions. So reporting into the corporate center are functions, business units, and geographies. The organization design challenge is balancing power and authority across the three-dimensional structure. The resulting power distributions will be driven by the global portfolio strategy (Galbraith, 2000).

The fourth strategy stage begins with a focus on the customer (Galbraith, 2005). Driven partly by demands from global customers like Walmart, companies such as Procter & Gamble, IBM, and investment banks are adding global customer or customer segments to their structures. Another contributing factor is the conversion of products and services into digital offerings. In the digital world, everything talks to everything else. Vendors, like IBM and Accenture, can combine digital hardware, software, and services into smart solutions for their customers. They can easily customize and codevelop applications with customers for customer segments, like financial services and utilities. This solutions strategy is best executed by organizing around the customer or customer segments called verticals. So in these solutions-oriented companies, we find customer segments reporting into the corporate center along with business units, countries, and functions. The challenge for organization designers is to integrate four dimensions into a one-company strategy and organization. Integration becomes the task of the company's processes. As we will see, the more complex the structure is, the more important are the processes.

Inevitably, the question that comes up is, "Is there a fifth stage?" In the concluding chapter, I speculate about a fifth stage. It appears that the forces around big data, meaning the increased volume, complexity, variety, and velocity of available data, may very well manifest themselves in a fifth strategy and organizational dimension.

Drivers of New Strategies

It is natural to ask why companies are continually changing their strategies. What is driving this movement through the stages? Usually managers prefer to keep things simple, so why are they moving to ever more complicated strategies? There are at least two reasons. One is the pursuit of growth. Many companies are driven by a growth imperative. And the other is the continuing fragmentation of the stakeholder environment.

Growth

Every publicly traded company wants to grow and drive its stock to trade at a premium price. If there is no growth, the company's stock is flat and trades like a bond. A high stock price makes it easier to attract capital and reward employees. The elevated stock also can serve as a currency to make acquisitions. More important, talented people want to join a growth company that has a bright future. But while growth is desirable, it also faces limits. A firm can grow only so much in its core business and its home country. So when growth in the core business slows, firms diversify into adjacent businesses and become multibusiness companies. When growth slows in the home country, firms expand across borders and become multinationals. This pursuit of new growth opportunities causes firms to change strategies and move through the stages.

Fragmentation of the Stakeholder Environment

The other driver of strategic change is the movement from mass markets to ever smaller market segments. In the twentieth century, businesses used mass production to supply mass merchants to serve the mass market. Now, with ever-increasing data, firms can focus on ever smaller customer segments. Consulting firms can now identify 650 microsegments in the food market. Some of these microsegments are declining, some are flat, and others are growing. So food companies are focusing on these growth microsegments, like Hispanic moms and senior foodies. Both the growth imperative and market fragmentation lead to customer-focused strategies.

So it is largely the growth imperative and market segmentation that drive firms to continually evolve their strategies. But not all companies progress through all of the stages. Some companies, like utilities and defense firms, remain domestic enterprises, and some family-owned companies remain in a single business. Andersen, Marvin, and Pella focus largely on residential windows and doors. Most companies, however, become three-dimensional, multinational enterprises like General Mills, Pfizer, Siemens, Canon, and Johnson & Johnson, while others, like Experian and Nike, progress or are progressing through four or even five stages. My point is that different strategies drive different organization designs. It is not size or industry that is the primary shaper of different organizational forms. Size, industry, and nationality all have their effects, but in this book, I start with strategy to begin the design process.

The other point about strategy stages that is important for organization design is that the strategies are cumulative. Chandler called this feature concatenation. That is, a multibusiness enterprise also has stage 1, single-business strategies that guide its business units. And when the stage 2 enterprise expands across borders, it adds third-stage international strategies to its stage 2 multifunction, multibusiness strategies. This cumulative stage-wise progression is what increases the complexity of organization designs and gives organization design its challenge and its priority to create high-performing enterprises.

Drivers of Organization Designs

There are three major shapers of organization designs. The first is the one that we have been discussing: the diversity and variety of units that must be coordinated for the company to execute its mission. The second is the degree of interdependence between these diverse units. Usually the units in a company are not independent but require coordination, and the amount depends on the degree of interdependence. This interdependence results from the initial division of labor into functional specialties that are needed to execute the business's activities. The third factor is the dynamics of change associated with a business. The dynamics consist of the rate or pace of change combined with its predictability. The predictability of change is the key. Even if a business is subject to constant change, if that change is predictable, a company can use plans and schedules to coordinate interdependence among units. If each unit can meet its planned goals and delivery schedules, the organization greatly reduces the amount of ongoing communication that it needs to coordinate its work. It is when change is constant and unpredictable that plans and schedules need constant revision and renegotiation. These organizations require designs that permit high levels of communication, flexibility, and adaptation.

Variety and Diversity

It is actually the interaction of the three shapers—variety, interdependence, and change dynamics—that drives organization designs. To illustrate, let us start with a single business that conducts its affairs through seven functions: development (of products and services), operations, marketing, procurement, sales, finance, and human resources. These seven functions must coordinate their efforts to conduct normal business for the existing product already in the market. They must also synchronize their activities to launch a new product, and they probably need to agree on the priority and features of the next product in development. The communication and decision making to arrive at the plans and schedules for the existing product in a seven-function organization must take place across twenty-one interfaces. (Links = $\frac{1}{2} n [n - 1]$. Thus, $21 = \frac{1}{2} \times 7 [6]$.) Communication and collaboration must also take place across these same seven functions and twenty-one interfaces for the launch of the next product and yet again for the initiation of the new product. The process repeats itself for each product that is added to the single-business, functional organization. So variety, as measured by the number of products in this case, increases the volume of information processing and decision making that a single functional organization must execute. And every functional organization has a limited capacity for communicating and deciding. Then when the growth imperative causes the single business to follow a diversification strategy, it will add one or two new businesses. At this point, the coordination task exceeds the company's capacity to coordinate. As a result, it will move to a stage 2, multibusiness company and multibusiness structure. The functional organization does not have the information-processing and decision-making capacity to manage multiple businesses within a single functional structure.

Dell is a good example. Dell started with a single product line of desktop personal computers. In order to maintain its growth, it added desk-side computers and laptops. Then it added new businesses of personal desktop printer, personal desk-side storage, and low-end servers. It also migrated from a single personal computer business into a multibusiness unit, multiprofit center company. It changed its name from Dell Computers to Dell. Each profit center was a functional organization capable of managing a single business, like personal computers, printers, storage, and servers.

Interdependence

Interdependence is the degree to which activities in one organizational unit affect the activities and goal accomplishments of other units. Interdependence has been a driver of coordination since the work of Thompson (1967), who identified three types of interdependence, which increased in magnitude. These types are shown in figure 1.1. The simplest interdependence is pooled interdependence whereby field units, shown in figure 1.1a, share the same pool of funds and talent resources. Other than sharing resources, these field units, like sales units, perform their work completely separately. There is a minimal need to coordinate and communicate between one another. The next type, sequential, shown in figure 1.1b, indicates a higher level and greater amount of interdependence. In sequential interdependence, the output of manufacturing is a necessary input for the performance of the sales function. In order to achieve successful performance, company management must coordinate the flow of work across sequentially interdependent units. The sequentially interdependent units, however, also possess pooled interdependence. The greatest amount of interdependence exists when units are reciprocally interdependent, as in figure 1.1c. The output of both is the input of the other. Engineering design groups are a good example. The reciprocally interdependent units possess the greatest amount of

Figure 1.1 Types of Interdependence

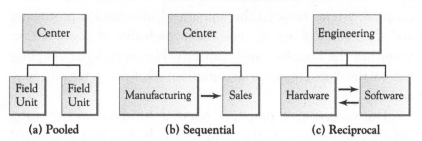

(a) Pooled   (b) Sequential   (c) Reciprocal

interdependence because they possess all three types. They require the greatest need for coordination as a result.

Interdependence is a variable that can be changed and can lead to different amounts of coordination. For example, the new product initiative referred to above may have greater interdependence among development, marketing, operations, and procurement than it has with the other three functions. Therefore, the interdependent four functions can form a core new product team, which has more limited communication with the other three functions. But when you add the other functions to the core team, it becomes the extended product team. One of the reasons that interdependence drives organization designs is that a principle of design is to create structural units based on the degree of interdependence. A designer should maximize the amount of interdependence and coordination that takes place within an organizational unit and minimize interdependence and coordination across units.

Today the most competitive management practices—lean processes, speed to market, and real-time decision making enabled by big data—increase the interdependence among functions. Previously companies reduced interdependence by using sequential work flows across functions. Between each stop in the flow of work were buffers like in-process inventories and order backlogs. These sequential work flows, called "loosely coupled systems," uncoupled the functions so that they could solve their issues independent of other functions. The loosely coupled systems reduced the amount of information processing and decision making so that the complexity of coordination fit within the business unit's capacity. However, loose coupling led to the barriers between functions that we refer to today as silos.

The competitive practices referred to above are creating tightly coupled systems that remove the buffers that uncoupled sequential flow across functions. And in their place, we need to create communication links across the interfaces between functions. We need to break down the silos. One of these practices began as lean manufacturing, such as in the Toyota production system. In lean manufacturing, all the buffers were seen as waste to be eliminated: they consumed resources and created no value for customers. From manufacturing, "lean" has progressed into services and now to the lean start-up (Ries, 2011).

The new product development process has been redesigned to reduce time to market. Previously the process was sequential. Engineers designed the product. They then gave the design to procurement, which contracted for the components and to operations, which designed the manufacturing process. Almost all manufacturers today use parallel processes called simultaneous engineering or concurrent design. The engineers still design the product, but they are joined by manufacturing engineers, quality engineers, and service engineers to jointly design a better, and more complete product, faster.

A third practice for speeding up decisions is the need to decide and act in real time as events unfold in social media. Nestlé has a digital acceleration team to constantly monitor social media conversations about its brands and categories, and then engage consumers in conversations. The team is not composed just of social media experts. It includes many functions like brand managers, consumer insights, legal, customer account managers, agency personnel, and food scientists if needed. The purpose is to act quickly on bad news before an incident goes viral. The digital acceleration team is a good example of a reciprocally interdependent group of functions.

All of these practices increase the speed of decision making and the amount of interdependence across functions. Usually to implement these practices, cross-functional teams are needed to short-circuit the hierarchy. The organizations take on a strong lateral or horizontal orientation. Many refer to these designs as networks. I address these in chapters 3 and 4.

Dynamics of Change

The predictability of an organization's work has been identified as a shaper of designs for a long time. March and Simon (1958) identified programmed decision making as the appropriate process for predictable tasks and unprogrammed decision making for unpredictable work. Burns and Stalker's (1961) case studies revealed two types of organizations that they called mechanistic and organic, with the appropriate organization depending on the work to be performed. If the work was predictable, a hierarchy or mechanistic form was appropriate. If it was unpredictable, an organic form was appropriate. By organic, the authors meant lots of lateral forms to foster coordination. The work of Lawrence and Lorsch (1967) was the most revealing. (Their results are shown in table 1.1.) They compared companies in the plastics, food, and container businesses and measured the amount of revenue in each company that came from new products introduced in the previous five years. This variable was a proxy for predictability of the work. Revenue due to new products varied from zero for containers (can companies) to 15 percent for food to 35 percent for plastics (packaging).

Table 1.1 Matching Strategy and Organization

	Plastics	Food	Container
Percent of revenue due to new products	35%	15%	0%
Coordination mechanisms used	Hierarchy Voluntary Formal groups at three levels Integrating departments	Hierarchy Voluntary Formal groups Integrating roles	Hierarchy Voluntary
Percent integrators/ managers	22%	17%	0%

This work was performed by functional organizations. The container companies were able to achieve cross-functional coordination with only voluntary or informal personal contacts across the hierarchy. These companies had the most predictable work to perform. Cans were a commodity, and the focus was on operational excellence. The food companies faced moderate amounts of unpredictability associated with 15 percent of their revenue coming from new products. The impact of more unpredictable work can be seen by the number of additional resources that were invested in cross-functional coordination. In addition to the hierarchy and informal contacts, the food companies employed integrators (product managers) and formal groups (cross-functional product teams). In addition to the managers in the functional hierarchy, the food companies used 17 percent more managers for coordination.

The results are even more striking with the plastics companies. These companies compete with new products and continually face new and unpredictable tasks. These companies employ integrating departments (product management departments) and formal groups at three levels (cross-functional product teams). They employ 22 percent more integrators to coordinate all of this cross-functional, new product coordination. So the effect of unpredictability on interdependent work flows is dramatic. When companies are designing, making, and launching new products, the effect of unanticipated issues causes them to make and remake decisions repeatedly. They must process information from all of the interdependent functional groups, which requires an organization designed specifically to execute a new product strategy.

The effect of unpredictable work is much less dramatic when the work is independent. A law firm may work on uncertain cases for different clients. Each case has a team working it, and each case is independent of the others. There is minimal pooled interdependence and minimal need for continuous decision making and information processing across the case teams. The law firm can function with a much less complex organization. So the design challenges come from the extreme values of the shapers of organization design. That is, the challenge is to design an organization that is providing a variety of products and services through an interdependent group of functions when change is rapid and unpredictable. But most companies have been following strategies that push us to the extremes of these design-shaping factors. These companies need the accumulating design knowledge to create the high-performing organizations they desire.

Summary

This book will follow a school of thought called strategic organization design. That is, we start with a company's or a unit's strategy and design the organization from the top down. This school of organization design follows from Chandler's work, *Strategy and Structure*. His model states that every twenty or thirty years, companies add a new strategic dimension to their portfolio. Not all companies follow this stage-wise progression, but many publicly traded companies do in order to pursue growth. In so doing, they adopt ever more complex strategies. This complexity is behind the rise of organization design to guide the choice of organizations with which to compete in global markets.

If growth creates complex strategies, it is diversity or variety, interdependence, and change that shape organizations. As a framework for the book, I describe the trajectory of a typical company as it evolves through the stages of increasing diversity and increasing complexity. To the extent possible, I provide examples of actual companies to illustrate the points being discussed. But before beginning the chapter on the single-business strategy and functional organization, I define what I mean by organization and use the Star Model for this purpose. I also identify the design factors that leaders can use to create the organizations that they desire.

2

THE STAR MODEL

Strategic organization design began with Alfred Chandler's *Strategy and Structure* (1962). Since that time, the topic has been expanded beyond structure to include several other factors: information and decision processes, reward systems, and people practices that make up the human resources function. Collectively they define what we mean by organization. In this chapter, I place those factors into the Star Model and describe their interactions. In so doing, I define what we mean by organization design.

The Origins of the Star Model

I created the Star Model on the basis of my experiences in trying to apply information and decision processes. My initial training was in the areas of production and inventory control. In 1967 and 1968, my colleagues and I had built a number of models that could make decisions about scheduling and inventory levels in a supply chain. We were quite proud of our models: our simulations showed that they would lead to some significant performance improvements in a number of supply chain applications. However, as we tried to apply the models to client problems, we always had a great deal of difficulty in convincing managers to use these models.

As we tried to uncover the problem, we discovered that the performance of managers in the supply chain was measured on the basis of accounting costs and standard costs. This was a problem because we always used economic costs in our models. We used variable and marginal costs, so the decisions that came from the models were different from what the managers would normally have decided to do. And since they were measured on the basis of standard costs and rewarded with bonuses on the basis of their decisions, they were not going to follow our models. In fact, they thought that our models would lead them to make incorrect decisions according to their metrics. In order to implement the kinds of information and decision models that we were creating, we would have to modify performance measurement and the reward systems under which the managers were going to operate.

The second issue we ran into was that we were also going to have to modify the structure of the supply chain. Decisions at the time were made in the factories at the level of the plant or the department. In order to profit from the information decision models that we were creating, the company would need to centralize those decisions so that they applied across its entire supply chain. The managers in the various companies with whom we worked found that they would encounter a lot of resistance from the current occupants of the roles in the structure, and so that became difficult.

The third issue was that if they implemented this model, the company would have to hire some new people—people with quantitative skills who could operate the model and reach the kinds of decisions that would be optimal for running the supply chain.

In the end, what we found was that if we wanted to make a substantial change in the information and decision processes of a company, we also had to modify its performance measurement and reward system, the structure, and the skill sets and mind-sets of the people. As we realized that we needed to change all of these factors in a way that reinforced one another, we learned to take a holistic or systemic view of an organization. We saw that we could not change organizations piecemeal. It is necessary to see the organization as a complex social system. The Star Model was the framework that allowed us to take a systemic view.

Figure 2.1 The Star Model

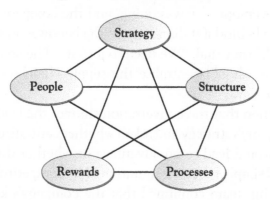

So this was the origin of the Star Model, which is shown in figure 2.1. It gives a holistic way of thinking about an organization as consisting of a structure, information decision processes, reward systems, and people. And this is the model that leaders and general managers need to refer to when they're considering changing their organization.

Some other models of organization are similar to the Star Model, including the McKinsey 7-S model. Today, in fact, almost every consulting firm has a model that looks something like the Star Model or McKinsey 7-S model. They all have a common set of messages.

First, these models say that different strategies lead to different structures for implementing them. That seems obvious, but in the heat of debate concerning organization structures, organization often follows fashion. For example, in an organization that consisted of four relatively autonomous business units, the conversation started at the corporate level about whether to centralize the supply chain. The debate started when several competitors had centralized their supply chain and another competitor was considering whether to do so. The fact that the competitors had changed their structure and others were going to change theirs seemed to be the compelling argument. The idea was that this was the trend in the industry: centralization was what everyone else was doing, and the company was going to be falling behind if it didn't get on the bandwagon soon. "This is the trend," they said. "We need to join it." The argument that the company should centralize the supply chain seemed to be carrying the day.

It was then that the conversation shifted: the leaders looked at the company's strategy and asked whether centralizing the supply chain would lead to an advantage or whether the company then would simply be a poor imitation of its competitors. Instead, the leadership team confirmed that the company's key strategy revolved around new product development. It was quite effective at taking new technology and getting it to the market ahead of its competitors and thus achieving a first-mover advantage. As a result, its supply chain was not centralized. However, some aspects of the supply chain were centralized—for example, the choice of some of the trucking companies that it used. Current practice involved over one hundred trucking companies, so some benefits were attained, but the company maintained its autonomous business unit structure. More recently, some of its competitors have been licensing technology from it. So different strategies mean different organizations. The lesson is that you start with the strategy and design the organization to implement the chosen direction.

The second point is that organization is more than just structure, yet frequently, leaders make changes that are structure only. They thus fail to make the compensating reinforcing choices around the kinds of people they need, the kinds of performance measurements that would be introduced, and the types of information and decision processes that would work across the structure. They are making the same mistake as my colleagues and I did some forty-five years ago when we were implementing new analytical models.

If companies use a matrix organization, they frequently spend inordinate amounts of time arguing over solid lines and dotted lines of authority. I will address this later when I consider matrix organizations, but there's very little value in having a debate about dotted and solid lines of authority. The time is better spent defining roles and responsibilities, investing in the planning and budgeting processes, and finding individuals who work effectively in matrix organizations. Thus, it is better to take a holistic view and design the whole organization than focus solely on the structure piece.

And finally, the third feature of the Star Model is that an effective organization is one that has all of these factors in alignment: they fit together and reinforce one another, and the people in the organization get a consistent message about the appropriate kinds of behavior. When the factors are not aligned, frictions develop, people are confused about the direction, and time and energy are wasted on unnecessary conflicts. So no matter which model is used, these are the three design principles to follow.

We are often asked why we chose this particular set of factors to include in the Star Model. There are basically two reasons. The first is that these factors are directly controllable by leadership teams. Leaders can decide on the structure, the processes they use to make decisions, the people they're going to recruit, and so on. And second, these are the factors that have an impact on people's behavior. If you measure and reward particular kinds of behavior, you're more likely to receive those behaviors. You're more likely to get cooperative kinds of behavior if you hire people who are naturally collaborative, and so forth.

The fact that culture is not one of the elements of the Star Model is frequently questioned, and the reason is that leaders cannot directly control the culture. They can change it, as we will see, but they do so by making changes to the four factors I've described. If the strategy is to become more customer-centric, the leaders choose to organize by customer segments, accentuate the customer relationship management process, reward people on the basis of customer satisfaction and customer retention, and hire people who are relationship oriented as opposed to transaction oriented. If the leaders make all those decisions, they're most likely to generate the kind of behavior that then leads to a culture of customer-centricity. The balance of this chapter describes each of the factors of the Star Model in more detail.

Strategy

Strategy is the direction in which the company is going to grow. It is set so that people in the organization know how they should be guiding their own behavior. Strategy is also important to determine and make choices. That is, the organization needs to decide what it's going to do and what it's not going to do because it has limited resources. The scarcer the resources, the more clearly defined the strategy needs to be. As a matter of fact, the only reason companies need a strategy is that they have very limited resources. Companies face an enormous amount of opportunity but limited resources. Therefore, each one must decide what it is going to do, and do well, and what it is not going to do. These choices then guide decisions about organization structure, rewards, processes, and people practices.

The Monitor Group has developed a framework for guiding the strategy of a business unit, a region, a function, and even the entire enterprise. Strategy consists of three pieces: what to do, where to play, and how to win. *What to do* refers to goals and objectives. As I said in chapter 1, all publicly traded organizations pursue growth as one of their goals in order to keep the stock price advancing. Other goals could be, for example, market share or, for customer-centric companies, customer share or a specific return on investment. These are some of the choices around goals and objectives for both short-term and long-term decisions. Most organizations are fairly effective at making *what to do* kinds of strategic choices.

The second element, *where to play*, is literally about the question, "Where in the world are we going to be present and do business?" There is a choice of countries in which to be present and also a choice of products. What will be the portfolio of products that we offer? Which markets are we going to address, and where in that market will we compete? Will we compete at the high end, the low end, or somewhere in between? Where along the value chain will we conduct business? Where will we outsource and buy services and products from other people? So for each type of industry, there are *where to play* kinds of choices in terms of segments and microsegments, products, channels, countries, and so on.

Companies continually add dimensions to their strategy, and therefore their organization. Initially they compete within their home country and then expand into a host country. They start in their core business and then add different products, customer segments, and so forth. The *where to play* decision is made continuously over time as the organization seeks out its growth objectives.

The third strategic element, *how to win*, is all about competitive advantage: What is our recipe for success? What's our formula to compete? This is a harder decision yet an important one, and it has a lot to do with the distribution of power in the organization.

Some companies are product-centric. Pharmaceutical companies, for example, focus on discovering, patenting, and introducing blockbuster drugs. The blockbuster strategy is a product-centric kind of strategy. Pharma companies would achieve a patentable position for some number of years, and that would give them an advantage. Today these companies are finding that that strategy is more difficult and are now becoming more customer-centric—that is, they try to address the health outcome needs of a population. In Australia, the government has given some companies specific populations to target, along with a fixed amount of money. In this case, pharmaceutical companies look at providing not just drugs but health information, hot lines, support groups, and other elements in the effort to become more customer-centric for a particular population.

Procter & Gamble has always been a good example of getting advantage through quite favorable views of its brands like

Tide and Pampers. But it also is able to maintain these brands by having greater insights into why consumers buy and behave the way they do. Citibank has achieved a competitive advantage by being located in more than one hundred countries. By taking deposits and making loans in local currencies, it allows companies that are its clients to avoid currency risks. The closest bank to Citibank is the Hongkong and Shanghai Banking Corporation (HSBC), which is present in fifty-six countries. Citi clearly has an almost unattainable advantage by its presence in so many countries. IBM has pursued the solutions and "Smarter Planet" types of offerings based on its in-depth customer knowledge and an ability to integrate hardware, software, and services around a customer's problems or needs.

It's also important to know how long a competitive advantage will last. All advantages are temporary, but they last for different time periods. It's safe to say that most industries are now seeing increasingly shorter-lived advantages. In fact, experts recommend that companies work continually on their next advantage rather than try to sustain a current one. It's also important to know how long a competitive advantage is likely to last, because that is how long the current organization will last. In fast-moving, high-rate-of-change industries, the organization needs to be capable of moving from one advantage to another and concurrently of moving from one organization to another.

Structure

The structure of an organization is about the distribution of power and authority across a hierarchy. All organizations that we know of have hierarchical forms. In this section, I describe the forms that that hierarchy can take: the functional organization, product or business unit organization, customer business unit, channel organization, geographical organization, hybrid structures, and matrix organization. Then we look at the other dimensions of structure, such as the distribution of power (both horizontal and vertical), the division of labor, and the shape of the organization. We start with hierarchy and then move to the other forms in which the hierarchy can be configured.

Hierarchy of Authority

Today there are discussions of choices between networks and hierarchies as a form of organization. In fact, a hierarchy is a network—a particular form of network, so it's best to think of hierarchies *and* networks. It's difficult to find an organization of any size that has existed over any length of time that is not a hierarchy. The reason is that for large numbers of people to act in an organized way, it's necessary to create some kind of division of labor. That is, people must simultaneously sell the products or services, while other people are producing and delivering those products and services. And at the same time, other groups of people are designing the next generation of services and products. Still other people are recording the transactions and receiving funding from sales of those products and services. Another group is looking for funds to grow the enterprise. And so on. There is a division of labor of a large number of people whose behavior needs to be integrated.

This large number of people cannot continually communicate among themselves and decide on what they're going to do. Instead, we select a few people and place them in a hierarchy of authority. They decide what directions other groups will take, what the prices should be, what the schedules should be, and so forth. A hierarchy arises because organizations do not have the information-processing and decision-making capabilities to get a consensus among a large group of people. A consensus is particularly difficult when the people are really quite talented and have minds of their own. It's even more complicated when they're facing uncertain futures with limited resources and high stakes.

The function of a hierarchy is thus twofold. First, decisions are made in a hierarchy in order to coordinate the behavior of a large number of people who cannot otherwise make timely decisions among themselves. Second, it is a path of escalation in order to resolve disputes among people about the direction of the enterprise. And the likelihood of disputes is high when there are strong people, high stakes, high future uncertainty, and limited resources. For these reasons, it is difficult to find a large, ongoing institution that is not a hierarchy.

One example is the US court system. The population of the United States would still be arguing over who won the 2000 election, Bush or Gore, without the Supreme Court, which debated the issue and then voted five to four. The justices chose Bush, and the country went about implementing that decision. Why did half of the US population decide to go along with this, even though they disagreed?

The reason is that the US Supreme Court has legitimate power that we refer to as "authority." It is the consent of the governed. That is, people eventually comply with a decision made by a legitimate hierarchy of authority, even if they disagree with the decision. And it is this dispute resolution power in a hierarchy of authority that allows collective action among a large number of people. Authority therefore enables collective action to take place in an integrated manner. Alternately, there is no hierarchy for fiscal policy in the United States. As a result, there has not been a budget for several years. Instead, we have sequestration and gridlock, which no one wants.

The lesson from the US legal system is that there is a hierarchy of authority: unpopular decisions get made, and everyone moves on. An important feature to note is that that it isn't always an individual who is at the top of the hierarchy. It can be three people, as in an appeals court, or it can be the Supreme Court of nine people. The decision process itself takes place within a hierarchy so that a decision can be made and action can take place within reasonable time frames.

It has been suggested that open source software institutions are an example of large numbers of volunteers who are creating a software program. While that is true, there is always someone who has the final approval of changes to the software program. At Linux, the software program that's widely used as an operating system today, Linus Torvalds, the founder of Linux, was the final arbiter of any disagreements on major changes to the kernel of the operating system of Linux. He then became a bottleneck to the decision process. There was an open revolt around 2008 among all of the volunteers who participated in the creation of Linux. The result was the addition of a decision-making body—a layer of committees—between all of the volunteers and Linus Torvalds, who still maintains the final word on important decisions. This layer of committees now makes decisions about parts of the overall program. When there are disputes and a time frame of action, hierarchy is the intelligent way to organize in order to get something done.

A hierarchy can be designed around different types of structures. A few of them are listed and described below.

Functional Organization. When firms have a large number of people, they divide the work into subtasks that can be performed simultaneously. Invariably, this initial division of labor is based on functional specialization. It results in a hierarchy of authority that is shown in figure 2.2.

Figure 2.2 Functional Organization

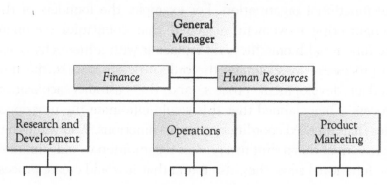

Most organizations have some people who are dedicated to selling the products and services. Others are dedicated to the delivery or the operations of the organization that delivers the product or service to the customer. People in finance track the transactions and fund the growth of the organization. There are people in human resources, information technology, legal, and product development who specialize in these particular tasks.

It is instructive to note that when any organization begins, it usually has a functional organization based around a single-business strategy. For example, when Google started in search, it used a functional organization. Nike, when it started with athletic footwear, began as a functional organization. Analog Devices, a semiconductor manufacturer, was a functional organization when it started with converters.

One of the reasons companies choose the functional organization, and have consistently chosen it, is that society itself is organized around those functional specialties. That is, business schools have departments of finance and accounting, departments of supply chain management, and marketing departments. Engineering schools have departments of electrical engineering and mechanical engineering. Law schools segment themselves into various domains of legal study. Society itself is organized around specialties, and people in society choose them as their career.

It has often been suggested that we should do away with the functional organization. For example, the founders of the reengineering movement suggested that companies eliminate the functional hierarchies and replace it with a hierarchy based on processes—for example, the order-to-cash process, the new product development process, and the customer acquisition process. They claimed that this would eliminate the functional silos that impeded coordination across functions. And while they were correct that a shift to a process organization would eliminate the functional silos, they also found that it would create process silos, which goes against the way society itself is organized. Today we may have process owners and a lateral organization based around the new product development process, but most organizations are still based on individual functions.

Many functions come and go. For example, we currently are looking at the trend toward big data. There's a suggestion that we should form a new specialty around data scientists and have a data and analytics department, and many organizations are doing this. Procter & Gamble combined procurement, manufacturing engineering, manufacturing, and distribution into a superfunction called product supply. Other companies call it supply chain. There are also many subfunctions. For example, within sales, many organizations develop a subspecialty of export sales. There's thus a continuing evolution of different types of specialties that are created within society and within universities. Organizations respond to this evolution by hiring and then organizing around these particular kinds of specialties.

Product Organization or Business Units. Companies that diversify usually move into adjacent markets or product lines. That is, when growth slows in their core business, they diversify by adding a new business in which they can continue their growth.

Procter & Gamble started out in 1837 by making candles and soap based on animal fats. It dropped the candles as a product line with the advent of the light bulb but was a very large soap manufacturer at the end of World War II. However, its scientists discovered synthetic granules, which became the basis of detergents. The company expanded into Crest and other toothpastes and later into paper products like Charmin and Pampers. In this way, P&G moved into additional industries in which it could grow. Each of these industries, however, is a consumer packaged goods product line. Each is based on a similar business model of selling through a system of brand management to mass merchandisers, where consumers make repeat purchases of fairly

Figure 2.3 Product Structure

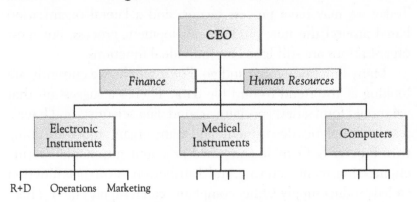

low-priced products. In this way, P&G created a product- or a business unit–based organization. Each of those product lines or business units was itself a functional organization. We can see that the negative of a functional organization is that it is difficult to manage variety within a single functional structure. Instead, we create multiple profit center structures, each of which is an individual business unit, as shown in figure 2.3.

Customer Business Unit. The third type of structure is customer-based or a customer business unit. Service businesses, as they expand out of their original core business, typically move into other customer segments. For example, there was a group of financial services organizations called savings and loans in the United States. They took people's savings and lent out these savings as mortgages to other people who were buying homes. That's all they did. Then they were deregulated and expanded into other consumer lending products like auto loans and home equity loans. They also expanded into commercial loans, that is, loans to businesses. Many banks have a set of lending products for consumers, as well as other products for commercial enterprises of various sizes. As a result, there are separate profit centers for small, medium-sized, and large businesses and another for national businesses. Thus customer segmentation is implemented throughout the entire organization. Each of these customer segments is often a functional organization. Other service businesses, such as telecommunications businesses, are also segmented by type of customer and organized into customer business units.

Channels. A fourth type of business structure is built around channels. Williams-Sonoma, for example, is organized around how people want to purchase their products. It has retail outlets—actual brick-and-mortar buildings where customers can physically go and buy and take away the products—a large catalogue business where it can function on a mail order basis, and an online business where customers can order over the Internet and take delivery through a delivery service. In addition, many retailers also have an outlet channel. Some of its products may have a defect yet are still valuable. These products are sold through an outlet channel at a lower price. So many retailers have a brick-and-mortar business, an online business, a catalogue business, and an outlet business. Each is often a profit-and-loss center and a functional organization.

Geographical Structure. The fifth type of hierarchical structure occurs when companies organize around geography. This is typical of a hospital, which has a radius around which it attracts patients and physicians. A multihospital type of an organization then replicates the full hospital in different areas. A cement company such as a CEMEX, where delivery is based on a radius around a cement plant, is organized on a geographical basis. A cement plant is no longer competitive after a radius of about 150 miles, so each of these units is replicated on a geographical basis. Each geography is a profit center and a functional structure.

Many services were also based on geographies, where people had to go to the store or clinic based on the proximity of the facility. Today the digital revolution provides things like online education, distance medicine, and online banking, where rather than going to the branch of a bank, you can now do business with the institution online. Some refer to this digital phenomenon as the death of distance. The digital revolution is reducing the need for many types of structures that were previously used by service providers.

Hybrid Structures. Often organizations combine one or more of the types of structures already identified. For example, Boeing structures its organization around the type of aircraft, as shown in figure 2.4. It creates product organizations for wide-bodied aircraft in one division. That is, the 747s, 767s, and 777s are in a single wide-body division. A narrow-body division designs and assembles the 737 and the 757. The 787 is in a separate organization for its design and assembly since it has new technologies. And there is another division as well: the central fabrication division. This unit makes all of the structural components like wings, spars, and struts. The manufacture of these components requires expensive, numerically controlled machine tools. Since each product division cannot afford to have its own, a separate fabrication unit is created that supplies all of the aircraft divisions.

Telecommunications operators use a similar kind of structure. AT&T and Verizon have their own customer segment

Figure 2.4 Hybrid Product and Function Structure

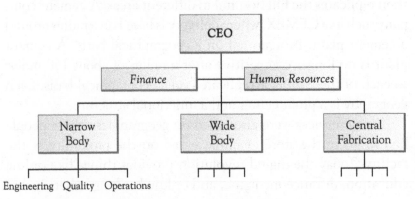

specialties focusing on consumers, small business, large business, multinationals, and so forth. These are their customer business units. However, all of these businesses share a common network. Originally this was a copper wire network, but it's also a capital-intensive network of communications that spans the entire country. Again, the reason for this special network is the scale of the investment that's necessary to create a network. Each independent customer segment cannot afford its own, so they share the central network. The result is a hybrid structure comprising a network and customer business units. Many organizations use this kind of structure when sharing a common, large-scale infrastructure.

Today many organizations outsource those requirements for economies of scale. Virgin Mobile buys network time from its competitors and then resells it. Many semiconductor design companies do not have their own fabrication facilities. A silicon fabrication unit today costs around $4 billion. So if you're a large manufacturer like Intel and you see an advantage in having your own fabrication units, you do the investing yourself. If you're a relatively new semiconductor company, like Marvell, which was founded in 1995, you do the design work for semiconductor products but go to Taiwan Semiconductor Manufacturing Company to do the fabrication. Taiwan Semiconductor incurs all of the investment for maintaining the state-of-the-art manufacturing facilities and invests up to $4 billion on new cutting-edge equipment. It can afford to do this because it provides semiconductor fabrication services for Marvell, Analog Devices, NVIDIA, and other semiconductor design companies. So sometimes a hybrid is adopted by an organization; other times, an organization outsources this highly specialized economy of scale-driven type of facility.

Matrix Organizations. A final kind of combination of structures is a matrix organization. In this case, the unit or company is simultaneously organized around two dimensions. The matrix began with American aerospace companies in the 1960s. These companies were organized around functions, primarily different engineering functions, manufacturing functions, quality, and a marketing or sales department (Galbraith, 2009).

When President Kennedy announced the goal of putting a man on the moon by 1970, aerospace companies adopted a second dimension of program management. There was a program manager who would be in charge of the Lunar Orbiter or the Saturn Booster—both different types of space vehicles or components. The program managers of major programs and the leaders of the individual functions simultaneously reported to the head of an aerospace company. The purpose was to pursue both cost and schedule priorities in the program, as well as technical excellence and design in the functions. The two initiatives were equally important and critical to putting a man on the moon and bringing him back.

A matrix is a two-dimensional organization where the company is simultaneously organized around two dimensions— functions and profit centers. This is different from a product or business unit structure, where there may be functions reporting to the CEO, along with the business units. In this case, the functions are usually coordinating units and are not placed in a matrix. More recently, these functional units have been strengthened as activities like the information technology group or human resources organization increase in their power and authority, and many of these organizations have also moved toward matrix structures.

•••

In summary, there are different types of hierarchical structures that companies adopt. Typically a company starts with a functional structure. Then as it diversifies, it moves into product lines and business units. If the company is a service business, it will move into customer segment profit centers. Or it may move into geographic profit centers or individual channels if it's a retailer. In each case, the company moves to a multiprofit center structure, and each of the profit centers is itself a functional organization. We also see different hybrids, where one of the functions of an organization requires significant scale or specialization or heavy investment. And finally, there are matrix structures or simultaneous structures.

Distribution of Power Across the Hierarchy

The distribution of power across the hierarchy has two dimensions to it: vertical and horizontal. The vertical dimension is the one with which we're the more familiar. The design issues are questions of centralization and decentralization. For example, the functional structure centralizes decision making in the chief executive, because this person is the first role that supervises all of the activities that are interdependent. All of the functional activities are sequentially interdependent as work flows across them from raw material to customer delivery. Operating decisions such as schedules and pricing are made by the chief executive and the leadership team.

If we move to a product organization or a regional organization, the functions report into the product managers or the regional managers at the second level of the structure. In these types of organizations, the power and authority to make these same operating decisions are decentralized to the product managers or geographic managers. The CEO does not make those operating decisions. Instead, he or she makes larger financial decisions such as capital expenditures above $1 million. The chief executive, along with the chief financial officer, makes those decisions, which are then centralized in the office of the chief executive.

Horizontal distributions of power receive less attention but are nonetheless equally important. Some companies are known as being marketing-dominated organizations, such as consumer goods companies. The chief executive of these companies comes up through the marketing function. In high-technology companies, the dominant function tends to be engineering. The CEO often comes up through the product development function.

These distributions of power change over time. In the consumer goods industries, the rise of retailers such as Walmart, Tesco, and Target has also created the rise of the sales department inside the consumer goods organizations. When an element in the stakeholder environment increases in power, the corresponding internal department that deals with that stakeholder should increase in power inside the company as well.

Similarly, for some consumer goods food companies, periodic droughts caused shortages of particular commodities. With shortages came higher prices; thus, procurement departments saw an increase in their power in the organization. The increased authority can be dramatic, as procurement can often influence the recipes of the product development department. The power distribution inside the organization should reflect the power distribution in the stakeholder environment. Changes to the power base of customers, vendors, and regulators should be met with corresponding increases in the power of the sales, procurement, and legal departments.

Division of Labor

The division of labor is the degree of specialization of the roles that are executing the work. Most work is divided into functional specialties and subspecialties, as mentioned before. These are the kinds of careers found in society as a whole. The greater the degree of specialization, the more effectively a company can execute particular subtasks. For example, technology companies that can bring greater expertise and knowledge to bear on designs of products and processes achieve better performance. But the greater the degree of specialization, the greater the degree of interdependence required between particular units. Specialization is thus a two-edged sword.

As a result, the choice of the degree of specialization is a key organization design decision. Some organizations choose generalists to be permanent members of the structure and then outsource specialties they need at particular times. If a specialty is key to the competitive advantage of an organization, those specialties will be incorporated into the organization and owned by the organization itself.

Another factor that permits specialization is the size of the company. Greater scale permits much greater specialization. It's usually an advantage to be more specialized in many situations. Larger consulting firms and larger financial services firms can begin specializing around customer segments. They will, for instance, specialize in verticals like retail, distribution, government, high technology, and pharmaceuticals. In this way, they can speak the language of the customer and bring greater expertise to bear on that particular customer's problems.

Shape of the Organization

The shape of the organization is determined by the number of levels and the spans of supervision that are used in the company's levels and departments. A span refers to the number of people a manager has reporting to her or him. The number of levels and spans is certainly influenced by the number of people in the organization, but there is also some discretion in how wide a span the organization designer chooses.

The trend today is toward much wider spans and flatter structures (fewer levels). As we move away from command-and-control styles of leadership, managers can lead larger numbers of people. Thus, the hierarchy becomes flatter because fewer people are needed to supervise others. The flatter hierarchies lead to faster decisions, leaders who are in touch with organizational members, and lower overhead costs. But what is the optimal number of subordinates for leaders to be able to provide help and training to while still making accurate judgments about their work?

The Conference Board, a group that conducts research on organizational structures, recently surveyed spans of supervision among its members. With thousands of observations from work

, the distribution ranged from 0 to 127 people. The distribution was trimodal, with modes at 7, 17, and 75. (The *mode*, as distinguished from *mean* and *median* as descriptors of central tendency, is the value that occurs most frequently.) In this case, three numbers frequently occurred; hence, there was a trimodal distribution. How could this happen?

The traditional organization model typically used spans of about seven people, plus or minus a couple. To communicate with subordinates, coordinate their work, and evaluate them, managers had time for only about seven people. But this span can be increased depending on the nature of the people and the task. For example, a leader can have a much wider span of control if the leader and the group members are all highly experienced people. They need to have less communication and training involved while conducting the work. Second, you can have wider spans when all of the employees do the same work. In this case, you can use group coaching and group communications, and the leader needs less scope of expertise. A leader can also have a wider span of control when each employee's task is independent of the others because it is less likely to have disputes or overlaps in authority. And finally, the leader can have a wider span of control when the task is easily measured and easily observed. The leader can set goals and let the goals do the managing. A group of fifteen to twenty salespeople, all doing the same sales work but each with an independent sales area that is measured by quotas, can be supervised by a single leader. In contrast, a tightly coupled software design group, which has a rapidly changing type of task, will probably consist of only around five people. Thus, the span of control will vary with the nature of the people and the task that they are performing.

Delegation of work by the leader to the group also results in wider spans. Indeed, some organizations actually widen spans to encourage more delegation. Some organizations monitor the spans in their organizational units and set goals to widen them progressively. As people join and leave, leaders widen the spans at these opportune moments. Organizations train their managers to adopt more of a coaching style and less of a controlling style, which means that spans of about seventeen are quite possible.

A different kind of organization is needed for spans of seventy-five people. An example is a factory with a plant manager and seventy-five blue-collar workers. The workers are organized into three teams of twenty-five people each, with a team for each of the three shifts. Each team is self-managing. It selects, trains, disciplines, and rewards all of its own members. These teams schedule the work and propose capital investments. The plant manager advises the teams and spends most of the workday communicating with people outside the plant. Thus, the more that managerial work is delegated to work teams, the less need there is for direct supervision. These kinds of teams lead to the elimination of levels of supervision and the complete elimination of command-and-control styles.

So in summary, it is quite possible to observe companies following the traditional management model choosing spans of about seven. More delegation and more goal setting can lead to spans of around seventeen. In companies with policies of self-managing teams, spans of around seventy-five are possible.

It is important to follow the Star Model, however. In order to create these kinds of teams successfully, the organization needs different kinds of individuals, different types of reward systems, and measurable outcomes. It requires a complete organization design to create these self-managing teams.

Information and Decision Processes

Information and decision processes are the ways in which work gets done in organizations. It's often useful to think of the structure of the organization as the anatomy and the processes as the physiology. There are three kinds of information and decision processes that I will highlight. The first are the informal, or voluntary, kinds of processes—the old grapevine or water-cooler talk that we used to refer to and now takes place over social networks. The second are business processes—the generic business processes that almost all companies have. And the third are management processes for allocating the scarce resources that are applied to the various opportunities facing the company.

Informal Processes

Let's start with the informal. The informal organization is one that's been around for a long time. These are voluntary behaviors that individuals enact to perform their work and carry on social conversation. Today these informal processes are often referred to as self-organizing processes. They are often bottom-up processes, where people work together naturally and spontaneously around a set of issues. These processes can be influenced primarily by changes in physical location. That is, project organizations would often physically locate people together when their work interacted or was dedicated to a specific project. This proximity increased the likelihood of face-to-face conversations and information transfer.

Today the informal processes have changed dramatically with the advent of e-mail, social media, and software programs. Collectively these processes are referred to today as Enterprise 2.0. There is a whole group of different software packages called enterprise social software, which is very much like Facebook and Twitter in the social world. There are equivalents of Facebook now available for the enterprise world called Chatter and Yammer. There are wikis and various Microsoft software products like SharePoint. There are many ways of working together that encourage different kinds of spontaneous behaviors, community formation, and linking together communities of interest. Software providers predict a great future in being able to exploit these opportunities for the communication, coordination, and decentralization of work.

Currently these social software processes are not anywhere near as developed inside the company as they are outside, for a number of reasons: normal habits, the inability of the top people to trust their employees, and the usual organizational silos. But in the future, there's a great deal of opportunity to use self-organizing processes for managing the increasing complexity of organizations.

Business Processes

The second type of information and decision process is business processes. These processes are often programmed and therefore automated because they are predictable, understandable, and replicable and take place quite frequently. These generic processes are the new product development process, the order-to-cash process, the customer relationship management process, and so forth. Some of these processes are enterprise-wide, and some are within a function. Some of them link together a couple of functions like the sales and operations planning process. For the most part, these are cross-functional processes. They are the means of coordinating the interdependent functions within a business. They are increasingly sophisticated, expressed in software and automated.

The example that's often given is the Cisco Configurator process, which takes place with a Cisco salesperson and a field applications engineer working with a customer design team. The design team can create its own configuration of a network of Cisco routers and switches and all of the digital networking that underlies the customer's digital systems. Once this team has determined the configuration and size of the order that they wish to place with Cisco, they simply press a button, and the configuration is entered into the Cisco system. It then passes through the Cisco system to Cisco's contract manufacturers, which produce the required items. These items are sent directly to the customer, as is an automatically generated invoice, which the customer pays by electronic transfer to Cisco's bank. Cisco's entire order-to-cash process takes place with very few people participating directly. It's completely automated.

And of course, this replaces the old manual or partly automated systems. When an order was placed in the old system, it went into the order entry system, where order entry clerks manually posted the order into the system, and it would be checked. Then it would go to a credit department to see if the customer was credit-worthy for the size of this order. Following that, it would go to the production scheduling group, which would then try to schedule this with the contract manufacturing team. The logistics people would plan for the transportation from emerging market countries and do the necessary paperwork for export or import. Finally the finance people would send an invoice. All of this required a lot of human interaction. In today's system, after the salesperson and field application engineer work with the customer, the order takes place without any human intervention. The only people who actually touch the order and participate in its transmission are workers at the contract manufacturers.

Today we're looking at more and more of this kind of automation. Machine-to-machine communication and information processing is increasing by quantum leaps. These business processes are an important means by which companies can now manage increasing complexity. Much of the interdependence that comes with work flows can be anticipated and programmed and then placed into software. The work that remains is professional work like projects and initiatives. The organizations that are the most effective in managing complexity are those that have been able to create robust business processes for handling much of the routine, predictable kind of work.

Management Processes

The third type of information and decision process is the management process. Management processes are for allocating the scarce resources to the opportunities that the organization faces. These processes are the means by which it executes strategy.

The strategies that we articulate tend to be the intended strategies that the company would like to accomplish. However, it is the de facto strategy, the resulting strategy, that occurs from the actual allocation of resources. A few years back, Hewlett-Packard articulated an impressive e-commerce strategy for Europe, but it could be implemented only partially. The reason was that there were only ten people in all of Europe who could program secure transactions over the Internet. And while every bank in Europe wanted to do an e-commerce project, none of them would sign a contract with Hewlett-Packard until they saw which of those ten experts was going to be working on their project. The resource availability was the limiting factor in how effectively Hewlett-Packard could implement its intended strategy.

The importance of these management processes arose with the creation of the multiple profit center model of organization. When companies were a single business, the key challenge was coordination across functions, and so the effort was on business processes like scheduling, pricing, and forecasting. Once those were mastered, then organizations moved to allocating financial resources. After World War II, General Electric, Westinghouse, ITT, and others moved away from single-business strategies to diversification and multibusiness strategies. A number of the processes for allocating resources, capital, and expenses arose at this time. These were processes for allocating resources across a portfolio of opportunities.

One of the best known was the Boston Consulting Group's (BCG) strategy of identifying businesses that were cash cows, stars, and dogs, which were to be eliminated. BCG's model was really a way of allocating resources by identifying businesses that were growing (thus cash users), and funding them from other businesses in the portfolio that were cash cows (cash generators). The criteria for allocating the resources were determined using the growth share matrix. That is, on one axis you had the growth of the business and on the other the market share of the business. High-growth, high-share businesses were the ideal. The allocation from cash generators to cash users is a permanent feature in the management processes of multibusiness companies.

As we move into more complex organizations of multiple businesses, multiple countries, and multiple customer segments, the importance of this resource allocation process also increases. The more complex the structure is, the more important are the management processes. These processes accomplish a couple of things. First, they achieve an alignment of goals within the company and across its different dimensions. That is, companies have one set of goals arising from the businesses and another set of plans and goals coming from the countries. Managers eventually want these plans and goals to be aligned so that there is a single, consistent, aligned plan for the company. If these plans and goals are not aligned, the people representing the different dimensions are going to be arguing about the conflicting goals throughout the year. Today many companies have an event whereby regional leaders, business leaders, and functional leaders interact with one another to arrive at a single, consistent company plan. This master plan is aligned across the three dimensions.

The second important reason that these management processes have been implemented is to achieve alignment on the setting of priorities. If there's a single issue where the corporate leadership has experienced difficulty, it is in determining a set of priorities for the company. It is the same as choosing a strategy for the corporation. While companies are becoming more and more effective at generating business strategies and country strategies, an overall corporate portfolio strategy is usually much less well developed. A solid corporate portfolio strategy is necessary to choose among opportunities for applying resources across the company.

Priorities are important precisely because of the resource scarcity. If we had plenty of money, we wouldn't need priorities, but when times are tight and the economy is in a difficult position, it is increasingly important to make priority decisions.

Regions, business units, and functions all have different ideas on how to spend the limited funds. The management process for allocating money and talent is the arena within which these conflicts are managed and discussed. It is the process by which decisions regarding how to allocate the scarce resources are made. The purpose of a strategy is to allow the company to say no to a good idea. Weaker leaders tend to say yes to many ideas and then underfund them. They spread the funds like peanut butter across all the ideas.

A challenge in this process is to identify the scarce resource. Historically we've assumed that money is the scarce resource. Thus, we spent time on the capital budget, the advertising budget, the R&D budget, and so forth. Today the limiting factor that prevents companies from implementing their intended strategy is talent, or various types of talent. Most software companies in Silicon Valley are experiencing a shortage of people who can create software applications for mobile devices. You do not just shrink an application software package running on a desktop computer to make it work on a smart phone. The talented software developers are in short supply and limit how quickly companies can implement mobile strategies.

The economically rational course of action is to maximize the returns on the scarcest resource. It used to be that there were never enough SAP programmers. The scarce resource often changes, so the important decision process that underlies the management process is the one for allocating the scarcest resource, that is, the strategy-limiting resource. Therefore, some consultants have suggested using return on skills as a criterion for allocating resources or choosing which opportunities to pursue. McKinsey has pursued return on employees as a criterion. There are currently a number of efforts to develop logical criteria for allocating the scarcest resource. The point is that more and more, the scarcest resource is talent, and particular kinds of talent.

In summary, informal processes, business processes, and management processes are the types of information and decision processes we need to complement our choices of organization structures. The next major factor in the Star Model is reward systems.

Reward Systems

The purpose of the organization's reward system is motivation. Organizations consist of a number of individuals, each with his or her own private and personal goals. The reward system is designed to align the goals of these individuals with the goals of the organization. Recall that the organizations that interest us are formal ones, which are purposeful entities. In order to accomplish the organization's goals, leaders must motivate individuals in the organization to behave in ways that will lead to successful execution of the strategy.

Organizations have created several tools to motivate its members. In this section, we examine the use of compensation, promotions, recognition systems, and job challenge.

Compensation Practices

The motivational value of compensation varies with the form that the compensation policy takes. Most organizations offer a fixed salary. However, a fixed salary is not something that motivates performance. It motivates people to join and stay in the organization, but not to perform at a higher level. Typically people receive the same amount of salary regardless of their performance.

The next level of motivation occurs when companies offer a fixed salary plus a merit increase. This merit increase too has a limited amount of motivation value. It has a recognition value—people are motivated because they get an increase. However, by the time a merit increase of 3 to 4 percent is divided by 12 and the taxes are taken out, the person can hardly see how much additional salary he or she is receiving.

The third level of motivational value is a fixed salary, plus a merit increase, plus a bonus. The bonus has the highest leverage in motivating behavior, depending on the size of the bonus and the value that the person places on monetary compensation. Some jobs, like sales jobs, are 100 percent commission: all of the person's take-home pay is variable compensation. Others, such as investment banks, have somewhere between 70 and 90 percent of take-home pay consist of a year-end bonus. For many companies, the bonus of the top managers will be somewhere around 20 to 50 percent. Usually the higher you go in the organization, the greater the amount of variable compensation. These large year-end bonuses have the most leverage in influencing the decision-making behavior of the organization's leaders. The particular behavior being motivated depends on the design of the bonus system.

First, bonuses are a flexible and adaptable form of payment. They can be adapted to the issues of the day to motivate particular kinds of behavior. For example, in order to motivate more of a customer-focused policy, the leadership team at Microsoft received bonuses based on customer satisfaction, measured by a Gallup survey taken with its top customers. Another example of a customer-focused incentive is the bonus for Sun Microsystems' leadership team. Sun Microsystems sold computers to eBay along with a maintenance contract. After eBay's website went down for more than twenty-four hours, Sun Microsystems changed the bonus metric for its managers. The new leadership team bonus was based on the up-time of eBay's website. So bonuses are quite flexible and can be used to reinforce temporary initiatives and goals.

Second, the bonus usually varies with the strategy of the organization. For example, a single-business functional organization probably has a management bonus based on the company's profit for that year. Managers of a multibusiness company have some different types of bonus practices. Typically the bonus pool is based on the company's overall profit for that year. Thus, if you are a corporate leader, your bonus is based on the company profit. If you are in a business unit, often your bonus is based half on the profitability of your business and half on the profitability of the company as a whole. The proportion of business-corporate profit will vary depending on whether the company's strategy is a conglomerate or a related business portfolio. We explore the portfolio strategy concept in chapter 8 on multiple businesses.

Usually the more complex the business becomes, the more the bonus is based on total company profit. The reason is that it becomes more and more difficult to isolate and independently measure the profit contribution of a business, a country, or a customer segment. If leaders are rewarded only on their own profit-and-loss in these complex forms, dysfunctional behaviors can result.

There are other factors to consider as well when designing a bonus system. One of them is whether the bonus is based on short- or long-term performance. Typically the short-term performance is profitability within a particular fiscal year. Some other organizations that work on longer cycles have a longer performance measurement that underlies their bonus. At one point, IBM's account managers for its very large clients were measured on a five-year moving average of the revenue obtained from that particular client. Typically there was a bonus based on this year's performance and then a form of compensation for long-term performance, usually in the form of a stock grant. In this way, the manager participated in the performance of the company over time.

Another dimension is the degree to which the performance measurement is objective or subjective. Is the measure a single, narrow dimension of performance or a complete or total assessment of performance? Many organizations believe in the power of a single, measurable goal, such as this year's earnings before interest and tax (EBIT) number. Normally a clear, objective single goal will produce a great deal of motivation. People can understand it and can see how to connect their behavior to their own performance and bonus. However, the clearer, the more objective, and the narrower the goal becomes, the more that dysfunctions are likely to creep in. For example, if all of the people working in a retail store are salespeople on 100 percent commission, the store will have trouble getting those people to stock the shelves, clear the aisles, and wait on a dissatisfied customer who is returning merchandise. So you get the specific behavior that you're measuring, but not the total behavior needed for effective performance.

One of the ways companies have tried to adjust is by using multiple goals, subjective goals, and contextual assessments made by the leader. Subjective goals and assessments are seen to reduce the amount of dysfunctional behavior that a person would engage in, but it tends to reduce the motivation because the goals are not quite as clear. They are subjective, and the managers do not always see a direct link between an employee's behavior and the desired performance outcome. A number of organizations make the trade-off and choose to have a strong, clear, objective goal based on an EBIT number, along with some subjective personal goals. Other companies reduce the amount of variable compensation, perhaps to 20 percent of total compensation.

Professional services organizations are particularly interesting in their practices around compensation. Some have a direct bonus tied to the amount of revenue that a partner would bring in within a year. These organizations are often referred to as an "eat what you kill" company. They attract people who are individual performers and can produce at a high level. These people are often called rainmakers. The danger very often is that these types of people can also go to another organization and take their clients with them. This practice is usually known as a star system, and a number of professional services organizations operate under this kind of a compensation system.

Other professional services organizations are known as "one company" types of firms. They have a strong identity between the professionals and the company itself. Normally a client doesn't hire an individual; rather, he or she hires the company. Clients would hire McKinsey to do a particular engagement with them. Companies like McKinsey, Bain, Boston Consulting Group, and Goldman Sachs in investment banking and Latham & Watkins among large law firms are all organizations that embrace full and fair assessments of performance that determine the bonus and promotions.

By "full," I mean that the performance assessment examines multiple dimensions of performance. One of the dimensions is the amount of revenue that the consultant generates and the kind of customer service that the professional delivers. These are typically measured by revenue and customer satisfaction. These firms also measure the amount of contribution to the intellectual property of the firm. There are various projects like the McKinsey Global Institute, which builds the firm's intellectual property. Another dimension is how well a consultant attracts and develops talent. Many professionals return to their alma mater to recruit new talent to join the company.

Some companies use a measure called "partner-like behavior." This is assessed largely through subjective interviews. They ask other partners about a consultant's responsiveness. That is, they interview people in the London office and ask, "Is Jay Galbraith responsive to requests for help that you send to him?" These are measured largely through interview questions that are very structured. They're usually called "rigorously subjective questions." They ask for identifiable behavior that the interviewee has perceived. Responsiveness is one. Reaching out is another. That is, "Does Jay Galbraith bring leads to you from clients whom he's encountered somewhere else? Does he reach out without being requested to do so?" And, "To what degree does Jay Galbraith balance individual interest versus firm interest? Does he always try to get the most credit for himself, or does he see that credit is apportioned according to what actually happened with the client?"

All of these factors make up a full assessment of a professional's performance, and this assessment is done by a fellow partner, usually someone a little senior, who takes as much as a week of his or her time to interview customers, peers, and people who work with the professional under scrutiny. The assessing partner will read the exit interviews of people who have left the company and try to get a complete 360-degree view of the performance of the professional in question. All of the questions asked are tested over time, and they're very specific. The goal of the questions is to seek observed behaviors on the part of other people.

All of these professional organizations take the performance review process seriously. They commit a lot of time to doing a serious and complete assessment of people's performance, so they dedicate people to collect the data. The people charged with these assignments take the assessment seriously and make the time available to participate. These are all very busy people, so the values and norms of the company support this rigorous approach to subjective assessment.

Following the data-gathering phase, the individual assessments are combined and discussed within the compensation committee. Each of these large firms has compensation committees for various parts of their global organizations. The attempt is to have not just a full assessment but also a fair assessment. It's very easy for partners in Asia to see if the partners in London and New York are getting the lion's share of the bonus pie, and when they do, their perceptions generate trust problems. The purpose of the compensation committees is to have comparable fair and equal bonus shares to professionals across the organization. These bonus allocation decisions are then posted. There is transparency at a macro kind of level. They don't identify bonuses to individuals, but post the overall bonus picture with highs and lows. They show the total amount for Asia, for the Middle East, and so forth. This is a performance management system that creates a full, fair, and transparent assessment. It does require an enormous amount of time from busy people in order to do it right. Thus, subjective assessments without dedicating the time required are not very effective.

In summary, compensation systems vary from those that give a fixed salary, a fixed salary with a merit increase, and a fixed salary with merit increase and a bonus (usually for top executives). These practices are used to motivate the kind of strategic behavior that is desired. The design of the bonus system is key. It varies considerably on the kinds of behaviors it motivates, the timing of long or short, whether the performance measures are objective or subjective, and whether single or multiple goals are used. Collectively these make up the design of the compensation system.

Promotions

The second element of the reward system is promotion practices, which encompass the selection and development of individuals who should advance to higher levels. Again, professional services organizations are key on this particular dimension of promotion. Most people join professional organizations with the goal of advancing to become a partner. In academic institutions, professors want to be promoted to a position of a full, tenured professor. Often it's easier to make an assessment of a person's performance over a longer time frame. In this way, a partner's behavior can be assessed over three or five years. Professional services firms apply the same kind of rigorous and subjective assessments to determine who gets promoted. Some organizations have a combination of a very specific, narrow goal of an EBIT performance measurement for this year's bonus, but then use a thorough examination every three years for a longer-term assessment. They use a full and fair assessment of a person's performance prior to recommending him or her for promotion.

Recognition Systems

A third type of reward organizations use is a recognition system. We have all seen photos in hotels and retail establishments of the "employee of the month" and "employee of the year."

All of these are recognition systems that identify and reward outstanding performance. These systems can be quite extensive. For example, on the basis of extraordinary performance, an employee might be given a dinner for two at a nice restaurant, a day off, or a gift card. Many of these types of recognition rewards do not cost a lot of money. They do take a lot of effort, but can be quite meaningful.

For some sales organizations, the recognition systems are quite extraordinary. Companies like Amway and Mary Kay are sales organizations that are known for elaborate and motivational corporate meetings. People are singled out and publicly praised for having met high-level goals. Almost everybody gets recognition for something. The truly high performers are anointed to the 100 Percent Club, win a trip to Hawaii, and more. The specific recognition practices vary substantially.

But for the most part, recognition systems are probably underused and should be used much more frequently than is the actual practice.

Job Challenge

The fourth type of motivation boils down to the challenge of the job. The three prior motivational tools of compensation, promotion, and recognition are known as extrinsic rewards: they're externally applied to the behavior and are not a natural result of it. In contrast, an intrinsic reward is satisfaction that is internally generated from a job well done. There are a couple of dimensions to this. One is that some organizations are fortunate in serving an attractive purpose. Hospitals have this attribute, as do some pharmaceutical companies. Other organizations have attractive missions. An automotive company can attract car enthusiasts. Anita Roddick, founder of the Body Shop, attracted talented employees with her mission of using natural products and helping people (mostly women) in Africa to grow and harvest ingredients. A number of companies have the ability to provide rewarding work because of their industry. Other dimensions come from the attraction some people have to continuous learning and developing their own skills. Many people find personal satisfaction in being perceived as an expert in their field. Thus, organizations that recognize and enable employees to develop additional skills will attract and retain more people than those that don't.

Many people are attracted to professional organizations because they find that the work itself is challenging. These professionals want to work on the next challenge, the next state-of-the-art advance in technology, or the current hot topic. Companies can use this to motivate people. By doing a good job, professionals have an opportunity to work on the next challenge. Thus, through the challenge of the job or the attractive mission of the company, organizations can motivate people to perform.

•••

In practice, companies use a mixture of all of these practices: compensation, promotion, recognition, and job challenge. Certain items, such as job challenge, are probably best suited for professionals who are tackling interesting work. For salespeople, compensation and bonuses are particularly attractive. Naturally, the design of these reward systems is also driven by the strategy of the organization. We discuss this in later chapters when considering the multibusiness enterprise.

People

The people dimension of organization design focuses on choosing the skill sets and mind-sets that align with the company's strategy. For example, companies today are looking for data scientists who can extract insights from the vast amount of data that companies are collecting. When these companies expand internationally, they look for people who have international experience and global mind-sets. There is a continual search for the skill sets and mind-sets that match the strategy the company is trying to execute.

The tools that companies use for changing skill sets and mind-sets are recruiting, selection, development, rotations, and promotions. These are HR practices, but they're also the responsibility of the business leaders.

Three key practices characterize today's search for and development of talent. The first is "hire hard, manage easy." The expression is pretty straightforward: if you work hard on recruiting and selecting and get the right people in the door, then you're going to have more success with these people in performing their work.

First, you need to know who the right people are. Many organizations have studied the success of leaders in their company and traced the origins of where these people came from. They use that as a blueprint to seek out people with similar characteristics. For example, 3M is famous for hiring good engineers from solid schools in the Midwest. It searches for the number three, four, or five graduates of engineering schools from Iowa, Illinois, or Minnesota. The company has found that people who are number one in their class at, say, MIT or CalTech tend to have big egos and are often difficult to work with. But the third- or fourth-ranked engineer in the graduating class from, say, Purdue, is a good engineer who wants to do good product development. Cirque du Soleil is another example. It searches for gymnastic talent around the world and looks for the number four or five finisher in gymnastic events like the Olympics. If it chooses the number one or two person, it tends to get the big egos of people who have achieved a lot of fame. By choosing number four or five, Cirque du Soleil gets someone who is almost as good as number one but is a lot easier to work with and is still hungry.

So if you know the kind of people you're looking for, you work hard to find them and look for different ways of finding and recruiting them. For example, Quicken Loans has a lending program for mortgages. The recruiters go to T.G.I. Friday's and Houlihan's after work and observe the wait staff who serves them. The employees who are very friendly, outgoing, and attractive people are the ones whom they then recruit. This process of recruiting allows Quicken Loans to see people in action when they're not performing or faking any particular kind of behavior or answers to tests. It's a real situation that allows recruiters to find the kind of people they think are going to be good salespeople in their mortgage business.

Another example is the Mayo Clinic. A nurse who had eighteen years of experience wanted to work at the clinic and assumed she could walk right in the door and be hired. She was hired, but after about twelve interviews. The Mayo Clinic uses team interviews with a physician, a nurse, and an administrator to jointly interview applicants. There are multiple interviews and active communication between the interview teams. The process also includes behavioral interviews. If they're interviewing a physician, for example, and that person has a condescending attitude toward the administrator, that physician is not given an offer. The clinic knows the kind of people that it is looking for and goes to great lengths to find, select, and attract those people.

The second practice is called "hire for fit, train for skills." This means that organizations try to match the personality of the individual being recruited with the culture of the company. The features of a culture change very slowly, while technical skills and jobs change quite often. So rather than selecting for immediate technical skills and jobs, the first priority in selecting and recruiting individuals is the fit with the culture of the company. Certainly one would like employees to have good skills, but the thinking is that you can always train the individual. It is easier to fix a job-skills gap than it is to fix a person-culture mismatch.

Organizations that are most interested in people who fit with their culture are those that require collaborative types of behaviors. More and more companies are moving to matrix types of structures or multidimensional structures that we have touched on. Key to being effective at the interfaces of these multiple dimensions are people who can collaborate effectively with others. Today most matrix organizations are searching for this kind of individual.

The third practice, using rotational assignments, is probably the most difficult one to implement. Rotational assignments are crucial to developing people who will have a total perspective of an organization that has multiple dimensions. So, for example, the typical new employee at Procter & Gamble joins a function. Very often it's as a marketing specialist. The first job may be at the corporate headquarters, but then the person would be moved to a part of the marketing department in a global business unit, then to a customer team, and then on to a market development or regional organization. The strategic movement of people around the organization gives him or her a total perspective as to how the complex organization at Procter & Gamble actually works. These assignments also build managers' personal networks.

BMW is another company with an interesting type of career system. BMW calls it a "knight's move." Like knights on a chessboard, people move up and then they move over, up and over, up and over, and so on. In this way, managers get a multifunctional career. BMW still has specialists in corrosion and other engineering functions who stay put, but those who are targeted for leadership roles rotate from one function to another.

Rotational assignments today require special effort. It's best to make it known to people when they're hired that the company is seeking people who will take on international assignments. It's also good to have people make international moves early in their careers. Today's two-career couples make it more and more difficult to have these rotational assignments later in life. Some companies find ways to match the assignment with the timing in a person's life, when perhaps a spouse is between jobs or they have an empty nest. Other companies maintain a list of people who are interested in rotational assignments, but just not now. In any case, it's hard to find a successful organization that implements a matrix or a multidimensional structure that does not have an effective rotational assignment practice.

Summary

In this chapter, I've described the Star Model, the basis for thinking about organizations and organization design. I briefly described the strategy, the structure, information and decision processes, reward systems, and people practices that make up the design choices that a designer has. For each of these factors, I identified the tools to use in designing the structures and the information and decision processes and so forth. In the area of structure, we looked at the hierarchy of authority, the type of hierarchy, and the distribution of power. On the process dimension, we identified the informal processes, formal business processes, and management processes that an organization designer has available. Reward systems, another lever, consist of compensation, promotion, recognition, and job challenge. Under the people dimension are recruiting, selection, development, and so forth. These are all of the tools that leaders can use in designing their organization.

In the following chapters, I start with the strategy and then describe the kind of structures and processes used in these organizations and emphasize the structure and process side. I note reward systems and people practices less often because there are books and specialists in each of these areas where a more in-depth treatment can be found.

3

SINGLE-BUSINESS STRATEGY AND FUNCTIONAL ORGANIZATION

The functional organization is the most common of the organizational structures. In fact, all companies begin as functional organizations, whether it is Google in search, Apple in personal computers, or Amazon selling books online. Even when companies diversify or expand internationally, they maintain their functional structures as both a foundation and a key dimension of the organization. Other companies maintain their functional structures even as they grow. BMW is an 80 billion euro company that is managed through a functional organization. The reason is that it is a single business: a passenger car company. The factories, including the one in South Carolina, report to the vice president of manufacturing in Munich. The sales and marketing departments around the world all report to the vice president of sales and marketing in Munich. But they use cross-functional teams extensively for the 300 Series, the new 400 Series, the 500 Series, the 800 Series, and so on. It is the single-business strategy that shapes BMW's organization, not its size.

Other companies return to the functional structure after diversifying and creating divisional structures. Cisco started as a functional organization and then divided itself into three business units. It designed and sold routers and switches of different types to the telecom operators like AT&T, large-scale enterprises like Citibank, and many small and medium-sized enterprises. But in 2001 after the dot-com bust, when it lost $2.3 billion and laid off a large percentage of its workforce, it returned to its initial functional structure. The divisions had created three of everything. The functional structure permitted Cisco to consolidate and reduce the unnecessary duplication.

In this chapter, we begin the analysis of the functional organization. There are as many variations on the basic structure as there are single-business strategies. We begin with start-ups and small businesses and follow them as they grow into fully functional structures. We continue with three types of single-business strategies: cost-centric, product-centric, and customer-centric. Then we look at the concept of the lateral organization, which is used by many companies including BMW.

The Evolution from Start-Up

Companies do not actually start off as fully functional organizations; rather, they evolve into them. As start-ups, they begin with very little structure and organization and often with a few founders. Nike was founded by Phil Knight, a runner at Oregon, and his track coach, Bill Bowerman. Most running shoes at the time were made in Germany out of leather and metal spikes for traction. The two founders thought they could design better, cheaper running shoes and source them from Asia. Bill designed the shoes and Phil and some salespeople sold them. They opened a store in Santa Monica, California, and discovered that consumers liked the shoes. Good running shoes were also very comfortable. They added some fashion, and the business took off.

Today the model of a start-up is referred to as the lean start-up (Ries, 2011). This model avoids the practice whereby the founders have an idea, perfect that idea into a product, and then launch it. This practice requires a lot of upfront work prior to actually taking the product into the market. Instead, the lean start-up creates a bare-bones product and gets it in front of a customer or customers very quickly. It then gets a reaction to the product and redesigns it. It repeats this process until its leaders discover a viable product and a business model with which they can make money. The lean start-up process is a learning process that minimizes risk and uncertainty and engages customers in the actual product design. It's an iterative cocreation process.

The start-up, whether lean or traditional, has a minimal structure at this point. As a matter of fact, structures are probably an impediment, even an unnecessary evil, at this point. The organization consists of a small group of generalists who can move quickly. They can respond to new information and adjust their strategies appropriately while consuming a minimal amount of resources.

One of the realities of start-ups is that a new hardware or software product based on a new technology rarely hits the initial target market. As new information comes in, the organization is prepared to transition toward a new direction to follow what appears to be a newer, attractive market niche. The lean start-up people call this the *pivot*.

So the start-up organization is lean, it's fast reacting, it's customer driven, and it results in a viable product with minimal resources. And at this time when its leaders find an attractive product and business model, the revenue begins to arrive and the start-up begins to add people. At this point, they begin building an organization.

Initial Organization

The growth imperative also begins at this point. The company begins to move through its developmental stages. These first couple of stages are driven by size, however. Once a company attains the size of a couple or several hundred people, the future transitions are driven by the strategy.

Attaining this initial structure is often difficult. The reason is that transitions from one type of organization to another are often resisted by the founders. It's as if success at one stage leads to resistance to change to go to the next stage. People often like the initial stage with its small size and lack of formality. The founders like the original garage-like atmosphere that they believe is responsible for their initial success.

Many new companies resist change until a crisis forces it on them. One organization failed to build the necessary infrastructure until a crisis actually occurred. This company was a hardware product company that was successful with its initial product. Then management believed that they could grow faster if they shifted from outright sales of the product to a rental or a leasing model. They knew that this would slow their cash flow, so they arranged for the appropriate levels of financing. What they didn't anticipate was that the transition to a rental model meant that they would have to send an invoice to their customers every month. The result was a twelve-fold increase in the number of transactions going through their accounting system, which lacked the capacity to handle the increased volume. The result was a major slowdown in cash flow and a major crisis.

Many of these transitions are also painful. That is, the initial founders are often young people with no particular experience other than working on the product. Very quickly, they can get in over their heads as the sales volume increases and the number of people in the company grows. As these start-ups ramp up, jobs increase faster than the skills of the people. Sometimes one or more of the founders may need to be replaced. Again, it takes a crisis in order to force the other founders to replace their peers and move on to the next stage (Greiner, 1998).

These initial stages are driven primarily by rapid increase in size. As the number of people in the company increases, two things happen. First, larger numbers of people require an increase in the number of levels in the hierarchy, and so communication becomes a new challenge. The other major change is that greater size leads to a greater division of labor. Instead of generalists doing an activity, it is now possible to add two or three specialists. The discussion usually starts, "We need someone who knows something about ..." export sales, taxes and depreciation, or whatever other in-depth specialty the company requires to maintain its effectiveness. What the increased specialization does is increase interdependence. Rather than a single, self-contained task performed by a generalist, we now have a task that's performed by three or four specialists, all of whom need to coordinate their behavior.

The increase in size also creates a couple of barriers. One arises between levels. Communication becomes more difficult between workers and bosses. The second barrier crops up between departments. That is, engineers have difficulty communicating with marketing or salespeople; each has its own special language. Unless efforts are made to reduce these barriers, poor communication can often become a major impediment to continued growth.

The increase in size from a small start-up to a formal organization structure—a formal functional organization—takes place in two steps. The first is a transition from a system of personal and informal control to a system of more formal, impersonal control. As long as the number of people in an organization is fewer than 100 or 120 people, it is possible for everyone to know everyone else. You can use personal contact and personal control by assigning people to problems. When the size increases above 150 or 200 people, it is impossible to know everyone. At this point, formal processes and activities replace the informal processes. The company begins using tools to forecast demand, uses a budget, and adopts a company-wide salary structure. There are legal requirements too: the company can be sued for wrongful discharge or discrimination, so it starts to bring in people who have knowledge and experience in these formal activities.

The founders and the old-timers often resist the newcomer specialists. The old-timers prefer the small, garage-like atmosphere and the ability to turn quickly on a dime. They see the new formal controls as bureaucracy and impediments to their behavior, thus reducing their ability to respond. They don't typically embrace the controls as a foundation on which a larger enterprise can be built. Therefore, the transition from personal to impersonal is one of the changes that takes place in start-ups that successfully move on.

The second step is the conversion from a centralized hub-and-spoke system of decision making to a more decentralized, cross-functional team approach to making decisions. New products and services need to be managed differently from the existing and now mature products and services. Normally the founders maintain control through a hub-and-spoke kind of system. Under this model, all decisions, new employees hired, and expenditures must go through the founder. Size forces the company to decentralize some decisions because of the increased interdependence among specialists and the increase in the variety of existing and new types of products. Eventually the firm arrives at a more formal, functional organization structure.

The Functional Structure

The successful start-up becomes a small business and organizes itself around the functional structure. An example is Rovio, a Finnish company whose success began with the popular mobile game Angry Birds. In 2003, long before Angry Birds, three students at the Helsinki University of Technology entered a contest sponsored by Nokia and Hewlett-Packard to produce games. They won. Encouraged by this win, they formed a company called Relude, which was a studio to produce games. Meanwhile, their original contest-winning game was sold to another game company. The proceeds from that sale financed their start-up, Relude. Along the way, they received some funding from a business angel in 2005. At this point, they changed their name to Rovio, which is Finnish for "bonfire," and they introduced their famous Angry Birds game in December 2009 for the iPhone. The rest is history. The game has been downloaded over 1 billion times. It is the most-downloaded paid gaming application of all time.

Since then, Rovio has introduced a whole portfolio of Angry Bird games. Angry Bird Star Wars is the latest. Bad Piggies is an offshoot of Angry Birds. They've also expanded the business and are willing to sell other people's games, so Rovio will form partnerships with developers and distribute their games. Angry Birds has become a popular brand. They now license that brand to producers of merchandise like T-shirts, coffee cups, and key chains. There appears to be no limit to the possibilities.

Rovio has become a highly successful business. In 2011, the company raised another $42 million in venture capital and changed its name to Rovio Entertainment. In addition to video games for mobile devices, the company now also produces full-length cartoons and features for their various characters.

In 2013, Rovio became a company of some $200 million in revenue. It has 650 people, with studios in Helsinki, Stockholm, and Shanghai and has organized into a functional organization. That organization is shown in figure 3.1. The figure shows a chief executive officer, as one would expect, and then functions for R&D, marketing, operations, development, sales and strategic partnerships, as well as the normal support functions of the chief financial officer and chief legal officer.

The head of R&D, one of the three founders who wrote the original game, continues to look for new technologies and platforms, along with other ventures to continue developing Rovio's products. The chief marketing officer is now in charge of the Angry Birds brand and how it's used in various media promotions. Rovio also has a channel on YouTube through which it conducts most of its promotions.

Figure 3.1 Rovio Functional Structure

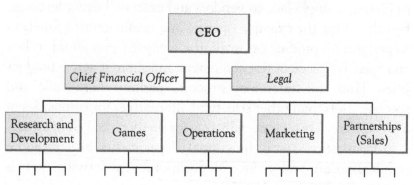

io continues to grow and is similar to Walt Disney. That is, it bases growth around the intellectual property of its characters, in this case, Angry Birds and perhaps some additional ones in the future. It also takes Angry Birds into various games, cartoons, publications, and publishing; the YouTube channel; and licensing of merchandising. It sells advertising where advertisers can insert an ad into an Angry Bird game of various types.

Rovio thus began from a single product—a game—and turned itself into an entertainment company that profits from the intellectual property of its characters. It has become a single-business functional organization. In June 2013, Rovio hired a chief operating officer who was previously an executive at Nokia. With this addition, Rovio is continuing its developmental journey by acquiring a leader who has the knowledge and experience about how large companies operate.

Now we can see why it is that companies that are single-business start-ups all begin as functional organizations. The reason is that the functional organization provides several advantages. First, gathering together all workers of one type—R&D people, for example—allows them to transfer ideas, knowledge, and contacts among themselves. Second, it allows them to achieve a greater level of specialization. When two hundred or so software engineers are pooled, the company can afford to dedicate a subset of engineers to such specialties as programming for the iPhone and Android. Third, using the example of a single purchasing function in operations, pooling the workers allows the company to present a single face to vendors and exercise buying leverage. Fourth, taking the example of using one manufacturing function to perform all production work, the company can afford to buy an expensive piece of test equipment and share it across product lines. Thus the functional structure permits more scale and specialization than other structural alternatives for companies of a certain size. This is especially true for smaller-sized companies.

Organizations with functional departments also promote standardization and reduce duplication. An activity that is organized functionally is performed in the same way and (presumably) in the best way throughout the company. The functions adopt one system or one policy for everyone rather than have each department invent its own. The functions adopt a single computer system, inventory control policy, absenteeism policy, and so on. Companies like Cisco often revert to the functional structure to reduce the proliferation and duplication of systems, standards, and policies that result when independent units do not manage to share or cooperate.

Every organization structure has its strengths, but it also has weaknesses. The functional organization has two weaknesses that frequently lead to the adoption of alternative structures. The first becomes apparent if a company has a variety of products, services, channels, and customers. In chapter 1 I described Dell Computer, which used a functional structure in its early days when it designed and sold laptops and desktops. Dell changed its structure after adding product lines for desktop printers, storage, low-end servers, and computer services. This kind of variety overwhelms the decision-making capacity of the general manager and the functional leadership team. Thus, Dell, like other companies in similar situations, abandoned the single functional structure.

The functional organization is best at managing a single product or service line. When strategies involve product or service diversification and market segmentation, the functional organization is either changed by organizing departments around products and markets or enhanced by introducing lateral processes. (The latter are described in chapters 4 and 5.)

The other weakness of the functional structure is the barriers created between different functions, inhibiting cross-functional processes such as new product development. When a company has only one product line (which does not change often) and when long product development cycles are feasible, the functional organization can manage the cross-functional processes and simultaneously deliver scale, expertise, and efficiency. But product variety, customization, short product life cycles, and rapid product development times overwhelm the functional structure. The strategy of product variety is first handled with lateral processes like cross-functional product teams before a company evolves into fully structured product divisions.

Thus, the functional organization is appropriate for small companies and for those that need proprietary expertise and scale. It is appropriate if product and market variety is small and product life and development cycles are long. It is declining in popularity as a basic structure because in many industries, speed is more important than scale, and responsiveness to variety from any source is a condition for survival. And where scale is important, it is possible to outsource the scale activity. But the functional structure is always present as an overlay or matrix on top of other structures.

Types of Single-Business Strategies

Not all single-business strategies are alike. Different single-business strategies lead to different types of functional organizations. Michael Porter (1985) identified two types of business strategies: low cost and differentiation. Using the differentiated strategy, a company pursues low costs but invests in brands, new products, and other features to differentiate the business from competitors. Later, Treacy and Wiersema (1997) described two ways to differentiate a business: customer intimacy and product leadership. In this section, I describe the organizations that are designed to execute the low cost or operational excellence strategy and the product-centric and customer-centric strategies.

Operational Excellence. A company pursues the operational excellence strategy when it strives to become the low-cost provider in its industry. Southwest Airlines and Jet Blue try to be the lowest-cost airlines, and Walmart and Dollar Stores try to be the lowest-cost retailers. In so doing, these companies pursue the lowest-cost policies and most efficient practices in everything that they do. They organize around the functional structure and build scale and expertise in all activities. A complete and completely aligned Star Model is shown in table 3.1. It is clear from the table that the organization design is a holistic and low-cost model.

Product-Centric. A product-centric strategy is one where a company tries to find as many customers as possible for its product. The best example is the pharmaceutical companies that search for a blockbuster drug. The ideal is to get a patent monopoly for a number of years (twelve to fifteen). Pfizer had such a position with Lipitor. At its peak, Lipitor was a $12 billion per year product. Most food companies also pursue branded food products that are unique, like FiberOne bars and V8 Fusion drinks. A complete and completely aligned Star Model for a product-centric company is shown in table 3.2.

Nike began as a company designing and manufacturing running shoes, then expanded into a full line of running shoes. Next it diversified into basketball shoes, soccer shoes, tennis shoes, women's fitness shoes, and so on. It became a multiproduct, but single-business athletic shoe company. It was organized as a functional organization with cross-functional product teams for each type of athletic shoe. The management focus at Nike was all about new products. Managers spent a good deal of energy on the new product development process, competitive products, new features, customer insights, and new materials for products. They tried to differentiate themselves from competitors by offering better, newer, and more comfortable shoes.

Customer-Centric. A customer-centric company tries to find as many products and services as possible for its customers. An example is a private bank. A private banker will offer stocks, bonds, options, real estate investment trusts, foreign exchange

Table 3.1 The Cost-Centric Organization

	Cost-Centric Company	
STRATEGY	Goal	Lowest total cost
	Main offering	An acceptable product at the lowest price
	Value creation route	No-frills offering for the middle of the market
	Most important customer	The value shopper
	Priority setting basis	Find the most efficient way to do everything
	Pricing	Guaranteed lowest price or everyday low price
STRUCTURE	Organizational concept	Strong centralized functions to standardize, economize, and achieve scale
PROCESSES	Most important process	Order-to-cash
		All transaction processes are efficiently reengineered
REWARDS	Measures	• Detailed measures of all costs
		• Total delivered cost
		• Constant improvement and cost reduction
PEOPLE	Approach to personnel	Power to discoverers of how to use scale and leverage
		• Highest rewards to the discoverers of cost reduction ideas
		• Best fit is the frugal person who prefers Motel 6
	Mental process	Lean thinking: *How to eliminate time, waste, cost?*
	Sales bias	Anything that increases constant, level volume
	Culture	Constant search for improvement of costs through eliminating waste and variety and implementing repeatable processes

Table 3.2 The Product-Centric Versus Customer-Centric Organization

		Product-Centric Company	*Customer-Centric Company*
STRATEGY	Goal	Best product for customer	Best solution for customer
	Main offering	New Products	Personalized packages of products, service, support, education, consulting
	Value creation route	Cutting-edge products, useful features, new applications	Customizing for best total solution
	Most important customer	Most advanced customer	Most profitable, loyal customer
	Priority setting basis	Portfolio of products	Portfolio of customers—customer profitability
	Pricing	Price to market	Price for value, risk
STRUCTURE	Organizational concept	Product profit centers, product reviews, product teams	Customer segments, customer teams, customer P&Ls
PROCESSES	Most important process	New product development	Customer relationship management and solutions development
REWARDS	Measures	• Number of new products • Percent of revenue from products less than two years old • Market share	• Customer share of most valuable customers • Customer satisfaction • Lifetime value of a customer • Customer retention

(continued)

Table 3.2 (*Continued*)

		Product-Centric Company	Customer-Centric Company
PEOPLE	Approach to personnel	Power to people who develop products • Highest reward is working on next most challenging product • Manage creative people through challenges with a deadline	Power to people with in-depth knowledge of customer's business • Highest rewards to relationship managers who save the customer's business
	Mental process	Divergent thinking: *How many possible uses of this product?*	Convergent thinking: *What combination of products is best for this customer?*
	Sales bias	On the side of the seller in a transaction	On the side of the buyer in a transaction
	Culture	New product culture: open to new ideas, experimentation	Relationship management culture: searching for more customer needs to satisfy

trades, private equity opportunities, and many other products to the wealthy customers. The banker will also offer competitors' products if they suit customers' needs better than the bank's own products. Private bankers do not work on commission and do not churn customers' accounts. Instead of a commission, they receive around 1 percent of the assets that the customer has on deposit with them. The banker's incentive—along with the customer's—is to grow the assets, so the bankers' and the customers' interests are aligned.

The private bank is a functional organization. It is segmented by the net worth of their customers. The bankers work on a relationship model rather than a transactional model.

•••

All three of these single-business strategies use a functional organization structure. The cost-centric strategy uses the pure functional structure like the container companies shown in table 1.1. They invest in no other organizational units. The product- and customer-centric strategy companies invest in cross-functional teams for new products and customer segments. They are organized like the food and plastics companies shown in table 1.1. They make extensive use of the lateral organization. We now turn to the types of lateral coordination mechanisms that companies use to coordinate across functions.

The Lateral Organization

Most of the activity in an organization does not follow the vertical hierarchical structure. As continuous change becomes the natural state in most industries, lateral processes become the principal means of coordinating activities.

Lateral processes are information and decision processes that coordinate activities spread out across different organizational units, providing mechanisms for decentralizing general management decisions. They accomplish the decentralization by recreating the organization in microcosm for the issue at hand. That is, each department with information about—and a stake in—an issue contributes a representative for issue resolution, as shown in figure 3.2.

No matter what type of hierarchical structure is chosen, many activities require coordination across departments. Most organizations deal with a complex world. They do business with multiple customers, multiple partners, and multiple suppliers.

Figure 3.2 Lateral Processes Across Functions

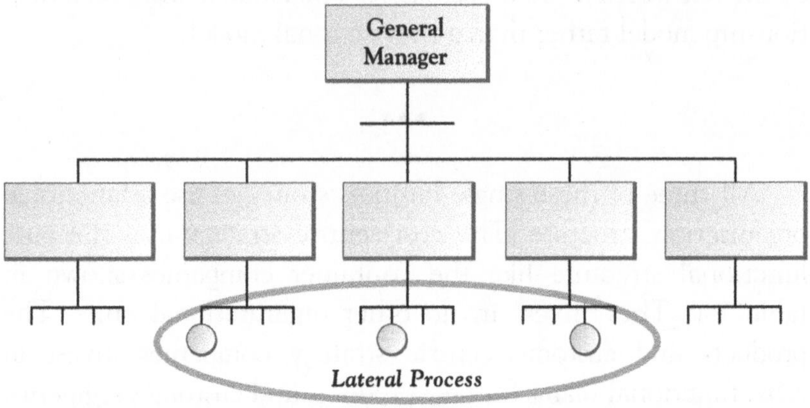

They compete with rivals in many areas of the world. They deal with governments, regulators, distributors, labor unions, and trade associations. They employ different skill specialties and use multiple technologies while producing a variety of products and services. If a company creates an organization to maximize its effectiveness in dealing with one constituency—for example, customers—it fragments its ability to deal with others—for example, vendors. All the dimensions not handled by the structure require coordination through lateral management processes.

These other dimensions are increasing in number and importance. In addition to focusing on more powerful and knowledgeable customers, a company must leverage its own buying power, concentrate its R&D investments on its leading technologies and core competencies, and become a good citizen in regions where active host governments negotiate relationships. Companies must focus simultaneously on governments, customers, functions, vendors, and products. Lateral processes are designed to provide the company with the networks and capability for addressing all of these concerns. Today a company must create a multidimensional organization built around its basic structure. A company must be flexible in addressing whatever unpredictable issue arises, whether it presents a threat or an opportunity.

Lateral Coordination

The organization designer must match the amount of lateral coordination needed to execute a multidimensional strategy with different types and amounts of lateral processes. To learn how to match coordination needs and lateral processes, let us examine a single-business functional structure and its cross-functional lateral processes. The functional structure is the most common organizational structure. (For a discussion of lateral processes across subsidiaries and business units, see Galbraith, 1994b, 2000.)

The management challenge for a functional organization is to coordinate the cross-functional work flows and common contact points with customers, suppliers, and other shared constituencies as indicated in figure 3.3. Coordination across functions—to create and deliver products or services—is the responsibility of the general manager and the functional management team. As mentioned in chapter 1, this coordination is most easily accomplished when the company produces a single line of products or services

Figure 3.3 Work Flows Across a Functional Structure

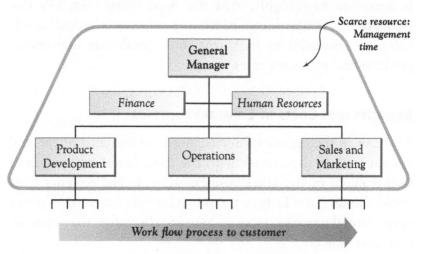

for a single customer type and when product life and development cycles are long.

But the need for lateral coordination will exceed the capacity of the team at the top when a company's strategies and tasks involve the following:

- Diversity and variety
- Rapid and unpredictable change
- Interdependence between functional units

To deal with these forces, management may have to change the entire structure of an organization. Another alternative is to enlist lateral processes, which may be thought of as "general manager equivalents." These processes offer a more subtle approach to decentralizing decisions and increasing decision-making capacity. The types and amounts of lateral processes used will vary depending on the relative importance of the three organizational shapers, as discussed in chapter 1. Collectively these three forces determine the need for cross-functional coordination and the correlating amount of cross-functional lateral processes. It is important to recognize that the need varies from low (for companies manufacturing beer or producing classical music titles, for example) to high (for those producing multimedia products and rap music titles).

Benefits and Costs of Lateral Processes

The task of the organization designer is to match the type and amount of lateral processes with the cross-functional coordination required by the firm's business strategy. The designer must avoid choosing too little or too much lateral processing. Up to a point, lateral processes produce benefits; thereafter, they increase costs and difficulty.

The benefits of lateral processes involve permitting the company to make more decisions, different kinds of decisions, and better and faster decisions. Because these processes decentralize general management decisions, they free up top management for other decisions. Thus they increase the capacity of the organization to make more decisions more often, and the organization is more adaptable to constant change. Different types of decisions are made and can address the multiple dimensions of a business environment. Companies decentralize choice to the points of product and customer contact where decisions can be made and implemented quickly because these groups may have access to current and local information available only to them.

A business may have a functional structure, but by enlisting lateral processes, it becomes capable of forming new product teams, customer teams, and process teams for reengineering. The business is therefore flexible, no matter the issue at hand.

Lateral processes can also create costs. The decentralized decisions may not be better than those of top management, for example, and the people at the front lines may not have the perspective and experience of top management. These costs can be minimized, however, by making the organization's total database available, training people, and providing the correct incentives.

Another cost is the time of the people involved. With today's flat and lean hierarchical structures, employee time is at a premium. Time spent on a reengineering team is time not spent with customers or developing new people. The more time spent on teams, the greater the cost is. Lateral processes can be seen as investments of management time to create shorter cycle times.

The third cost comes in increased level of conflict. Cross-functional teams are made up of representatives who see issues differently. Much of the time involved in cross-functional processes is devoted to communicating, problem solving, and resolving conflicts. The company that is skilled at conflict resolution can lower the costs and time needed to reach decisions.

Thus, the designer needs to find the point of balance between the benefits and costs of lateral processes. This balance can be struck by matching coordination needs with the different types and amounts of lateral processes.

The Five Types of Lateral Processes

There are five basic types of lateral processes, as shown in figure 3.4. They vary in the amount of management time and energy that must be invested in them.

Informal or *voluntary* lateral processes occur spontaneously. They are the least expensive and easiest form to use. Although they occur naturally, organization designers can greatly improve the frequency and effectiveness of these voluntary processes.

E-coordination involves using Internet and social technology to communicate and coordinate across departments. These electronic links may combine the efforts of people working on a new product using three-dimensional computer-aided design, now called product life cycle management, or serving the same customer using customer relationship management processes.

Figure 3.4 Types of Lateral Processes

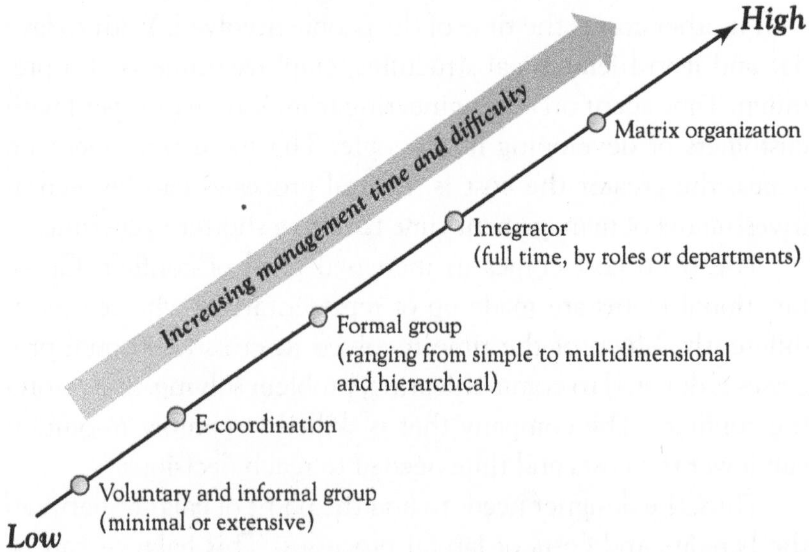

Today much can be accomplished through social technologies like Yammer.

The next type of lateral process, which requires more time commitment, is the *formal group*. Teams or task forces are formally created, members appointed, charters defined, and goals set for the cross-functional effort. Formal groups are more costly than voluntary groups because they are the creation of management and do not occur naturally. They require some team building and maintenance for proper functioning. Formal groups are also more costly because they are used in addition to the voluntary groups, not instead of them. The organization needs both voluntary efforts and formal groups to supplement the general manager's coordination across functions. The simpler forms are still needed but are insufficient by themselves to achieve the integration the strategy requires.

The fourth level of commitment to lateral processes comes with appointment of *integrators* to lead the formal groups. At some point, full-time leaders may be required. Leaders may be product managers, project managers, process managers, brand managers, and so on. They are all "little general managers," who manage a product or service in place of the general manager. They are enlisted because there are many products, new products, and rapid life cycles.

Using integrators is the most costly lateral process. In addition to the cumulative costs of the voluntary processes and the formal groups that must already be in place, integrators require hiring a group of full-time people whose task is to integrate the efforts of others. The integrator role is also the most difficult to execute. Integrators introduce confusion over roles and responsibilities and add an element of conflict. However, the cost and difficulty may be judged appropriate because the strategy requires functional excellence and rapid generation of new products or services.

The last and most difficult form of lateral process is the *matrix organization*. To create a matrix, the integrator role becomes a line organizational position. The person in the functions who works on the products or project team acquires a second boss. The company then has two line organizations. The matrix is used only when there is a need for a power balance. The R&D function, for example, is typically organized around projects and functions in a matrix model. (For a complete description of matrix organization designs, see Galbraith, 2009.)

The organization designer must match a company's cross-functional coordination requirements with the appropriate types and amounts of lateral processes. Figure 3.5 illustrates how the three shaping forces create a need for varying levels of lateral processes.

The remainder of this chapter describes how the organization designer can foster voluntary processes and e-coordination. The other types of lateral processes—formal groups, integrators, and matrix organizations—are discussed in depth in chapter 4.

Fostering Voluntary Processes

An organization characterized by voluntary coordination across units is usually referred to as an informal organization because the

Figure 3.5 Matching Coordination Needs with Lateral Processes

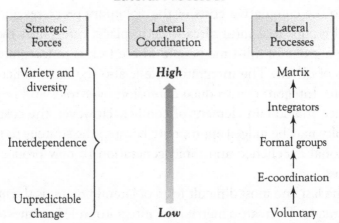

process seems to occur naturally and spontaneously. For example, a discussion between a salesperson and a customer leads to an idea for a product change. The salesperson and an engineer make a preliminary design. The design is sent to operations and marketing for their ideas. A new product modification results a few weeks later, all because of the voluntary cooperation of people in different units.

Such acts may occur hundreds of times each day and can be a source of great strength for the company. But great weakness occurs when the voluntary acts do not happen. In many cases, these acts do not occur because of cross-functional barriers.

Today there is great interest in removing barriers and encouraging voluntary cooperation. Leaders can employ a number of actions to elicit voluntary cooperation:

- Interdepartmental rotation
- Interdepartmental events
- Colocation
- Mirror-image departments
- Consistent reward and measurement systems

All of these forms of activity create networks of relationships. People cooperate voluntarily when they have relationships with people in other departments and are comfortable working with them.

Interdepartmental Rotation. The most powerful tool of the organization designer for creating voluntary lateral processes is the interdepartmental assignment of key people. Rotational assignments have two important effects. First, they train and develop people in all facets of the business. People who are successful at rotational assignments learn how to learn; they do not simply gain the specific knowledge of the business. The rotated managers can more effectively participate in cross-functional teams, can chair the teams, and grow into integrators. Rotations create generalists and the general management capability that is at the heart of lateral processes. Individuals become more flexible, and if we are to create flexible organizations, we need flexible people. These people also develop relationships in the various departments, which then can be used later in lateral coordination attempts.

Thus, rotational assignments create a lateral communication network across the company (see Galbraith, 1994b). Taken together, the trained individuals and the relationships they have cultivated create the organizational capability for lateral coordination. Rotational experiences simultaneously develop the individuals and build their relationships, thereby developing the voluntary organization. The task of the organization designer is to make sure that relationships are created at key work flow interfaces where coordination is required.

However, rotations also create costs. People are less effective when they are learning new roles. When managers are reluctant to give up good people and train newcomers, effort and time from the leader is needed to keep the rotation process in motion. When filling an international position with an expat rather than someone from the local area, the costs are two to three times as much. But the cost of rotations should realistically be considered an investment instead of an expense as it develops individuals, creates a network of relationships, and builds a flexible, lateral capability.

Interdepartmental Events. Voluntary processes also result from events such as training courses and conferences. Indeed, training budgets are as justified by their networking effects as by their developmental effects. The organization designer needs only to decide who should attend. Also, like rotational assignments, events are most effective when they create relationships across the key work flow interfaces.

The importance of training in strategy provides an opportunity for developing people and the organization's networks.

When companies rely on informal, voluntary cooperation and e-coordination, the people need to know and participate in the creation of the company's strategy and priorities. Training in and participation in the strategy is a great way of preparing people with direct customer contact to know how to serve customers appropriately.

Colocation. Proximity of employees is an important factor in fostering productive relationships. There is good evidence that reducing distance and physical barriers between people increases the amount of communication between them. Engineering firms colocate everyone working on a project. As projects come and go, the firms reconfigure the organization and the office layouts.

The organization designer needs to give careful thought to location patterns. For example, if a marketing group is located close to an operations group, perhaps it is not located close to engineering. Once again, the designer needs to know the key interfaces where communication is most necessary and relationships most likely to be productive.

Mirror-Image Departments. One of the greatest barriers to lateral processes is the sheer number of interfaces across which people must communicate to gain a consensus for action. Usually each function organizes according to its own logic. For example, in one consumer packaged goods company, over twenty interfaces would have to be worked for a salesperson and an engineer to modify a product. The sales function is organized by geography, marketing by brands, manufacturing by site and process, engineering by product, purchasing by commodity, and vendor. It would take an engineer an unrealistic amount of time to communicate with and gain support from each function.

In response, some companies have organized their functions as mirror images of one another. Figure 3.6 shows how an airplane manufacturer has organized each function around major sections of the aircraft. A manager of the wing, for example, has

Figure 3.6 Mirror-Image Functional Structure

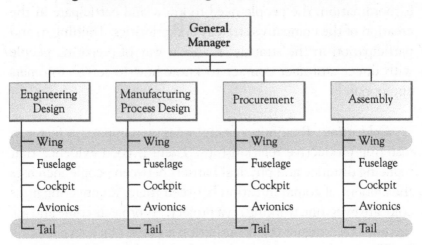

an interface in each other function. Each person has to work only five or six interfaces in order to get complete support. These five or six people can form the equivalent of a general manager for the wing, tail, avionics, and so on. Decisions can be decentralized to these groups, with each group assuming end-to-end responsibility for its section of the aircraft. It is an easy next step to formalize the group and have it set group goals for cycle time, quality, and cost improvements.

The mirror-image structure creates a clear line of sight across the entire organization. It can facilitate the establishment of relationships by simplifying the interfaces across which lateral processes take place. The managers get to know one another and spend less communication time getting an end-to-end commitment to a decision. The likelihood of voluntary cooperation is much higher.

However, there is a cost to this structure. It is tantamount to organizing by product or process at the level below the functional manager. It creates the costs that are associated with those structures, such as loss of scale, duplication, and so on. Often the costs are accepted in order to get the coordination and cycle time reduction. Or the designer can create a hybrid structure within the function.

Consistent Reward and Measurement Systems. One of the keys to creating voluntary processes across units is to align the interests of the parties involved. Often, functional measurements designed independently of each other create incompatible goals, causing another barrier to cross-functional cooperation. A task of the leader is to test for cross-unit consistency of goals and to design supporting reward systems. Performance measurement and reward systems are useful tools for creating aligned goals and objectives. Often a common goal, like cycle time reduction, can apply across all functions, or there may be a customer for the cross-functional work. The group can start with what the customer wants in order to generate measurement criteria. But in any case, clear and consistent measures, goals, and correlated rewards are needed to promote voluntary cooperation across units.

E-Coordination

The potential of Internet technology—and now social technologies—for linking previously independent departments is approaching realization. Although the use of social technologies inside companies lags their use outside the organization, there are some positive examples. There are also some lessons learned.

E-Coordination with Mobile Devices and a Service Contract on the Web. International Service Systems (ISS) is the largest provider of cleaning, security, and catering services in Europe. Recently it has been signing national and regional agreements with customers who outsource these services to it. In one national agreement a UK manufacturer has outsourced its cleaning to ISS at all of its UK sites. It is a customized agreement for cleaning. For example, the offices are to be cleaned every night with special attention to PCs and keyboards. The back hallways and fire escapes are cleaned once a month, and reception areas and conference rooms are to be cleaned on demand. This contract and its application to various sites is placed on the ISS website. It is accessible to the cleaning crews by wireless mobile devices.

The cleaning crews check their assignments and the cleaning criteria that apply to the areas assigned to them. When an area is complete, a sign-off signal is sent and registered at the website. Any comments can be noted. The site supervisor and national account manager can observe whether all areas at all sites have been serviced. The next day the customer site managers register their satisfaction with ISS's performance and give the crews a score. The site supervisors' and account managers' bonuses are determined by this score.

The on-demand cleaning is also registered on the website. When a request is registered on the site, an alert is sent to the cell phone of the site supervisor, who calls the crews. Some crews are cross-trained to provide cleaning, catering, and security services so that there is a quick response capability. Other requests can be registered as well. For example, say Prince Charles and members of the press will visit a factory in Southampton on Friday afternoon. The highest level of cleaning is needed on all areas of his tour. In this manner, the website coordinates the behavior of various crews at multiple sites throughout the day.

Social Technologies. The McKinsey Global Institute (2012) predicts some substantial increases in productivity that will result from a shift to using social technologies. The gains will result from a shift from one-to-one channels of communication (e-mail and phones) to many-to-many channels (social media). Their study shows that the use of e-mail and short message service declines when people use Facebook and Twitter. In addition, McKinsey suggests that a huge amount of company knowledge is locked up in peoples' e-mail inboxes, which are not searchable.

Making this content and expertise available to everyone would be valuable. Surveys support this optimistic view (McKinsey Global Institute, 2012; Kiron, Palmer, Phillips, and Berkman, 2013). Large percentages of managers see a bright future for technologies, but everyone sees some current barriers.

A number of companies have already seen that installing Yammer and Chatter and then mandating their use does not work. Social technologies are voluntary, bottom-up processes. They are not top-down installations like SAP. One company tried incentives. All managers were to make five posts per week to the company's social network. Naturally the company got their five weekly posts from each manager, but they were of dubious value. Many organizations are repeating the mistakes of the past. Before, they installed software systems and assumed people would use them as intended. UPS has launched a social networking platform that allows drivers, packers, and managers to post comments, questions and ideas about health and safety (Schectman, 2013). The company is encouraging feedback and wants "constructive dissatisfaction." The Teamsters union is not supporting the new platform. They say that a grievance procedure is already in place for these dissatisfactions. The union says there are multiple complaints and ideas in the system. They believe management just does not want to spend the money. Instead, the company replicates online all of the company's dysfunctional behavior offline. If there are silos between functions offline, there will be silos online too. For these reasons, the adoption of social media outside organizations is much faster than its adoption inside the company.

There are some successes. When implementation is part of a change program, social technology can succeed. Consultants advise that success can be achieved by selecting a process like "order to cash" and then set some goals like "ten days cycle time." When people are trained, leaders participate, daily improvements are widely reported, and people join in. Some companies try to make it fun. People vote for the most innovative idea for change or which posts resulted in the most learning. Prizes and badges can be given to the winners of the vote.

Another example is the experience of a marketing head in a business unit of a global company. The marketing executive wanted to share information and ideas about products and promotions in real time over the company's social platform. Many of his peers were not interested, however. There was no history of sharing, many of the marketing heads did not know one another, and many saw no value in the initiative. The marketing executive nevertheless did not give up. He called a face-to-face meeting with all of his peers to debate the issue, get to know one another, and plan some next steps. It took some support from IT and the analytics group, but eighteen months later, the collaborative network was up and running. This is a good example of the time and energy it takes to create a network to serve business purposes when the current culture is not supportive.

The social platform created by GE's Colab receives a lot of attention. It was built internally and uses a lot of the software from Facebook and Twitter, so many people are familiar with the system. It was created to be GE-wide in scope and to be used by all levels of management. The designers launched Colab in January 2012 by getting GE's "power users" to use it. Following the concepts of the agile software development, they released a minimally designed system. Then, on the basis of feedback from users, they added features. They still release updates every two weeks as they link Colab to other systems like Salesforce.com and Chatter. Users can go to these other systems and not leave the Colab platform. More people join with each new added feature. As of spring 2013, about half of GE's 300,000 employees were users.

GE has an advantage. When Jack Welch was the CEO, he launched an initiative to create a culture of boundarylessness. Colab can therefore enable self-organizing activities more easily. One example is the Australian country manager who initiated a mining network across GE's businesses and regions. Starting with informal teams, the network addressed common customer problems over social platforms. The network is now addressing product and services and is becoming a complete mining business network.

The social platforms can become more powerful when combined with employee network analysis (Cross and Thomas, 2009). Using network analyses, organization designers can visualize networks throughout the company. They can see the group of people who spend time on the Walmart account, for example, or who contribute to a particular new product. The organization designer can see holes in the network where conversation should be happening but isn't. Then working like the marketing manager described above, the organization designer can introduce people, make connections, and get them active on the social platform. In this way, partially formed networks that have been self-organized can be completed and strengthened by some organization design tools.

Not surprisingly, all of the articles claim that social networks will not be successful without top management support. The sophistication of social platforms at Dell is attributed to Michael Dell's active participation in them. There is also a person in charge of social networks in the communications function. At GE, a manager was appointed to a position as the new head of a business unit. He had been active on Colab in his old job. But he found that only thirty people in his new unit were on Colab, so he started communicating with them through Colab. Now about eight hundred of his more than one thousand employees use Colab. Clearly the usage becomes contagious when the leaders start using the social platforms.

In summary, it appears that social platforms can become powerful enablers of the informal organization. Organization design can help forge networks with network analysis tools and the building of relationships among network participants. In other cases, champions like the Australian country manager are needed, along with an organizational change initiative to support them, as in the case of the marketing manager.

Summary

In this chapter I described the origins of the functional organization from start-up to a full-fledged single-business strategy. A variety of single-business strategies and a corresponding variety of functional organizations are needed to implement those strategies. Some businesses are cost-centric, some are product-centric, and others are customer-centric. In the case of the latter two types, the functional structure is challenged by the variety of products and market segments. As a product-centric company grows, it often needs to reorganize into product divisions. But in order to ensure a smooth transition, it uses cross-functional product teams. This type of lateral organization is also used for cross-functional segment teams. Lateral capabilities are important in all types of organizations to coordinate the requirements from a variety of stakeholders and initiatives that companies must satisfy. Finally, I introduced the concept of the informal organization. Social networking platforms are particularly good at enabling this form of informal, lateral organization. Organization designers, using network analysis, can enhance self-organizing networks to include people who would not otherwise be included but are necessary for implementing a particular task. The next chapter addresses the more formal types of lateral processes.

4

DESIGNING THE LATERAL ORGANIZATION

In this chapter, we complete the design of the lateral organization, which is used in all types of organizations, and apply these lateral designs to single-business strategies that require them. The voluntary processes described in chapter 3 arise spontaneously; they are a form of organization from the bottom up. With formal lateral processes, the leader is more directly involved in the creation, staffing, funding, and setting of goals. Thus, there is more organization from the top down.

There are several reasons for a more active role by the leader in the design of the lateral processes. If an issue arises and no voluntary process forms in response, management must create a group to deal with the issue. Management, from its perspective, may in fact become aware of an issue before it even appears to be an issue at the lower levels of the organization. Or management may want to augment or modify a voluntary process already in existence.

From a more global perspective, management shapes a lateral process to make it more compatible with other efforts, resources and priorities, and the overall strategy. For example, at the grassroots level, an issue may be seen as a sales and marketing problem, while from management's viewpoint, the issue may be larger, involving operations as well. Thus, management may want to increase or change membership in a cross-functional team. It may add a person who would profit from the experience or an experienced person who could commit more resources.

Finally, management must set priorities about the types and amount of lateral processes it wishes to undertake. With limited resources, a company cannot simultaneously undertake product, customer, process, vendor, and twenty-five improvement teams at the same level of the organization. Management must set priorities about where talent and other resources need to be invested. These priorities should set the strategic direction and focus the organization.

In this chapter, we complete the discussion of the five lateral forms. First, I discuss the group or team designs, which vary from simple to complex multidimensional designs. The integrator or team leader role is important. The power and authority of the role vary from a lightweight to heavyweight position. The integrator becomes a powerful equivalent to the line management role when dual authority is attained. The dual focus becomes the matrix organization.

Formal Groups

Formal groups augment the efforts of voluntary processes. When there is a need for more decision making, a team, task force, or council is created to focus on a set of issues. However, rather than being a substitute for voluntary processes, formal groups are used in addition to them and, indeed, build on the same capabilities. There are some important design issues.

Design of Formal Groups

All groups, no matter what type, are subject to the same design choices.

Bases. The bases for lateral processes are the same as the bases for structure, that is, function, product, market, geography, channel, and so on. If one is chosen for the structure, the others are candidates for lateral processes. Each candidate has the same positives and negatives as the structural type. Just as strategy drives the choice of structure, it should help set the priorities here. The organization designer should also decide how much time and effort should be devoted to each.

Charter. The scope, mission, and authority of the groups must be defined. What issues are to be addressed? What resource levels can the group commit? Management should define the groups' charters so that they are compatible with the charter of the hierarchical structure and supplement it. In addition, management should look for overlapping efforts among various groups and define conflict resolution processes.

Staffing. The people who participate in a group are central to its efficient functioning. A representative should be chosen from each affected unit. All should have a position within their unit that gives them access to the information relevant to the issues they will address and the authority to commit their unit. If the group is to be a unit making decisions in reasonable time frames, members must possess both information and authority. The roles created by mirror-image structures are ideal for this purpose.

The mirror-image structure also creates roles in which the manager's job in the vertical hierarchy is consistent with the job in the lateral processes. A less-than-ideal situation is when the managers of a company are spread across thirty to thirty-five teams, each one with four or five team assignments in addition to a full-time job. Very little will be accomplished in these teams. Organization designers should strive to staff groups so that managers are given only one or two cross-functional team assignments. Furthermore, the team assignment should have as much overlap as possible with the full-time job.

Conflict. Conflict management is a required skill in an ever-changing world. The group needs a way to manage the inevitable differences in points of view constructively. Individual members need group problem-solving and conflict management skills. The purpose is to use different points of view to stimulate information exchange and learning. Although each member will see a portion of a situation, the group problem solving will afford a total view.

Rewards. Participants will have little energy for confronting conflict and solving problems if they perceive little reward resulting from their efforts. Therefore, their team performance should count as much as their line job performance in evaluations. The team performance component can be gauged from the meeting of team goals such as cycle time and evaluations of other team members or of the team leader.

Leader Role. There is an emerging view that teams may not need a formal leader. And indeed, for groups with a reasonable number of members and some self-management experience, a designated leader may not be required. Instead, a different leader will emerge depending on the issue at hand and those in the group most capable to handle it. Most organizations, however, designate a leader to plan agendas, convene the group, lead discussions, and communicate the group's decisions.

Rather than creating a full-time integrator role, a leader may be chosen from the function most affected by the group task or from a dominant function. Boeing design-and-build teams are led by design engineers; Procter & Gamble brand teams are led by marketing brand managers. In both cases, the natural work closely resembles that of the leadership task.

Another option is a rotating leader: the leader changes as the function most affected changes with each successive stage of the group's work. For example, Dow-Corning rotates the leadership of new product teams. Initially the leader comes from R&D, then from manufacturing, and eventually from marketing as the product nears distribution. Over the product development cycle, the group gets a general management leader, but through sequential handoffs from one function to another.

Simple Group Structures

The design of lateral group structures can vary from simple ones that have only a few cross-functional product teams to complex multidimensional and multilevel structures. The coordination needs of the strategy dictate how complex a form is necessary.

The use of simple teams has been a management strategy since aerospace companies began using cross-functional teams in the 1960s. Today companies are focusing on work flows and creating cross-functional work flow teams to gain speed and reengineer processes.

In all simple structures, the designer tries to create ah end-to-end task so that the team has a complete piece of work. In this manner, the team controls most of the factors that influence its performance outcomes. The team can then be independently measured on its performance and held accountable for it. Management can give considerable decision-making power to such a group.

In the electronics industry, new products are introduced sometimes annually or sometimes every six months and last only eighteen months. Companies use cross-functional teams dedicated to the product for the entire eighteen months. The team develops the product, introduces it, manages it, and takes it off the market; the more complete the task is, the more control the team has. It is thus easier for the team to generate a plan and for management to delegate decision making to it. The team is measured on total profitability over the product's life cycle, making it easier to reward the members for the team's performance.

Complex Group Structures

Teams can become complex for three reasons. The first is the complexity of the task being managed. The auto industry uses cross-functional teams to design new products called *platforms*. A platform team consists of all the leaders of the design groups designing the platform. It is then further broken into its components—chassis, power train and engine, interior, exterior body, and so on. Each component has a cross-functional team designing that component to become part of the overall platform, so there is an overarching platform team managing the subteams for all the components. For large, complicated products like autos, large computers, aircraft, and the like, the team structure reflects the architecture of the product itself and becomes a hierarchy of cross-functional teams.

A second reason for complexes of teams and subteams is the number of people participating on the teams. When fifty to seventy-five people are involved in designing a component for an automobile, the team is usually split into a core team and extended team to include all the other participants. In the 1980s, engineers designed the car and passed the design to manufacturing. Today auto companies use simultaneous engineering. They follow initiatives with titles like "design and manufacturability," "design for quality," "design for serviceability," and so on. These initiatives mean that people from manufacturing, quality, service, marketing, and sales, and even customers, are part of the design process. These initiatives create very large cross-functional teams.

Teams also become complex when the business has multiple dimensions. Although the Boeing 787 design-and-build teams are created around sections of the product, Boeing also forms customer teams for customers like United Airlines or All Nippon Airways. The difficulty arises because the design-and-build teams want every plane to be the same so as to reduce costs and cycle time, while the customer teams want the planes to be different for each customer. Hence, there is a need for dialogue and conflict resolution. Complex structures become necessary when teams are interdependent and possibly in conflict. With complex team structures, the organization designer must solve two problems. First, the designer must create processes to coordinate and communicate across teams. Second, the designer must create a process to resolve interteam conflicts. An example illustrates these concepts.

Multidimensional Team. A personal computer business is organized by function and uses cross-functional product teams for notebook computers, laptops, desktops, and tablets. The product teams manage the product variety and reduce the time to market for new products. New products, which used to take two to three years to develop, are now created in one year or less and last about eighteen months. Speed is one of the bases of competition.

This business has also become cost driven, and many components are contracted out to low-cost producers. But component costs are volume driven. Thus, if each product team chooses the same component and the same vendor, the volume from the business can be concentrated with a single vendor, and lower costs obtained. To agree on a common component and vendor for each component on each product, the company created component teams for keyboards, liquid crystal displays, printed circuit boards, and several other potential common components.

The issue to be managed in this example is the potential conflict between the component teams and the product teams. Conflicts can surface in two ways. First, the product design engineers usually prefer components that optimize the performance of their product, but common components means that a component will fit all products and optimize none of them, so the design engineers may fight the idea of using common components at all, or they may disagree about which component should be the common one. The other point of conflict may involve the attempt to reach consensus across the product and component teams; this process can constrain the speed of the product design team. Top speed is attained when each team makes design decisions independently. The design of the team structure and the guidance from top management are the keys to achieving common components and speedy launch of new products simultaneously.

Top management of the computer company has articulated a strategy that places cost as the primary criterion for resolving conflicts. The strategy shifts the burden of proof to the engineers to show how a unique component will result in a substantial price and performance difference. Management also challenges the engineers to achieve high performance while using standard, common components. Top management's strategy is to provide criteria for decentralizing decisions to product and component teams. The same criteria serve the dispute settlement process across the teams.

The organization design of the product teams and component teams is shown in figure 4.1. Each product team is a cross-functional unit led by a product manager from engineering. Engineering and purchasing representatives working on printed circuit boards and keyboards are members of both the product teams and the component teams and thus serve as the links between the two teams. They are joined on the component teams by their counterparts working on other product teams. Component teams are chaired by technically trained managers from purchasing. In

Figure 4.1 Product and Component Team Combination

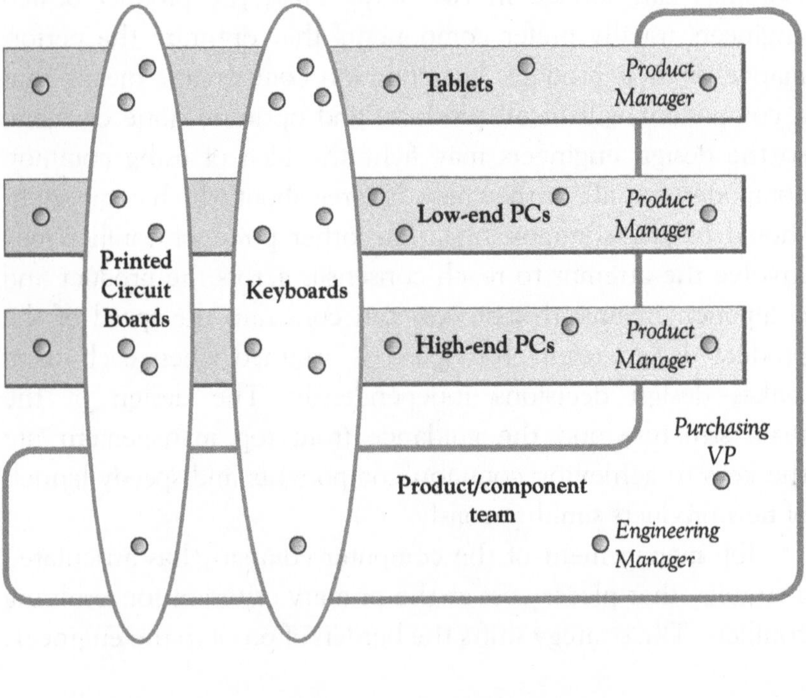

turn, the component team leaders, product team leaders, and product managers all form a conflict resolution team chaired by the purchasing vice president. A manager from engineering, usually a computer architect, participates as well.

The key features of the design are the linkages. The engineering and purchasing representatives who participate on both teams are central to the coordination and communication between the teams. The other links are the people who serve as leaders of the two teams. Collectively, they constitute the conflict resolution team, linking the team efforts with a thorough but rapid appeal process.

In this example, the teams permit a functional organization to focus simultaneously on products and on component vendors. With purchased components accounting for 70 to 80 percent of cost of goods sold and with product speed and cost central to the customer purchase decision, the business chooses to manage new products with the complex team structure. Each product requires a general manager as does each component. The intention is to generate a family of new, low-cost products rapidly. The speed of the product teams is constrained by the use of common components. But the more effective the participants are at communicating, sharing databases, and resolving conflicts, the faster they can generate new and low-cost products. The ability to execute a multidimensional decision process becomes a competitive advantage in the marketplace.

A Spectrum of Design. Thus, the organization design of teams can vary from simple to complex. The easiest design to manage is a series of simple teams, each with end-to-end responsibility for its task. Because each team controls its own destiny, the most freedom can be granted and the best speed in execution obtained. The teams get more complicated when the number of participants becomes too large for a single team to execute end-to-end responsibility. Teams are also more complicated when a business wants to be responsive with products but must simultaneously respond to vendors and customers. The size of the group and multidimensional responsiveness both lead to the design of linkages across groups and a hierarchical conflict-resolution process. The ability to execute multidimensional team processes rapidly contributes to responsiveness and achieves a competitive advantage.

E-Coordination of Teams

One of the factors that is permitting larger and more complex teams to work together is the placement of the new product development (NPD) process on the Web. The auto industry has always automated the NPD process by using systems for computer-aided design (CAD), computer-aided manufacturing (CAM), and computer-aided engineering (CAE). These separate systems are being migrated to the Web, integrated, and extended to include suppliers in what are called product life cycle management systems. When connected, the new system permits cross-functional teams to view a component or a whole car on their screens and communicate by voice. Each participant can then suggest changes that the whole team can see. These three-dimensional systems will also contain analysis packages to compute the cost, weight, and space implications. With a digital design, the car can be simulated for noise, vibration, and harshness and tested on a virtual track using simulations.

Success still depends on teamwork. This integrated system needs to be matched with an integrated organization capable of e-coordination.

In the examples discussed thus far, team leaders were put in place without much explanation of the integrating role. The next section discusses the design decisions in choosing the type of integrator and integrating roles. These roles are adopted when the teams need a full-time—and often neutral—leader. The teams require leaders when coordination is challenging, the performance targets are difficult, and the team efforts are high priority.

Integrating Roles

The most complex aspect of the lateral process is the creation of full-time leaders. Integrating roles create the truly multidimensional organization. There is a need for these roles when a company wants to attain functional excellence, generate new products and services, and be responsive to customers. This capacity is a requirement for some businesses in a complex, changing world.

The flexibility to deal with customers, vendors, and processes comes at a cost. First, there is the obvious investment in salaries for people who are to coordinate the work of others rather than produce work of their own. The investment, however, should yield faster time to market or better customer knowledge and relationships. The second cost is the time spent resolving conflicts. Managers for customer segments, products, and functions all see the world differently. Disagreement and the inability to resolve it effectively can slow the company responses and turn the focus inward rather than on customers.

In contrast, the ability to deal with controversy and different views increases the company's ability to respond to a variety of opportunities and threats, an important advantage.

Design of Integrating Roles

The organization design issues for integrating roles revolve around the power base from which the integrator will influence decisions. Managers in the hierarchical structure have authority and control of resources, but what is the power base of the integrator? How much power and influence does the integrator need? The power base of the integrator will be shaped by these factors:

- Structure of the role
- Staffing choice
- Status of the role
- Information systems

- Planning processes
- Reward systems
- Budget authority
- Dual authority

Structure of the Role. The ideal structure is to have the integrator report directly to the general manager. The three usual practices are shown in figure 4.2. Because there are usually several

Figure 4.2 Product Manager Variations

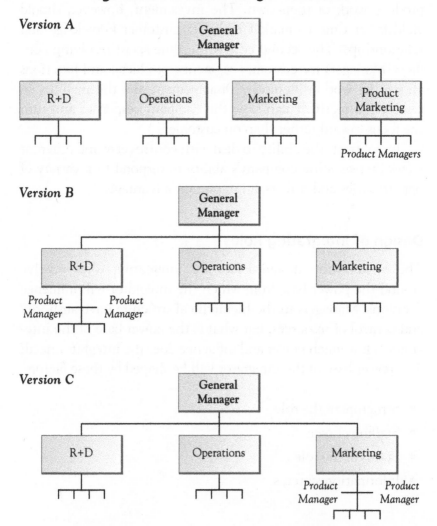

product lines, product managers report to a product management function, as shown in version A of the figure. The product management function may have some additional people working on costs and schedules of product programs.

In a variation of this practice, the product managers report to the R&D or engineering manager. Version B shows this method in high-technology industries and version C a variation seen in consumer packaged goods industries, where products and brands have long life cycles. Both versions B and C place the product manager in a function that is dominant for the industry. The variation in version A shows a more powerful, more neutral, and more general manager–like structure, because it is not associated with any function and has direct access to the general manager. The variations are appropriate for businesses that are technology driven (version B) or market driven (version C). Other variations are also possible (Galbraith, 1994a).

Staffing Choice. The people who play the integrator roles are the key factors in implementing the multidimensional organization. Few people who can play the general management role also have the skills to influence without authority. The key is to select people who have the interpersonal and networking skills to be personally persuasive. Technical skills are desirable but secondary.

The best way to find these individuals is to develop them internally. People who experience rotational assignments early in their careers, create their own personal networks, participate in lateral groups, and then chair a lateral group are usually ready to play a process integrator or project manager role. This process creates generalist skills, builds the person's network, and teaches influence skills early on. Management's role is to select the successful participants in the company's lateral processes because these people become the best integrators.

Status of the Role. There is a better likelihood that integrators will be able to influence if the role has status. What constitutes status varies with the culture of the company. Usually status can be bolstered by increasing the rank of the integrating role or locating the office of the integrator on the executive floor. Alternatively, the status of the role can be enhanced by staffing it with senior people with good track records. Whatever type of status enhancer is used, its purpose is to increase the ability of the integrator to exercise influence, even if the role has no authority.

Information Systems. Multidimensional organizations require multidimensional information. It is a real advantage to have the capacity to convert data into information on revenues, costs, and profits by customer, product, geography, and function. This information arms integrators with facts and knowledge they can use to influence others. The integrators can also contract with the line organization and then monitor the contractual agreements. Such rich data give the integrator a cross-company visibility into a product, customer, or process that no one else has, and this visibility and facts confer substantial influence on the integrator.

In contrast, a lack of integrated information systems presents a large impediment to companywide integration. Many reengineering projects to move processes to the Web attempt to obtain visibility across units and build databases so everyone works from the same information.

Planning Processes. The multidimensional information system can be used to support a multidimensional planning process. When based on valid data, the planning process can become the arena for focusing the natural contentions of the different perspectives for resolution. An example illustrates this point.

A telecom operator has created market segment business units. The planning matrix for the business unit serving medium-size companies is shown in figure 4.3. The functional organizations are listed across the top. The market segments managed by integrators are listed down the left side. The planning process amounts to a series of discussions between segment managers and functional

Figure 4.3 Planning Matrix for a Telecom Operator

	Sales	Marketing	Information Technology	Install and Repair	Network Operations
Health Services					
Financial Services					
Governments					
Distribution					
Manufacturing					
Other					

managers. The managers must agree on revenues, costs, and investments in each of the rows and columns because there are always more requests for resources than resources available. The business unit general manager sets initial guidelines, facilitates resolution of crucial disputes, and manages the entire process by convening all participants. When it is completed, the planning matrix allows all managers to shoot for the same targets, and their goals are aligned.

This planning process requires information to support it, participants skilled at problem solving in conflict situations, and a general manager skilled at managing the process and comfortable with managing conflict.

Reward Systems. The step from the planning process to the reward system is a natural one. The managers on either side of the planning matrix have now agreed on their goals. It is important for all the managers to make the goals in all of their individual cells in the matrix, not just in the total of all the cells (traditionally the normal practice). Then they become jointly accountable and are responsible for the same goals. The information system, planning process, and reward system form an integrated package of management practices that support the multidimensional organization.

Budget Authority. Another way to enhance the integrator's role is to give it control over the budget for its product, process, or market. The organization designer specifies which budget categories and amounts are involved in order to enhance the integrator's execution of the coordination task.

Dual Authority. The final step in creating a power base for the integrator is to give that person authority over the people in the function. This step creates a matrix structure that contains two reporting lines. Usually one person is selected as a subproject manager, as shown in figure 4.4. The person is jointly selected by both bosses and works for those two bosses. The dual authority is implemented by having both bosses participate in the joint setting of goals and joint performance assessment for the subproject manager.

Figure 4.4 Matrix Structure with Dual Authority

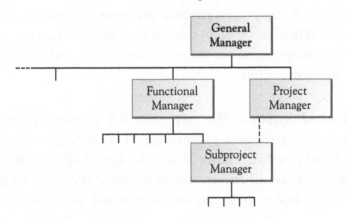

Only organizations that are skilled at lateral processes should attempt the dual authority step. It creates a power balance between the dimensions of the structure but can generate its own set of conflicts. The situation can easily produce more disagreements and confusion than flexibility (see Galbraith, 2009).

How to Decide

The discussion has described a continuum from low to high power for the integrator in decision making. How does the organization designer choose how much power the integrator needs to execute the strategy? There are two factors. The first is the strategic priority of the organizational dimension that the integrator is implementing. If the integrator is a product manager in a product-centric company, he or she will have a high degree of power. The chief risk officer in a bank used to make recommendations to the loan officers, who would make the final lending decision. But since the financial crisis, the risk officer can veto certain loans as too risky. So the risk officer has been elevated in power to match the current strategic priority.

The second factor is the difficulty of implementing the strategy. The difficulty is related to the organizational drivers. For example, a product manager will receive more power when he or she is managing many products or a high variety of products across the functions. The higher the interdependence between functions or a product program, the stronger the product manager must be. Speed is particularly important. The shorter the times to market, the stronger the product manager must be. Similarly, when a product based on a new technology is being introduced, the product manager will also be stronger. The new technology means that there will be more uncertainty in the project, so many new, unpredictable, and frequent decisions have to be made in the arenas of schedules, scope of work, and resources required. The product manager must be strong and powerful enough to engage the functional leaders making these decisions.

For other types of integrators (such as a segment manager or project manager), the organization designer must weigh the same considerations of strategic priority and organizational difficulty to determine how strong the integrator role needs to be.

At the moment, the choices in organization design are an inexact science. We do not know exactly how much power an integrator needs. In practice, organization designers judge the power base and then slowly increase it as needed. It is usually easier to increase the power of an integrator than to overshoot and subsequently take power away. Designers can fine-tune the power base of teams and integrators to match their ability to coordinate across functions.

Summary

The formal lateral processes of groups, integrators, and matrix are powerful methods to use when management must take a strong role in the lateral organization. Through these processes, a multidimensional organization is created, intended to increase the company's flexibility in responding to vendors, markets, technologies, governments, and so on. The organization is more likely to be capable of extensive communication and cooperation, as well as rapid escalation and resolution of conflicts.

The next chapters present some additional examples of combinations of structures and lateral processes. First are some examples of single businesses that have differentiated themselves by becoming product-centric and customer-centric.

5

TYPES OF SINGLE-BU
STRATEGY

In this chapter, we apply the general principles of lateral organizational design described in chapter 4 and present examples of product-centric, customer-centric, and real-time organizations. All of these examples are companies that are pursuing single-business strategies using the functional structure. They implement their differentiation variations but with lateral cross-functional processes.

Product-Centric Strategy

The first variation on the single-business strategy is the product-centric model. We use Nike, the US athletic shoe company, as the example. I referred to Nike in chapter 2 on start-ups. Recall that it entered the US running shoe market with high-quality Japanese shoes that were cheaper than the current German-made competitive products. Bill Bowerman, one of the founders, continued to develop new ideas for improving running shoes, and eventually Nike designed its own shoes and went to Asian manufacturers for its supply. Bowerman started the tradition of innovative product designs, and Phil Knight, the other founder, started the innovative marketing campaigns like, "Just Do It," and celebrity endorsements like that of Michael Jordan.

Nike positioned its product as high-performance shoes with high-technology features. It developed the waffle sole and air-cushioned sole systems under Nike Air. A number of new ideas came from an R&D facility in Exeter, New Hampshire, specialists in biomechanics, exercise physiology, advanced materials, computer simulation, and related fields were hired. Nike created research and advisory committees to review its research and development programs. These committees were made up of athletes, coaches, trainers, podiatrists, and orthopedists. Product innovation was thus at the heart of the company's values and its competitive advantage.

The Nike Air running shoe was soon joined by Air Force 1 for basketball and Air Ace shoes for tennis, product line extensions that leveraged the company's technology by entering new markets. As it grew, Nike became an athletic shoe company with over two hundred models of shoes in different sports.

In order to execute this product-centric strategy, Nike used a functional organization with cross-functional product teams (see figure 5.1). The usual corporate functions like CFO, legal, and HR report to the CEO, as does a special corporate function, sports marketing. Sports marketing is responsible for Nike's position in big sporting events like the Olympics and also leads

Figure 5.1 Nike's Functional Structure

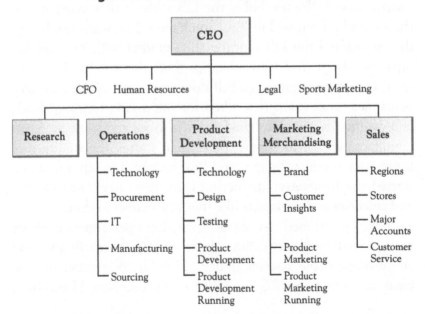

corporate-wide initiatives. The operating functions also report directly to the CEO, as does the research functions. The operations function chooses and manages all of the contract manufacturers and implements the necessary logistics. The product development function develops, designs, and tests the products, working directly with research on new technologies and with marketing on new products. The marketing and merchandising function is responsible for the Nike brand, consumer insights, and product marketing for each of the product lines. And finally, the sales function is organized by regions for small distributors and retailers, major accounts like Footlocker, Nike's own stores, and customer service and call centers. The center of activity revolves around the product development and product marketing teams.

The product management team for running shoes is shown in figure 5.2. The core team of product marketing and product

Figure 5.2 Nike's Cross-Functional Running Shoe Team

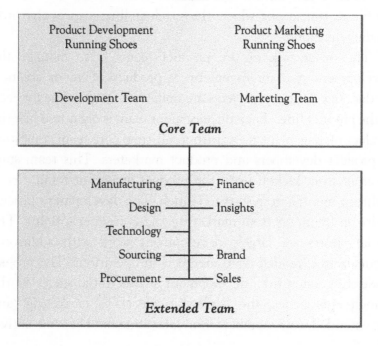

development works full time on the team throughout the year. They plan all the product launches, product improvements, and product marketing initiatives, managing the product line as if it were an end-to-end business. Members of the extended team from the other functions join the team throughout the year for planning and budget creation. There is a team for each product line, like running, basketball, tennis, soccer, and women's fitness, each one preparing a budget with inputs from the other functions. The planning process uses the spreadsheet tool to match functional resources with the product opportunities and sets companywide priorities. Leadership of the teams comes from the product marketing function, although long-experienced product developers have taken the lead on occasion.

The planning and budgeting process required that finance create accounting systems for tracking product revenues and costs. The cross-functional teams require an infrastructure of accounting systems, budget processes, and new product development processes. These infrastructure investments lay the groundwork for future transitions where the product lines can evolve into product divisions.

The other task of the product teams is to manage the development and improvement of products. Five or six new product development projects are under way at any time for each of the product lines. Each development team is organized like the product management team with a full-time core team consisting of product developers and product marketers. This team stays together from kickoff until the product arrives at retail, about eighteen months from start to launch. The development process is driven by inputs from marketing and consumer insights. The initial efforts are largely development work with additional inputs from extended team members in operations. The project leadership comes from development at this initial stage. As the launch approaches, the leadership passes to marketing, and the extended team members from sales and brand become active.

When the product is launched, the team members move on to the next new product effort.

Nike has designed an organization that executes its strategy of product-centricity. Its strategy is to meet the needs of top-performing athletes in various sports with technically superior shoes. Technically superior shoes are also very comfortable shoes, and when these shoes added fashionable design, they became very popular. The structure of the company is a functional design that places decision-making power and authority in the functions that are central to the product superiority: product development and product marketing. For long-run technical superiorities, the R&D function is also a major player.

In order to leverage technical innovations like the air-cushioned sole, Nike entered new sports markets, which gave it the scale to afford the R&D expense and attain advantages over competitors. The new markets added variety to the functional structure. In order to manage the increased complexity, Nike decentralized product management and development decisions to cross-functional product line teams. These teams form the hierarchy in which several product development teams reported to the product management team. The leadership of the development teams rotated from product development in the early phases to product marketing in the later phases as the product was launched in the market. The leadership of the product team was usually the product marketing head for the product line.

The key business process was the product development process, which supplied a full pipeline of new products. Each product took eighteen months to bring new fashion and technical ideas to market. At a company level, Nike managed the product development opportunities and its functional resources with a spreadsheet-based planning and budgeting process. The product and function goals were the basis for evaluating and rewarding the team members for their performance.

The people who staff the company bring the usual functional skill sets. Nike needs good marketers, like any other consumer goods company does, and it needs supply chain talent who can source and transport products from Asia. But Nike has an advantage: most of its employees are current and former athletes. They're customers as well as employees who identify with the mission of the company. The high performance of the products attracts specialists who want challenging work and competent colleagues. Nike has thus designed an organization using a complete and completely aligned Star Model for a product-centric company.

Customer-Centric Strategy

A second type of differentiation strategy is for a business to become customer-centric. A good example is the Retail Bank of the Royal Bank of Canada (RBC). The retail bank was one of four businesses at RBC. The others were insurance, wealth management, and corporate and investment banking. A fifth unit was a central transaction processing service center. The retail bank focused on consumers, small businesses, and small farms. Throughout Canada's banking history, the six largest banks enjoyed an undifferentiated and friendly competitive market, but in the late 1990s, changes began to appear on the horizon. Internet banking was now feasible, and the Canadian government was in favor of permitting more competition in banking. ING, a Dutch bank, entered the Canadian market with its Internet banking subsidiary, ING Direct. Then one of RBC's competitors began to white-label (private-label) consumer banking services through Loblaws, Canada's largest supermarket chain. RBC decided it was time to rethink its retail strategy and begin to differentiate itself for the coming competitive market.

The strategic rethinking began with a large survey conducted by the marketing group at the retail bank. It was an eye-opener: what was most important to customers was customer intimacy factors like trust, reassurance, a feeling that the bank wants their business and understands their needs. The retail bank, however, was busy providing ATMs, extended opening hours, shorter lines, and 24/7 Internet access. The study thus identified a whole new area of differentiation at which none of the existing banks excelled. RBC decided to pursue differentiation through customer-centricity.

The customer-centric strategy was built around a segmentation framework based on life stages. If the bank needs to understand the customers and their financial needs, a person's stage in life is the best way to do that. The original framework was four segments: first, youth (less than eighteen years old) and young adults (eighteen to thirty-five years old), single or married but with no children; second, builders and borrowers, with an average age of forty years old but with more loans than investment; third, wealth accumulators, people with more investments than loans; and fourth, wealth preservers, people who were living off their investments. Then the bank created many subsegments based on net worth, lifestyle, and relationship preferences. Lifestyle has an impact on financial needs, like sailors who buy boats and boat insurance and rent or buy marina slips and marina condos. There are skiers, who buy second homes in resorts in Canada, and Canadian snowbirds, who go to Florida in the winter and need housing, bank accounts, and American currency.

An example of segment strategy is the young adult segment. Marketing's analytical models identified customers' estimated lifetime value, which guided priorities for serving customers in the segment. One area of opportunity was identified as mortgages for first-time home buyers, where the new customer-centric strategy would be an advantage. First-time home buyers are young, inexperienced people who are anxious about a purchase of this magnitude. Because RBC could earn their trust and provide reassurance to them, the young adult segment developed a program to appeal to these customers and trained branch and call center people in the basics of the program. The information was placed on the website, where many young people were likely to search. The bank started forming a community of first-time home buyers and encouraged dialogues among the members. The staff of the segment also consisted of young adults who were themselves first-time home buyers. The segment then created a solution of complementary products, like mortgage insurance, automatic salary deposits into a bank account, and automatic withdrawal to pay the mortgage. The package was built to reassure customers and convey the bank's understanding of their situation. It was not just selling a mortgage.

The differentiation strategy was based on relationship management with customer interaction grounded in customer knowledge. The interaction was customized to the preferences, needs, and potential value of the customer. To implement the customer interaction program based on in-depth customer knowledge, the bank created segment units based on the framework, upgraded its data and analytics unit, and invested in technology to support a customer relationship management (CRM) system.

Customer knowledge is created from the analysis of the customer database, which consists of information from all customer accounts, external data provided by vendors like credit bureaus, from data collected in interactions with the customer. For each customer, the database contains his or her credit risk profile, transaction preference (fast, friendly, or Web), profitability, products bought, products likely to buy, likelihood to leave, and lifetime value or potential. All of the data are available to customer contact people at the moment of customer interaction.

The customer interaction is led by a personal banker and takes place through the CRM process. These bankers, formerly branch, marketing, and product specialists, coordinate all customer touch points for about two hundred customers who merit a personal banker. The bankers are arranged into the segments and interact with about twenty customers by phone and meet with ten others each week. They monitor all the touch points: branches, call centers, ATMs, e-mail, Web, and social media. To the extent that volumes allow, customer contact people in call centers and branches are specialized by segments.

The segment managers coordinate the activities of the customer contact people, who report to their individual functions, not the segment managers. The segments are responsible for training customer contact people, a major expenditure. The segments keep all the contact people up to date and provide input to their managers for performance evaluation.

The organization has been changed substantially to implement the new customer-centric strategy. Originally the retail bank was a product-centric functional structure that was not very differentiated. The organization consisted of sales branches distributed throughout the country, a marketing department that focused mostly on the brand, a shared services processing unit at corporate, and product management units for mortgage banking, credit cards, transaction services like checking and savings, loans, and investment products. This structure was left intact, but units were added to sales and marketing. The structure is shown in figure 5.3.

The sales function consists of call centers, redefined as interaction centers, regions of branches, and ATM infrastructure and commercial sales as before. Segments are the main addition and consist of people mainly from the branches, a previous central sales unit, and from the product lines. The product people were assigned to the segments most likely to buy the products. For example, mortgage bankers were assigned to the youth and the builders and borrowers segments, while the investment managers went to the wealth accumulators segment.

The marketing function consisted of the brand unit, consumer insights, and direct marketing (mail campaigns) as before. New units were added to implement and maintain the CRM process and for data and analytics. These new units and the segments signified a shift in the power and authority of the sales and marketing functions and a slight decline in the product management power base. These structural changes were necessary to execute the customer-centric strategy and shift from the previous product-centric orientation. The segments became

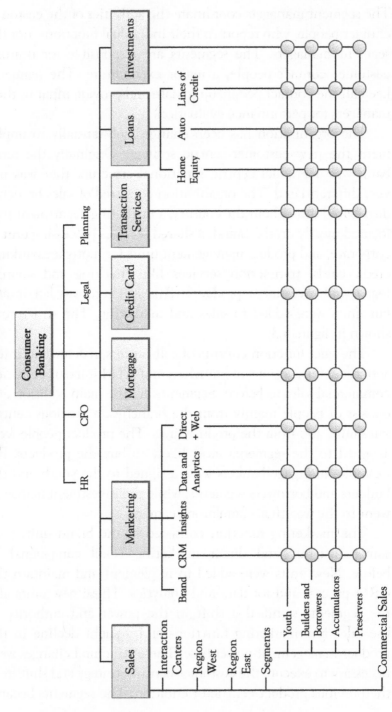

Figure 5.3 Retail Bank Structure

P&L centers, while the product lines maintained their P&L measures as well.

The other big change was implementation of cross-functional segment teams, led by segment managers from sales and staffed by marketing and product management as the volume of the product lines dictated. The segment teams are also shown in 5.3. These teams formulated the segment strategies (like first-time home buyers), built the three-year plans, and created yearly budgets. The bank used a spreadsheet as shown in figure 5.4 to match segment opportunities with product resources and set priorities. The spreadsheet was a central tool and process for managing the retail bank.

Each product management team was responsible for its product portfolio and new product developments. New product teams would create new products using cross-functional teams of product management people, segment representatives and the relevant marketing and branch managers. An active retail leadership management team was the conflict-resolving forum for segment-product disputes over scarce resources.

In summary, RBC created a retail banking business that differentiated itself with a customer-centric strategy. The basic functional structure was augmented with customer segments and marketing specialists in CRM, data, and analytics and Web design management. Decision-making power and authority shifted to the segments and was coordinated cross-functionally by segment teams, which drove the CRM process and the planning and budgeting processes. The shared goals from the spreadsheet development process became the basis for the performance management and reward system. People were shifted to the segment structure, and new skills were added in marketing for CRM and data and analytics. The biggest investment in people was the continuous training of call center and branch personnel to maintain the customer-centric experience at all customer touch points.

Figure 5.4 Retail Bank Planning and Budgeting Spreadsheet

	Interaction Centers	Branches	CRM	Data and Analytics	Direct + Web	Mortgages	Credit Cards	Transaction Services	Loans	Investments	Totals
Youth											
Builders and Borrowers											
Accumulators											
Preservers											
Totals											

RBC has been successful with the customer-centric approach because it created a strategy and designed a complete organization through which to execute the strategy. It did not just install a CRM system as an IT project.

Cost-Centric Strategy

The cost-centric strategy, like the others, makes use of lateral forms, but not as much. The ideal organization for the cost-centric company is the functional structure, where all specialties are gathered together and the work done with the fewest number of people. It allows management to centralize, standardize, and eliminate duplication. Usually all transactional activities, like payroll, accounts payable, accounts receivable, and so on, are centralized and consolidated into a shared services unit. Often the shared services are then outsourced to India or the Philippines. Management focuses on eliminating all non-value-added work, and the company focuses completely on cost reduction.

The problem with this type of functional organization is that it can be slow and unresponsive. There can be barriers between functions, and work must pass across multiple interfaces. Therefore, the leadership's other focus is on cross-functional processes. The high-leverage process is usually the order-to-cash process. The faster and the more error free this process operates, the more efficient it is. Usually a cross-functional team manages this process and continually searches for ways to eliminate or combine tasks to speed the flow and increase accuracy.

The team consists of a key player from each function that participates in the process. Then, rather than create a full-time integrator, companies usually appoint the head of operations or supply chain to lead the cross-functional team in addition to leading their function. This leader wears two hats. In addition to the team, the leader usually creates a process network. All people working on the order-to-cash process are linked together into the company's social network. The process leader, often called the owner, manages this network in addition to the cross-functional team.

The other process is the purchasing or vendor management process. For companies that buy a lot of materials and services, this process, often called the requisition-to-settlement process, is very important. Again, a cross-functional team and the network are created. In this case, purchasing or procurement usually leads the effort. These two operational processes receive a lot of attention because they have an impact on the cost structure. There may be other processes like new product development, but they are not central to the competitive success of the cost-centric company.

The Real-Time Business Strategy

Many businesses operate like the lateral organizations described, but others are being reshaped by digital forces like the Internet of Things (chips and sensors embedded everywhere), big data, software, and social networks. Combined, these digital forces are speeding the time cycles under which companies must operate. As more and more companies adopt these digital tools, they are becoming real-time organizations. Their cross-functional teams have to operate in continuous mode. Instead of periodic project meetings, today's teams meet continuously using a newsroom model—there is always breaking news somewhere.

Nike has been an early adopter of these digital tools and is using digital capabilities to extend its product differentiation strategy. As a result, it has been transforming its organization.

Nike launched its first website, nike.com, in 1998. It experimented with YouTube, MySpace, and other media sites. Then around 2005, it introduced NIKEiD, an online store. In addition to online direct sales, one of its features was that customers could design their own shoes, much like they could design their own computer on dell.com. Sales reached $100 million in a few years.

The big change came when Nike launched Nike+. Nike engineers became aware that virtually everyone was using iPods and approached Apple about a partnership. The idea was to embed a sensor in Nike running shoes that could link wirelessly to an iPod and then eventually to the iPhone and Android devices. The sensor could record distance, speed, and calories burned. The iPod could record these and provide music for running and other audio features. At the end of a run, the iPod could be uploaded to NikePlus.com and viewed and stored. The NikePlus.com website offered running tips, comparisons with others, and shared work-outs with friends on the Nike site and on Facebook and Twitter.

NikePlus.com built a following and in 2007 became the largest online running destination. Additional functionality was added to the website. For example, members could use the site to gather for group runs in many cities or could meet and gather after the runs. A Nike+GPS app was added to allow runners to map their runs. Then a database was built that now contains the largest collection of maps for running around the world. Users can ask for a suggestion for a steep course in Sonoma where it is possible to take a dog. Next came the Nike+GPS SportWatch. By 2013, there were more than 7 million members of the Nike+ community. The growth was 55 percent in 2011, with a sales growth of 30 percent in the running shoe business to $2.8 billion.

Nike is now in the software business. With embedded chips in shoes and digital sports watches and the website serving more than 7 million people, there is the expectation of new functionality arriving constantly to update the running program. To keep a constant supply of new software, Nike opened up NikePlus.com to outside software developers. Today companies like Nike are not just providing software products from their own software developers; they are building a software platform on which other developers can create apps valuable to the community. At some point, Nike could open the platform to advertisers of complementary products. The more and better the apps, the more Nike can differentiate its products.

The other big digital change for Nike has been its advertising: Nike spends more money on digital media than any other advertiser—about 80 percent of Nike's total ad budget. Nike's best customers are teenage boys, and they are on Facebook, Twitter, and NikePlus.com. Today, Nike does not become a sponsor of the Olympics; instead, it launches an Olympics campaign on Facebook and Nike's own networks. When a good ad goes viral, Nike now gets around 200 million views. However, like other companies, Nike learned that social media is not a broadcast medium but an interactive medium. Since the beginning, Nike has been building a conversation with its customers and community and, like other companies, is improving and constantly searching for how best to have these conversations.

The conversations, the uploaded running data, the Likes from Facebook, transactions on the website, and conversations from call centers provide a wealth of information to Nike about its customers, their running habits, and their views of Nike. Product development software developers then use this information for new apps, customer contact personnel, advertising, and managers of NikePlus.com. The information arrives in enormous quantities and in different forms—as texts, audio, photos, e-mails, videos, and transactions. And it arrives every second. In order to capitalize on the threats and opportunities revealed in the real-time data, the Nike organization also needs to operate in real time.

This increase in speed of decision making is a major organizational change required to implement the digital strategy. The change is made all the more challenging by the addition of new groups of digital talent to handle all of the incoming data and to make sense of it. There are software developers to create new applications and Web designers to update the NikePlus.com site. There are hardware engineers who understand sensors and embedded chips and who can select and manage hardware vendors that make products like the SportWatch. There are software evangelists who recruit and manage partnerships with outside software vendors. There are managers who can run e-commerce websites and social media experts who manage communities.

And finally, there are digital marketing experts who can manage the process of taking real-time data to the analytics group, which produces real-time insights for decision makers, who can make real-time decisions. So how does Nike organize to implement its digital strategy to further differentiate its products?

One way is to integrate the software and hardware engineers into the product development function and the digital marketing and social media experts into marketing. This alternative would maintain the current functional structure and would be favored by the current managers. Another alternative is to combine all of the new talent into a digital unit and keep that unit intact. Nike could make it into a new function in the business structure.

There are two arguments for a semi-independent unit. Operating independently, the unit can control its own activities and prove itself to the other units. As a new unit, it has to build its own capability and prove itself to others and earn credibility. A new unit always has a lot of trial and error as well until it arrives at its success formula. Also, a new unit is fragile and needs nurturing and development help from the leadership.

The second argument is that the unit is not just new but very different too. It contains different specialists, each with its own languages. But the real difference is the speed at which it has to operate. If it is a separate unit, it can operate at its own faster pace. If it is embedded in the other units, it will have difficulty increasing its speed of decision making.

But the unit cannot be completely separate because it is interdependent with the other functions. It must participate in the new product development process and pass ideas and information to consumer insights and brand advertising. As a result, the organization design is much more nuanced. The digital organization structure, along with marketing, is shown in figure 5.5.

The digital function consists of a community management unit, social media and mobile specialists, website management, hardware engineering, and a software function. These are all activities for which the digital unit is responsible. The units that

Figure 5.5 Nike's Digital Functional Structure

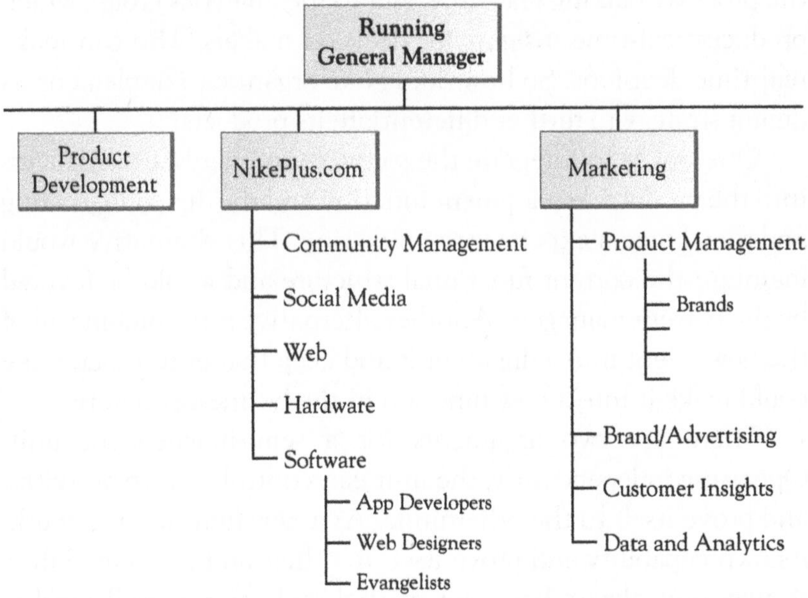

operate in real time are the software, the Web, and community management groups.

The software development group, like software developers everywhere, has been increasing the speed of product delivery. Originally software products were developed and launched in a year or more, but today developers follow the practices of Google and the agile software development process. Like lean start-ups, agile software groups create a minimally workable product and get it up on the Web and in front of users. There, users begin providing feedback immediately. The development group revises the product on the basis of this feedback through many fast iterations, until it is ready for product launch. In this manner, the products are codeveloped with interested users. Using this process today, companies like LinkedIn release new products and software three times a day.

Product development in software is continuous rather than a year-long project. The software is developed in project teams where members of other functions join for however long they are needed to contribute. The functions contributing vary with the project, as the interdependencies change with each project. Usually representatives from hardware, the Web, community, data and analytics, product management, other software vendors, and advertising join the team. A software development leader stays close to a product and initiates new activities when updates are required. Other developers move from project to project.

The software development process is a very different activity from the process for developing shoes. Software development is a continuous and interactive process, with users and external software developers. Shoe development is still a fifteen- to eighteen-month process. The organization design of the running business illustrates the design challenge of separating different activities yet integrating them when interdependencies exist. The separation is achieved structurally with a standalone digital function. The integration is achieved through multifunctional processes. In addition, people from different functions are used to staff the new functions and maintain cross-functional communication through the internal social networks. The design is a balance to enable working separately when it makes sense and working together when that makes sense.

The Web and community management groups work closely together. The Web group, which conducts itself like any other website management group, keeps the NikePlus.com site current with new product announcements and the latest running news. The community group, the new addition, keeps evolving, with its responsibilities and management tools expanding constantly. Some of the group's activities are to monitor the conversations on the Web, create subcommunities, launch initiatives, and continuously manage the communities. This group runs the newsroom. A 24/7 newsroom team monitors the conversation across all social media. If there's a positive or negative spike, the team swings into action. When a factory collapses in Bangladesh, for example, the team is quick to communicate that Nike manufactures no shoes in that country. If a positive spike occurs, the team investigates to see if it can be accentuated. In either case, the team explores what is behind the spike. They then ask, "What can we learn from it? Should we act on it now? Can we pass on the learning to others?"

The community group creates liaisons in all of the other functions with which it is interdependent. If an issue arises, it can call on all of the other functional resources that it needs. If it's a software issue, the software liaison tries to deal with the issue or find someone who can. The community management group has created an extensive internal liaison network across the business with people trained in community operations and kept informed about the communities' activities. When they get the call, the liaisons are prepared to swing into action. Some companies have a room in which digital displays can be accessed. Procter & Gamble calls its rooms "decision spheres." The newsroom team usually gathers in this kind of a room. The newsroom team and network is a real-time organization, acting on real-time information.

Sometimes the spikes can be anticipated. The running community is always active during races like the Boston Marathon, running events, and the Olympics. The newsroom gathers for these predictable events and starts listening and responding to the Twitter and Facebook feeds as the events unfold. In fact, the newsroom model is a new addition to the structure of many companies.

Another activity is to support the formation of subcommunities, many of these formed by runners organizing themselves. When community managers sense a new movement, they join in and build on it. One example is the women's running movement, especially outside the United States. Sensing the movement in spring 2013, Nike created races in eleven cities and countries in Latin America and Asia. The initiative was called "She Runs," and one event was "She Runs Bogotá." More than eighty-five thousand women participated in these races. In Europe, the initiative was scheduled after work hours and was called "We Own the Night." Prior to these runs, people suggested workouts on NikePlus.com, Nike held training classes for six weeks ahead of the run, and women could post their times on NikePlus.com. In London, Paula Radcliffe, the British winner of the 2012 London Olympics Marathon, participated in the event. There were other Nike-sponsored events before and after the race, coordinated through communities on NikePlus.com, facebook.com/nikerunninguk, and other country sites.

These community managers constantly listen to and converse with their community. They post articles, photos, and videos that they think are interesting to the members and run surveys on topics that the community is discussing. There are software tools that managers could use to analyze their community networks—which has the most followers, which are the community network influencers, and so on. The managers can carry on conversations with these particular community leaders. Community managers are looking for ways to work with these leaders and yet maintain their trust and the trust of the community. It is clear now why Nike thinks investing in social media is superior to investing in TV advertising.

Many companies believe that they have just scratched the surface in engaging their communities. Some companies see them as useful for crowdsourcing various types of initiatives. For example, Procter & Gamble will post a technical problem it's facing on a crowdsourcing website to gather new ideas. Other companies post new product ideas to the general public as a sort of crowdsource trial balloon. Harley-Davidson has in fact bypassed its regular ad agency and crowdsourced its next ad campaign to its user community.

A couple of other features are needed to complete the organization design of the digital function: a governance model and supporting HR practices. At Nike, the governance feature is a steering committee chaired by the running business head and consisting of the heads of marketing, product development, sales, and the digital function. At the beginning, they met weekly following the formation of the function. The purpose of the committee was to see that all of the cross-functional linkages were working, and if not, to fix them. Now it meets every two weeks and reviews plans, budgets, issues, and initiatives.

The HR practices are to support the community liaison network and provide for a process to assemble and disassemble newsroom teams. The liaison people need much more loosely defined jobs. They can be assembled in the newsroom for varying lengths of time so staffing policies need to be more like those of professional services firms—consultants who move on and off engagement teams and do not have jobs that need to be back-filled when one is called away. The performance of liaison people also needs to be incorporated into the performance management system. These practices complete the design of the structure, processes, rewards, and people practices of the digital function.

In summary, when a company extends its product differentia-tion strategy to include chips, sensors, and software in its products, it finds itself in the software business too. Part of the organiza-tion now has to move at the pace of the software industry. This pace approaches real-time and requires that cross-functional teams operate under the newsroom model.

Customer-Centric Real-Time Strategy

Companies differentiating themselves using the customer-centric strategy will follow a path similar to Nike's. In one sense, the transition to a real-time organization is easier. RBC and other customer-centric companies already organize themselves by communities or customer segments and subsegments. The retail bank's personal bankers are community managers who converse with customers and follow changes in the community or segment. Most social software companies have built-in links to existing CRM systems. So now the personal bankers and segment teams can manage their segments in real time. The subsegments can self-organize and converse among themselves. A first-time home buyer group on Facebook is exactly what RBC wants to create and cultivate participants. Customer-centric companies do not have to change structure to become real-time companies.

But they do need to change and speed up their processes and continue to change the mind-sets of their managers. Like product-centric companies, retail banks will need to gather their segment teams into newsrooms and establish extensive community networks that include functions with which the segment is interdependent. This interdependence will vary with the issue that becomes breaking news in the community's social network. Moreover, many of these newsworthy events can be predicted. The segments for wealth accumulators and preservers should gather in the newsroom each month for the Federal Reserve's announcements, which often move markets and interest rates. Therefore, the segment teams need to transition from periodic meetings and decisions to continuous meetings and real-time decision making. The bank will need to continue to promote the mind-set change not just to customer-centricity but also to fast and data-driven decisions. The leadership team of the retail bank needs to complete the organization design with a complete Star Model. Its members should speed up their own decision processes and reward segment leaders who adapt to the real-time culture. Employees from the leadership down need to increase their skills for making analytical, data-driven decisions. A number of companies have adopted standards for all of their managers to meet. Even if managers are not part of the data and analytics group, they need a basic understanding of data and analytics.

Summary

This chapter has described how companies following a differentiation strategy organize to implement it. Using the basic functional structure, Nike and RBC use lateral processes to implement a product-centric and a customer-centric strategy respectively. Nike's organization was described as it further differentiated its products by embedding sensors in its running shoes.

This change converted Nike into a high-technology company and a real-time decision making organization. The following chapters also look at some different strategies and how the companies have modified their basic functional organizations.

Notes

Material on the strategy and organization of Nike comes from annual reports and the following cases and their references:

Lyn Denend and Robert Burgelman, "Nike's Global Women's Fitness Business," case SM-152 (Stanford, CA: Stanford Graduate School of Business, April 2007).

M. J. Piskorskiss and R. Johnson, "Social Strategy at Nike," case 9–712–484 (Boston: Harvard Business School, April 2012).

A. S. Rao and D. Purkayastha, "Digital Marketing at Nike" (Andra Pradesh, India: IBS Center for Management Research, 2012).

Material on the strategy and organization of RBC comes from the cases below and their references, an investor presentation, and annual reports:

V. C. Naraxanon, "Customer Profitability and Customer Relationship Management at RBC Financial Group," case 9–102–072 (Boston: Harvard Business School, May 2007).

Royal Bank of Canada, "Investor Presentation" (2008). http://www.rbc.com/investorrelations/events-presentations .html

R. Slagmulder and D. Grottah, "Royal Bank of Canada: Creating Profitable Relationships with Small Business Clients," case 105–023–1 (Fontainebleu, France: INSEAD, 2005).

6

THE RECONFIGURABLE
FUNCTIONAL ORGANIZATION

The previous chapters have discussed single-business strategies that require cross-functional, lateral processes for their implementation. In this chapter, we examine a product differentiation strategy where product and other advantages do not last very long. The company uses an organization design that I called "reconfigurable" (Galbraith, 1997). Others have called the design an example of dynamic capabilities (Barreto, 2010) where the company combines and recombines its capabilities to create advantages. The company uses a functional structure as its foundation and then employs extensive lateral processes to reconfigure itself.

Every company needs an organization that changes as quickly as its business does. Otherwise it is falling behind. To keep this from happening, many companies are devoting enormous amounts of time and energy to change management. This task can be made less difficult and less time-consuming if some effort is focused on designing organizations from the outset to be more easily changeable. If change is constant, why not design organizations to be constantly and quickly changeable? It is this easily changeable or reconfigurable organization that is the subject of this chapter.

Competing with No Sustainable Advantage

Organizations have always been created to execute business strategies. As mentioned in chapter 2, different strategies have led to different organizations. But when advantages do not

131

last long, neither do the organizations that execute them. In the past, management crafted a winning business formula and erected barriers to entry to sustain the advantage. Then it created an organization structure around functions, products or services, markets, or geographies that was designed to deliver the success formula.

To complete the integrity of the organization, planning and budgeting processes, information systems, new product development processes, compensation systems, selection and promotion criteria, career paths, performance appraisals, and training and development sequences would all be designed and aligned with each other and with the organization's strategy and structure. Such an aligned organization would execute the strategy with as little friction as possible. This thinking resulted in concepts like the Star Model described in chapter 2, repeated for your convenience as figure 6.1.

In many industries today, that model of organization design is flawed: the success formulas it generates do not last very long (D'Aveni, 1994). The advantages around which the organization is designed are quickly copied or even surpassed by high-speed competitors, so every advantage is temporary. Therefore, to focus and align the organization is to become vulnerable. As a result, some people have concluded that alignment is no longer

Figure 6.1 The Star Model

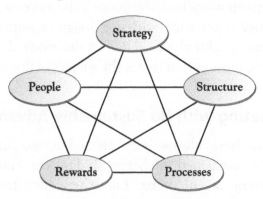

a useful organizational design criterion. I agree that alignment around a focused strategy can impede change to a new strategy, but it is the continued focus on a nonsustainable advantage that is the flaw rather than the alignment itself. The point can be made by focusing on the alternative: misalignment. Misalignment of strategy, structure, and processes will cause activities to conflict, units to work at cross-purposes, and organizational energy to dissipate over many frictions. Instead, we need a new, aligned organizational design with structures and processes that are easily reconfigured and realigned with a constantly changing strategy.

Thus, the challenge is to design organizations to execute strategies when there are no sustainable competitive advantages. When product advantages are not sustainable over time, the winners will be those who create a series of short-term temporary advantages. Under this scenario, the leaders will be future oriented and will continuously create capabilities that lead to customer value. They will move quickly to combine these capabilities to match and surpass current advantages (including their own), and they will outmaneuver competitors by stringing together a series of moves and countermoves as in a game of chess. Companies with the capabilities for flexible response and a variety of moves over the course of time will most likely win. The reconfigurable organization is the means for executing this continuous strategy shifting.

The Reconfigurable Organization

The reconfigurable organization results from the skilled use of three capabilities. First, the organization is reconfigured by forming cross-functional teams and networks across organizational departments. These lateral structures require an extensive internal networking capability as described in chapters 4 and 5. Second, the organization uses flexible accounting, IT systems, and planning and resource allocation processes to coordinate the complexity of multiple teams. And finally, the organization forms partnerships to secure capabilities that it does not have. These partnerships require an external networking capability, as discussed in chapter 7.

The three capabilities are best illustrated with an example. The example company is a manufacturer of consumer baking products—cookies, biscuits, crackers, and so on. The firm had competencies in brand management and distribution with a network of bakeries across North America and a logistics system that could deliver directly from the bakery to the retail store. Baking has always been a just-in-time business. This company's brands and its distribution system (only Coca-Cola and Pepsi could match it) had been its advantages and its barriers to entry.

In the 1990s, these advantages came under attack. Retailers and their private label suppliers could easily match the company's product quality at significantly lower prices. Also, the baker's products were high fat and high calorie. Hence, the company's products were being avoided by both the budget conscious and the health conscious.

The company's resurgence began with its discovery of a low-fat ingredient that maintained the product's taste. After the US Food and Drug Administration approved use of this ingredient, the company began reformulating its most popular brands and focused promotions on the health segment. The new products literally flew off of the shelves. The reformulation had revived the brands and created an advantage that the private labels could not match.

To capitalize on the products' popularity, the company expanded into all possible distribution channels. Different channels, however, require different packaging, so the company created partnerships with independent manufacturers (called *copackers*) to provide multiple packages. It now provides products in enormous boxes for discount club stores and single-serving portions for vending machines and convenience stores.

Next, the company took the new ingredient into new categories such as breakfast products and snacks, where it could create an advantage. It created new products for these new categories with partners and copackers because the products (like granola bars) were not baked. The expansion provided a new business in different aisles of the grocery store. The new products could also be kept fresh by using the company's existing delivery system. Other manufacturers of breakfast foods did not have this capability or the low-fat ingredient.

The company created partnerships (called *category management*) with two of its larger customers, which then turned the management of the entire cookie and cracker aisle over to the baking company. The baking company's skills in brand management, sophisticated analytics and big databases, social media experience, and knowledge of the cookie and cracker category allowed both customer and manufacturer to increase their respective profitabilities. By coordinating the product and cash flow from bakery to store, the partners could minimize working capital. The grocery customers are now interested in packaging that is unique to them. Here again, the baking company, with its packaging flexibility through its external network of partnerships, is able to meet its customers' needs.

In summary, this company created an advantage through its discovery of a low-fat ingredient that maintains product taste. Using its existing capabilities in logistics and brand management, it successfully targeted and dominated the health segment. It created a multichannel, multipackage capability to enlarge the population that its products can reach. It used the ingredient and its logistics to enter a new category (breakfast foods). The ingredient advantage will buy time for the company while it builds knowledge in the new category. And finally, its enhanced reputation, brand management, logistics, and flexible packaging capabilities made it an attractive partner for large retailers. The company has thus created a series of advantages by combining and recombining new capabilities and old ones to address new products, new segments, new channels, and new customer relationships. It is a good example of the continuous creation of advantages. The baking company creates and implements an initiative that gives it advantage. Then it quickly moves on to the next advantage.

The company has continued to develop new advantages in its approach to segments. For example, it initially focused on a health segment but now parlays that experience into other segments like Hispanics, a segment that continues to grow in numbers and in disposable income. The bakery focused on a dozen products and six major Hispanic markets, including the Mexican Southern California and the Cuban South Florida markets. The segment lined up copackers for packaging in the Spanish language and prepared ads for Spanish-speaking media.

The company also returned to the expansion of its existing initiatives. It expanded its partners in category management from two to five, with more being pursued. It entered the snack category with a partner. It avoided Frito-Lay, the dominant player, and positioned itself against the number three and four players in the market. The company also positioned itself as healthier because its products are baked rather than fried.

Any finally, the bakery has found a way to profit from its distribution capability. It has become a leader in collaborative logistics. Using the Web as a central coordination tool, producers, retailers, and truckers can share trucks and warehouses when going to and from the same locations. It has joined ten other manufacturers and its category management partners in a new venture in collaborative logistics. The venture has been a major source of savings and new revenue.

The company continues to create new sources of advantage from combining its new and old capabilities. It also knows that if it rests and does not generate the next sources of advantage, someone else will. As a result, it continues its search for new ingredients but also for new categories, new customers, new channels, new segments, and so on. It has become a player in the era of temporary advantages.

Creating Reconfigurability

This strategy of creating a series of short-term advantages can be effective only if the company has an organization that can execute it. Prior to the discovery of the low-fat ingredient, our example company was organized functionally around research and development, operations, marketing, sales and distribution, finance, and human resources. Like most other packaged consumer goods companies, it used cross-functional product line teams. These teams, shown in figure 6.2, are chaired by the product vice presidents from marketing. It had reasonably good cross-functional relationships. Quite a few of the top management group had cross-functional experience. In addition, for about five years, the company was encouraging project management experience. Almost all managers had attended the project management course, and almost all had worked on cross-functional project teams. The company built on this base to implement the continuous strategy shifts.

The first organizational change was the creation of a third team that was focused on the health segment and was to reformulate and relaunch the company's products. This team was chaired by a full-time marketing vice president. As with the two existing

Figure 6.2 Product Team Organization

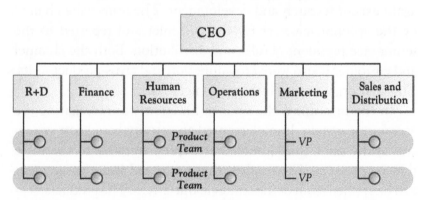

teams, each function contributed a representative who had the time (at least 50 percent), the authority to represent the function, and the information about the function use in problem solving. The main difference was that the segment team was both cross-function and cross-product.

The new category was addressed by another cross-functional unit chaired by a vice president from marketing. But this team was full time and dedicated to the effort of breaking into a new category. Several dedicated salespeople worked for the unit and created the new sales approach for the new category. This team reported directly to the CEO to get the attention and focus that a new business requires. The reporting relationship also gave it leverage with its partner.

A similar team was created for the new channels. A vice president from marketing chaired the team but reported to the senior vice president for sales and distribution. All functions, except research and development, contributed a full-time, dedicated manager. There was no research and development representation because no new products were involved. The channel team bought products from the factories and managed the relationships with copackers who packaged the products.

Following these changes, two more dedicated cross-functional units were formed for the two customer partnerships. These units also consisted of full-time, dedicated people from all functions, again except research and development. The units were chaired by the account manager for the customer and reported to the senior vice president of sales and distribution. Both the channel and customer teams were cross-function and cross-product units. This new organization is shown in figure 6.3.

In the meantime, the finance function was redesigning the accounting system. It implemented an activity-based cost system and at the same time installed enterprise software to automate that new system. The result is that profit and loss measurement can be applied to all of the strategic initiatives. The products, segments, categories, channels, and customers are all profit-and-loss

Figure 6.3 Multidimensional Organization

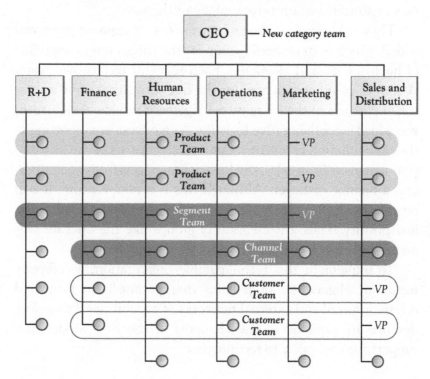

measurable. The human resources department is redesigning the reward systems to incorporate team-based rewards. Each of these teams is in fact a miniature business unit.

In this way, the example company has configured and reconfigured itself from a functional structure with brand managers to a multistructure based on functions, products, segments, categories, channels, and customers. It is a multiple profit-and-loss structure that can be flexibly changed to any dimension that will support the next strategic advantage. The company is creating the capability to organize any way it wants. Instead of choosing to organize by function *or* product *or* market segment to implement a sustainable brand advantage, the company is organized by function *and* product *and* segment *and* channel *and* customer to implement a series of constantly changing, short-term advantages. The company's second wave of new initiatives was also matched with new organizational units to implement them.

These additions are shown in figure 6.4. A segment group was added, which is an umbrella group for the three current segments of health, kids, and Hispanics. Each segment has its own team. A similar group was created for the five teams that serve as customer partners in the category management service. A new team was added for collaborative logistics. A vice president reporting to the sales function chairs the team, which consists of the distribution managers from sales, the logistics managers from operations, and a finance manager. Although this is a new venture, it still needs to keep the plants supplied and customers satisfied as the first priority. Thus, the creation of groups like the ones for segments and customers make the structure scalable.

To implement this reconfigurable organization, a company needs an aligned set of policies that permit it to form and reform internal and external networks of capabilities. I therefore describe in more detail the elements of the Star Model that support the capability to reconfigure.

Structure

The structure of the reconfigurable organization consists of a stable part and a changing part. The changing part was described in the course of the example as the company used cross-functional teams to configure miniature businesses around products, segments, channels, and customers. This changing part is the reconfigurable part, which flexes with shifts in competitive strategy.

The functional structure is the stable part, both home and host to the company's employees. It is home to the specialists and experts in food science, distribution, manufacturing technologies, data and analytics, and other competencies that the company has built. These people tend not to rotate across functions but do participate in the cross-functional teams. The functional structure is

Figure 6.4 Fully Reconfigurable Organization

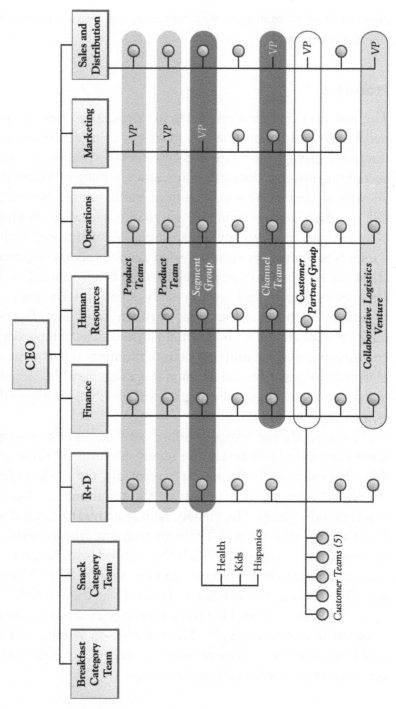

also the host to managers who move across functions on rotational assignments.

Processes

The first area, information and goal-setting processes, is often overlooked and underestimated in its power to define an organization's capabilities. The reconfigurable organization needs accounting systems, data structures, and planning processes that allow it to operate as a collection of miniature business units. All the data must be available to all the parties. In complex organizations, transparency is your friend. As mentioned earlier, the costs and revenues must be assignable to products, segments, channels, and so on so that profitability can be identified. Policies for transfer prices need to accurately reflect market prices to coordinate resource allocations between miniature business units themselves and with external partners. The complexity of coordinating all these miniature business units is aided by the use of flexible information and decision processes. Flexible, reconfigurable organizations must be aligned with flexible, reconfigurable accounting systems.

Constant change brings constant conflict, and the management team must be skilled at the timely resolution of these conflicts. For example, in the example company, the products from the health segment stole sales from the traditional cookie and cracker product lines. The management team had to do what was best for the total company. There are frequent priority decisions when resources are shared. Which channel and customers get supplied when the new products are in short supply? At its Monday morning meeting, the managers thrashed out these issues. The operations function head led these meetings. Attendance varied from ten to eighteen people. The information systems and the problem-solving management teams are necessary for the timely decisions in a reconfigurable organization.

The common processes are new product development, order fulfillment, and strategic planning. These are another source of stability. In the reconfigurable organization, the structure changes, but the processes are stable and common across the miniature business units.

And next, there needs to be a strong management team. There is really only one business and one profit-and-loss statement that counts: the company P&L. However, the strategy shifting and reconfiguring of the organization requires that it be decomposed into many miniature business units. In this way, each unit can pursue different initiatives, but they affect the company P&L both positively and negatively. The integration of all these units is the task of the management team, which must set priorities, allocate resources, and resolve the inevitable conflicts.

A joint project between the marketing and the finance functions has been launched to create modeling tools to help determine the profit impacts of initiatives in products, segments, channels, and so on. Marketing has the analytical tools and the databases, and finance has the financial analysis skills. These are to be combined into modeling techniques and simulations to support the leadership in launching and evaluating the miniature businesses.

Rewards

Finally, the reward system needs to be equally flexible and reconfigurable (see Ledford, 1995). Yet nothing turns a manager into a conservative faster than a recommendation to change the compensation system. Because of this conservatism, compensation systems are the greatest barriers to change and flexibility. At a time when pay plans need to be approximate, flexible, simple, and valid, they are instead precise, complex, quantitative, nonaligned, out of date, and rigid. It takes years to study a pay system, reevaluate jobs, pilot the new plan, and introduce it unit by unit. Far more speed and flexibility are needed.

At the example company, the new, nimble reward systems have far fewer grades or bands than their predecessors—three rather than the thirty pay grades of old. Salaries are based on a person's skills rather than job title. Today we pay the person, not the job. Jobs change too quickly. So do the people—but the more they learn, the more they earn. Often skill-based pay is given as a one-time bonus for learning because skills also come and go. Employees get fewer raises—annuity-style additions to their pay—and more one-time bonuses that reflect current efforts without generating an ongoing financial obligation for the company.

The appraisal process is also moving away from a boss's appraisal to a team-based appraisal or 360-degree feedback model. There is less ranking of all 220 engineers along a single dimension and less complexity in the performance rating scales. Some organizations have an appraisal day—an automated process that is done and completed in less than a day. It is done easily and quickly and can be repeated more often for quickly changing environments. Pay systems therefore are becoming more flexible in using more bonus and less annuity, simpler scales and grades, pay for skills rather than jobs, and encouraging faster changes and more experimentation.

People

Equally important is the area of human resources. The HR policies must be aligned to create the behaviors and mind-sets that support reconfigurability. The conflicts within a unit and between units over priorities and transfer prices can sap the energy of a miniature business unit. The participants need to be cross-functionally skilled, have cross-unit interpersonal networks, identify with the company as a whole, and be part of a reconfigurable culture. The various human resource policies are central to creating these skills and networks and the overall culture (see Lawler, 1994).

These HR policies start with hiring practices that recruit and attract people who fit the organization, not just the job. Jobs will change and new skills will be learned. But individual personalities and company values and culture are much less likely to change. Hence, a person-organization fit is key to the reconfigurable organization. Personality tests, work simulations, and extensive interviews are characteristic of hiring the person to fit the organization. For reconfigurable organizations, a fondness for working in teams, the ability to solve problems and handle conflicts, and the desire and potential to learn new skills are some of the sought-after personality attributes. For example, the baking company in the example uses a cross-functional interviewing process. Potential brand managers are interviewed by current brand managers and also by research scientists, manufacturing representatives, and sales managers with cross-functional experience. The company does not want a hot-shot marketer whose sole interest is a fast track through brand management. The person must also be acceptable to R&D and manufacturing. The intensive interview process selects people who will be effective in cross-functional work. This process also sends a message that "cross-function is the way we work" and helps build the reconfigurable culture.

Assignments and careers are also cross-functional for many managers. For example, R&D people often follow a new product they are working on into manufacturing and then into sales and distribution. At each step, they learn new functional skills and the new product development process. But just as important are the relationships they build, which add to their interpersonal network. The assignment process develops individuals and simultaneously develops the organization's network. The process builds the social capital on which reconfigurability is based.

Training is continuous and targeted at cross-unit participants. Project management training, for example, is given to cross-functional teams prior to beginning new projects. Other subjects are delivered to cross-unit groups consisting of people working at key interfaces. The purpose is always to simultaneously build know-how and know-who. The reconfigurable organization sees every training event, and especially social events, as opportunities to build know-who. The events are investments in building the company's social capital.

Collectively these people and reward practices build cross-unit skills, cross-unit interpersonal networks, and ultimately a reconfigurable culture. Such practices build the skills and mindsets to link functions, both inside and outside the company, into a miniature business unit. In this manner, an organization is better positioned to capitalize on an opportunity and build a new capability. These capabilities can be combined and recombined in interesting ways to create the next advantage. But the lasting capability, and possibly a more sustainable source of advantage, is the capability of an organization to reconfigure itself. Figure 6.5 shows an aligned Star Model with the various practices that constitute the reconfigurable organization.

Figure 6.5 Reconfigurable But Aligned Star Model

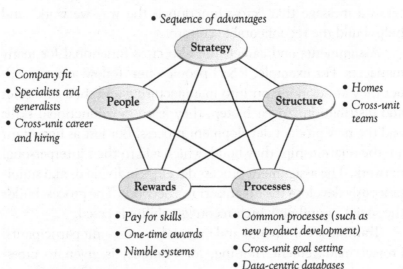

© Jay R. Galbraith.

The Cost of Reconfigurability

Reconfigurability, unlike quality, is not free. It takes time and resources to build the information systems and human resource practices. A significant investment in recruiting and training is required. Then there is the investment of management in coordinating work within and between miniature business units. It is a communications-intense form of organization.

It is also fraught with the potential for problems. Companies may not always be able to find people who can manage conflict and desire growth and development. Everyone is looking for team players. In addition, there is the potential for unresolved conflict. Transfer price issues can consume enormous amounts of time. As in matrix-type organizations, discussions in a reconfigurable organization can degenerate into endless internal negotiations that cut into the time available for customers. If all policies are not aligned, these internal frictions can absorb the company's energy. However, these costs and risks must be weighed against those of not being able to adjust to a reconfigurable competitor.

The reconfigurable organization is the companion to the continually shifting strategy. When competitive advantages do not last very long, neither do organizations. Instead, competitive advantage results from a string of short-term advantages delivered through a reconfigurable organization that consists of a stable functional structure around which projects and miniature business units are continually formed, combined, and disbanded. These units can focus on products, channels, segments, customers, regions, suppliers, technologies, and so on. The company can literally and simultaneously organize any way it wants to organize. The reconfigurability rests on three capabilities:

- Extensive internal cross-unit networking. This capability is built through aligned human resource policies. It attracts, holds, and develops the flexible people who create the flexible organization.

- An accounting and information system that permits an accurate and flexible determination of profit and loss on any dimension is the central tool underlying this capability. It is the planning and budgeting process for allocating resources across the portfolio of minibusiness units.

- External networking with partners to expand the capabilities that can be combined in creating new advantages. The same behavioral skills of cooperation, conflict management, and influence without authority that are used in internal networking are indispensable in managing external networks.

The final element is a top management team that sees its value added as designing and supporting the organization's reconfigurability.

Summary

When competitive advantages do not last long, neither do the organizations that execute them. In this chapter, we saw a bakery that created a series of advantages by creating, combining, and recombining capabilities. For each capability, a cross-functional team or minibusiness unit was created. These reconfigurable minibusiness units are the reconfigurable part of the structure. The functional structure was the stationary part and provided homes for the talent who cycled into and out of the minibusiness units. The remainder of the Star Model aligns with the structure and completes the reconfigurable organization. Some of the capabilities, however, were outside the bakery organization, so the bakery formed partnerships. The next chapter introduces the network organization, for which partnering is a way of life.

7

DESIGNING THE NETWORK ORGANIZATION

Another variation on the single-business functional organization is the network organization. Miles and Snow (1986) began describing this type of organization in the mid-1980s, when industries were transforming from vertical integration into horizontal industry models. It was also a time when companies were beginning to outsource activities and downsize. Many companies evaluated their supply chains as well. As they questioned their ability to perform activities along their value chains, they realized that they could not be good at everything along the chain, and yet to be competitive, they had to be good at everything along it. The network organization arose when a company began performing and owning only those activities at which it was superior. It would partner with other companies to acquire the other activities at which these outsiders were superior. Combined, this network of companies formed a superior business unit that performed all of the tasks along the value chain.

Two new organization design challenges came with the network organization. First, although the company has outsourced a function or two, these functions are still interdependent with the functions that the company owns and operates. So how do we design structures and processes to coordinate the cross-functional work flows involving multiple companies that we do not control? The company needs to acquire the capability to partner with other companies and understand the mechanisms of power and influence to coordinate its business along the entire value chain. Second, partnerships can leak intellectual property from one company to another. How do we design network partnerships to attain cooperation and share information and yet retain the intellectual property that sustains the company's advantages and valuable capabilities? We address these issues in the second half of the chapter.

History has also shown that as soon as a company decides what it is going to do and own, and what it is not going to do and own, the competitive landscape changes. It now sees the decision about what to outsource or where to play as a continuous one. It is a world in which all competitive advantages and the capabilities on which they're based are temporary. As capabilities come and go, partnerships may need to come and go as well. In this chapter, we review what we have learned about joining, forming, and exiting networks.

Probably the key learning is that the ultimate advantage goes to the company that can recognize over time which of its capabilities will capture the most value in the value chain. These capabilities are the ones for it to adopt, build, own, and keep. The others are the ones to outsource and discard. Our interest is in designing an organization and network in which the company can jump from one or one set of advantages to the next. Like the lateral organization, the framework for network organizations can be applied to any organizational stage. I describe it here in the context of the single-business functional organization.

The Network Organization Model

The chapter first explores the network strategies and industry structures that influence which capabilities to own and build and then focuses on organization design. It finishes with some examples of companies creating networks or ecosystems and how they manage those networks.

Network Strategy

A company following a network strategy and organization requires an extensive view of the competitive landscape. First, it needs to understand the entire industry value chain and where along that chain is the stage that captures the most value. This understanding is important because the value migrates over time in any value chain from one stage to another. This understanding should help a company avoid outsourcing and activity toward which the value will migrate in the next few years.

Second, companies' competitive landscapes include other industries that are converging with their own. The digital era is an era of industry convergence. Nike, for example, now competes with health care websites that give advice about exercise and with digital watch and device providers. Today a consumer can get news and entertainment from TVs, PCs, laptops, tablets, and smart phones. ABC and CNN never thought they would be competing with Google, Yahoo, Netflix, and Amazon to provide this news and entertainment. Therefore, strategists need to use a wide-angle lens when deciding where to play and how to win.

Strategic decisions in network organizations are being made more frequently and are more salient. The reason is that competitive advantages no longer last long. Not only is every competitive advantage temporary, but the half-life of advantages is getting shorter and shorter. The product development and life cycles of mainframes and large servers were very much longer than those of today's tablets and smart phones, and the development and life cycles of games and apps are very much shorter than those of operating systems like Windows 8.0. In these digital network industries, leadership teams are continuously deciding where to play and how to win: which capabilities to build and keep and which to outsource and discard and, at the same time, recognizing which are the capabilities that capture the most value and dominate the value chain.

Vertical and Horizontal Industry Structures. The 1980s saw a lot of downsizing and outsourcing and, with it, a shift to horizontal industry structures, but no other example caught people's imagination like the IBM PC start-up. An internal entrepreneur started the business with an interest in catching up with other PC start-ups and Apple. He moved the business to Boca Raton, Florida, so he could break all the rules of IBM. He could have moved anywhere as long as the distance from the Armonk, New York, headquarters was substantial. The key was to be "out of sight, out of mind," which enabled him to operate independently. He outsourced virtually all of the components, assembled them quickly, put the IBM brand on the product, and sold the PCs through IBM's distribution channel, as well as every other distribution channel. The product was an instant success and blew away all of the competitors except Apple. Most of us do not remember those first-generation PC firms, like Osborne, Sinclair, Atari, and Commodore.

The success of the IBM PC was immediately picked up by the business press and even business school professors hailed it as the model of the future. This model was, of course, the network model. Companies would no longer be vertically integrated like the rest of IBM. A company could simply design the product, manage the brand, and outsource the rest. It was suggested that IBM's PC division could even outsource the assembly. To bolster their argument, network enthusiasts pointed to Nike and Toyota. Both designed the product, managed the brand, and outsourced the manufacturing and distribution. Toyota, however, kept the assembly and ran it with the Toyota production system because it was a source of advantage for the company. Nike and Toyota, as we will see later, designed very different network organizations from the one designed by the IBM PC division.

The situation was quite different as the 1990s arrived. A new generation of PC vendors entered the market with IBM PC knockoffs. Compaq, Acer, Dell, Gateway, and HP all delivered new models faster and cheaper than IBM. They all used Microsoft Windows operating system, Intel microprocessors, and other components from IBM's suppliers. All of the value thus migrated from the PC product to the components from Microsoft and Intel. By outsourcing these components with no exclusivity,

IBM had converted the structure of the industry from vertical integration to a horizontal model. Andy Grove, Intel's CEO, represented the two models as shown in figure 7.1.

The vertically integrated model, followed by IBM and Digital Equipment Corporation (DEC), had given way to the horizontal model dominated by Intel and Microsoft. IBM and DEC had to be superior at all capabilities in the vertical chain. In the horizontal chain, each firm focused only on the component at which it was superior. Intel was best at microprocessors, Microsoft was best at software, and Dell was best at running a supply chain. The customer gets a superior product from the horizontal industry.

The move to the horizontal industry model also brought with it a move to network organizations. The reason is that the industry still needed to be integrated so that a complete PC came out at the end of it for the customer. If the industry was not vertically integrated by a single firm, it needed to be virtually integrated across many firms. Different forms of network organization arose as a result. Initially the PC value chain was integrated by the PC vendors like IBM, Compaq, HP, and Dell. They designed the product, assembled it, branded it, and managed the sales, distribution, and service. In this model, it was typical for the product designer and brander to become the captain of the industry team and provide the virtual integration. Nike, Toyota, and aerospace systems integrators like Lockheed and Boeing all followed similar models. The point here is that when there is a horizontal industry model, a network organization arises to provide the vertical integration of the industry.

The model to outsource and narrow product scope is not always desirable or followed. The research of Charles Fine from MIT (1998) shows that when an industry is either vertical or horizontal, pressures exist to move it to the other model. The computer industry serves as an example. The horizontal modular-product-focus strategy also arose in the commercial computing industry. By the mid-1990s, a computer customer could buy the digital infrastructure from Cisco, the servers from

Figure 7.1 Transformation of the Computer Industry

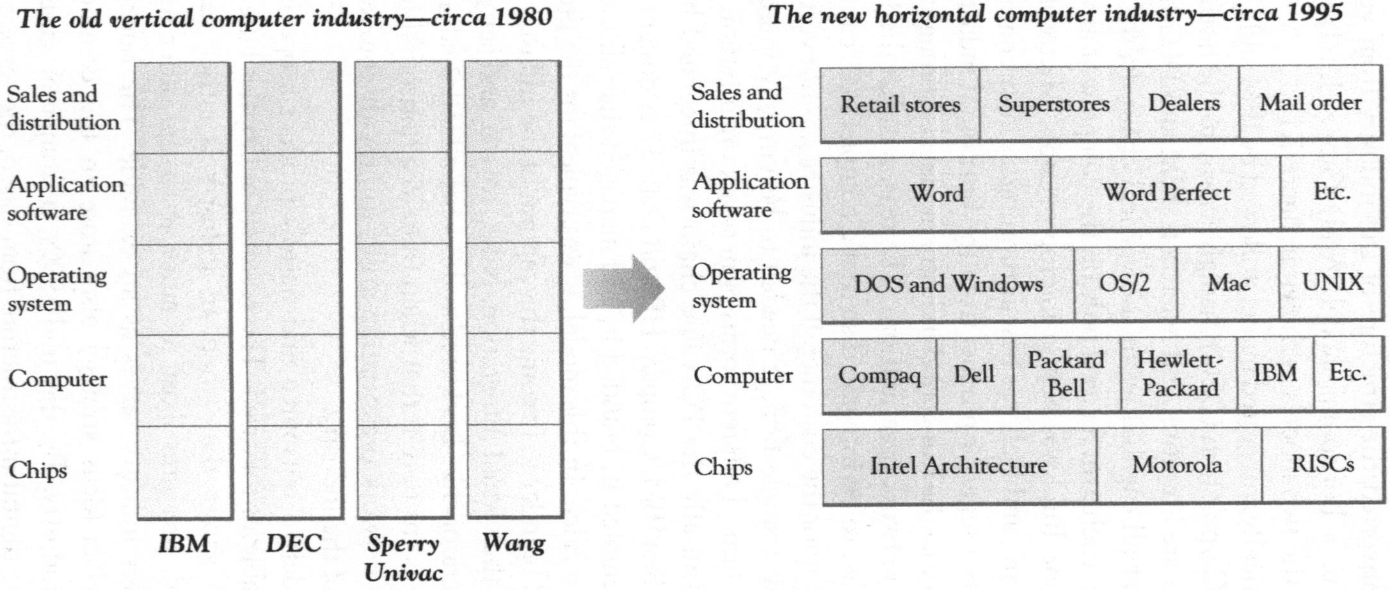

The old vertical computer industry—circa 1980

Sales and distribution				
Application software				
Operating system				
Computer				
Chips				
IBM	**DEC**	**Sperry Univac**	**Wang**	

The new horizontal computer industry—circa 1995

Sales and distribution	Retail stores	Superstores	Dealers	Mail order
Application software	Word	Word Perfect		Etc.
Operating system	DOS and Windows	OS/2	Mac	UNIX
Computer	Compaq	Dell	Packard Bell	Hewlett-Packard · IBM · Etc.
Chips	Intel Architecture		Motorola	RISCs

Source: A. Grove, *Only the Paranoid Survive* (London: HarperCollins, 1997), p. 44.

Note: The figure is not drawn to scale.

Sun Microsystems, software from Oracle, storage hardware from EMC, PCs from Dell, and printers from HP.

When Lou Gerstner took over IBM in the mid-1990s, everyone was advising him to break up IBM and compete with the focused-product horizontal model like everyone else in the industry. Gerstner said everyone was advising him to break up IBM except for the customers, who were saying that they could buy all these excellent products, but when they tried to put them together in a system, they did not work well. The customer had to do the virtual integration. A customer had to hire and pay Accenture, for example, to create software to get everything to work as intended. Instead, customers asked IBM to keep its businesses intact and get all of this equipment to work together under one firm. Keeping IBM integrated was another IBM choice that transformed the industry. This decision started to transform the computer industry back to the vertical model.

Today Cisco is still providing infrastructure but has added servers and software. Oracle provides software but has acquired more software types as well as the Sun Microsystems server business. Apple has shown that by owning and integrating both hardware and software design, it is possible to create higher-performing products. As a result, Google, Microsoft, and Amazon are acquiring, negotiating with, or partnering with hardware companies. Even the PC industry was reintegrated by Intel and Microsoft.

As more circuits could be put on the microprocessor, Intel did more of the product design. It then provided not just the microprocessor but also many of the surrounding chips in a chip set. It next put all of these chips on a printed circuit board called a motherboard. Intel did the branding as well with "Intel Inside." In addition to its Windows operating system, Microsoft provided all of the application software like Word, Excel, and Explorer in a suite called Microsoft Office. It did the branding with Windows 95 and now Windows 8.0. So Intel vertically integrated the hardware and Microsoft reintegrated almost all of the software.

The PC vendors simply snapped the modules together, applied their brand, and integrated just the downstream sales, distribution, and service.

The computer business has been partially reintegrated. The point illustrated is Fine's idea that when an industry moves to a more vertical or horizontal structure, pressures start to push the industry toward the other model. The newcomer to the industry through technological or business model innovation can start to move the industry in the opposite direction. It can integrate, separate, or bypass stages of the value chain and gain an advantage over the incumbents.

Strategic Network Decisions. Companies following the network organization model make two types of strategic decisions: what role in the network they are going to play and which capabilities they are going to own and control and which they are going to outsource and influence.

The choice of a role in the network varies between two extremes. On one extreme is the specialist who is superior at one capability, or a few, and becomes a player in all networks that need that capability. A good example is Dolby Laboratories for sound. At the other extreme is the captain of the network who coordinates all of the other players to deliver a complete business offering to the customer. An example is Nike, which outsources everything but product design and product marketing, but otherwise manages the whole supply chain from factory to retail.

The specialists are pretty straightforward. They have some feature like technology, scale, worldwide presence, or years of experience that gives them superiority over competitors. For Dolby, it is years of sound technology development. For Taiwan Semiconductor Manufacturing Company (TSMC), it is scale and process technology. In 2013, a state-of-the-art silicon fabrication facility costs somewhere north of $4 billion. Only a few semiconductor companies can afford that scale of investment, so most semiconductor design companies outsource the manufacturing of their designs to TSMC.

The captains and subcaptains take responsibility for coordinating the independent companies comprising the network or subnetwork (Lorenzoni and Baden-Fuller, 1995). The auto industry is an example. It was vertically integrated until the Japanese became competitive. In addition to its production system, Toyota contributed to the tiering of the industry value chain. For example, Nippondenso provided all of the electronics to Toyota as a tier 1 supplier. A tier 2 company may supply the components of the antilock braking system to Nippondenso, a tier 3 may supply parts to the tier 2, and so on. The system could extend to tier 5s. The tiering of the value chain converts the industry from a vertically integrated model to a horizontal model. Toyota then manages the entire network. For example, it gathers the total steel requirements for all members of the network. Then it negotiates a steel contract with Nippon Steel based on the total volume of the entire network. A small supplier receives steel at Toyota's price, far below what it could negotiate alone. However, if the small supplier provides only 20 percent of its output to the Toyota network, the contract covers only 20 percent of the vendor's steel requirements.

BMW plays a similar role in its network. It has identified all thirty thousand suppliers in its tiered network and follows all of them through social networks and news feeds. When it discovered an article in a local newspaper announcing that a small tier 4 supplier in Germany could not meet this week's payroll, BMW and its banks stepped in, met the payroll, and averted a strike or a work stoppage that could have disrupted BMW's supply chain. This kind of management is very important when supply chains operate on a just-in-time basis. The captain does whatever needs to be done to make the whole network effective. Similarly, the tier 3 supplier plays a captain's role for the tier 4s and 5s that are its suppliers.

The second strategic choice is the constant selection, building, and discarding of capabilities. These are the continual choices of where to play and how to win. A specialist can follow a couple of paths. Dolby Labs adds each new technological capability of sound to its repertoire. It started with noise reduction in professional sound studios. Then it discovered that film sound suffered from the same noise problems as the sound studios, so its technology migrated to every film, film studio, and movie theater. The company has since added stereo sound, surround sound, digital sound, digital sound compression, and more. Dolby Labs strives to be the best in the world at high-quality sound for the entertainment business.

Other specialists have added other capabilities and grown to play bigger roles in the network. Intel and Microsoft simply provided one chip and the operating system for the original IBM PC. They added more chips, more functionality, and software capabilities and finally dominated the industry. Another example is Honeywell. Originally it provided navigation systems for Boeing aircraft. Now it provides the entire flight deck. Through acquisitions, Honeywell built capabilities to handle an entire module of the aircraft, so it is now a captain of a major subsystem of commercial aircraft.

The captain's role is the one that has the key choice of which capabilities to own and perform and which to outsource. Usually the captain performs those activities that the customer finds important, those for which there are few outside suppliers, those that involve scale, those that integrate the members of the network, those that influence the brand, and those that give the firm an opportunity for competitive advantage. Commodities and input from plentiful or superior suppliers are contracted out. Contracting out to superior suppliers for capabilities that are quite essential then requires a company to design relationships with that supplier that reduce its vulnerability. These were the roles that were performed by many of the captains already discussed, like Toyota, Nike, and BMW. In addition, the most effective captains play whatever role is needed to make the network perform better. BMW saw the need to help a tier 4 supplier handle its payroll.

All of the captains have learned an important lesson from the IBM PC experience: not to outsource a key component without first taking steps to reduce their vulnerability. IBM should have negotiated an exclusive arrangement or should have developed its own capability to supply itself once the exclusivity ran out. Fine (1998) makes the point that a captain should outsource the capacity but not the knowledge that underlies a key capability. For example, Cisco outsources 99 percent of its manufacturing but still has five hundred people in its operations functions. It performs the other 1 percent and maintains a capability in manufacturing process design.

Nike has learned these lessons as well. Even though it has outsourced sales to retail partners, it always maintains a few stores in key locations and some showcase stores, like Niketown in New York City. These outlets give it direct contact with consumers as well as some locations where it can test products and promotions. The stores provide Nike as well with knowledge of the retail cost structure. Nike therefore hedges its bets through its retail knowledge and the ability to go direct. This gives it a better negotiating position with its partners.

Recently Nike introduced a direct-to-consumer channel using stores, like Apple stores, and e-commerce. It followed a similar policy with its outsourced manufacturing. Nike always maintained the capability in manufacturing process development and an expertise in different materials. Based on that, it has invented a new shoe manufacturing process, Flyknit, that creates a shoe that conforms to an individual's feet and gives easily when stressed. The manufacturing process, completely automated, is a good hedge as labor and exchange rates in Asia rise and shipping costs increase. Fine's advice to outsource the capacity but not the knowledge is sage advice indeed.

•••

In summary, the network strategy consists of a choice of role and capabilities. That role can vary from that of a specialist in one capability, to specializing in several, to becoming a captain of a subsystem, to being a captain of the industry network from raw material to end user. The second choice is which capabilities the company wants to own and control and which ones to outsource and influence. This second choice takes place continuously. When making this choice, the company moves to more or less specializing and more or less captaincy. The next sections describe the organization design decisions to manage the strategy.

Designing the Network Organization

The design of the network organization consists of four key choices: building the right types of external relationships, which companies to partner with, how to structure the partnerships, and determining the kinds of supporting policies that are needed.

External Relationships. Once a company has chosen its role in the network and decided which activities to perform and which to contract out, it needs to design processes to coordinate the activities performed by others. Communication and joint decision processes are needed to manage the interdependence between the companies in the network. These external relationships are similar in many ways to the internal lateral processes of a firm, and the types and amounts of coordination among them similarly vary. Thus, the task of the organizational designer is once again to match the types and amounts of coordination with the appropriate types and amounts of external lateral relationships.

The design choice is governed by the type of external relationships, which vary from a market relationship between buyer and seller, to contracts between parties, to sourcing and alliance arrangements, to equity relationships, to outright ownership. The continuum is shown in figure 7.2, where the relationships are linked with the amount of coordination required and the

Figure 7.2 Types of External Relationships and Coordination Requirements

Relationships	Relative Strength	Coordination	Dependence	Value Capture
Ownership	**Strong**	Very substantial	Very high	**High**
Equity		Very substantial	High	
Sourcing and alliance		Substantial	Moderate	
Contract		Occasional or some	Minimum	
Market	**Weak**	None	Zero	**Low**

amount of dependence on or vulnerability to the outside firm. The amount of coordination varies with the amount of interdependence between the partners and the amount of variety and unpredictable change. Dependence has two dimensions to it. First, how critical is the partner's contribution, and how many others could provide it? Clearly high criticality and few other providers mean high dependence. Second, how vulnerable is the company to leakage of intellectual property? The partners need to share information, so how vulnerable is the company if the partner uses that information to work with a competitor? The classic example is when Microsoft worked with Apple to develop Microsoft Office to run on the Mac operating system. Based on what Microsoft learned, the company released Windows 3.0, which duplicated the Mac. Apple then lost its competitive advantage. The more vulnerable a company is, the higher is the dependence and the greater the need for relationship strength.

The relationships at the bottom of figure 7.2 are the cheapest and easiest to use. As the designer proceeds up the list, the relationships become more complex and require more management time and effort. The designer should proceed only until the point where the coordination required by the partnering strategy is reached.

Another factor that influences the type of relationship between partners is value capture. For example, when Microsoft and Google form a relationship with a software partner, they often take a minority equity stake. The partner's stock will probably rise on the announcement of the partnership, so Microsoft and Google take an equity stake to capture some of that value. A different situation arises with biotechnology firms like Monsanto, DuPont, and Syngenta. They discover genes that can be inserted into seeds like corn or soybeans to help the plants resist pests and thus decrease the need for insecticides. But it's impossible to sell genes alone; the genes must be embedded in seeds that are sold to farmers. The value of the biotech firms' research can be captured only through the sale of the seeds, which motivated the biotech companies to take equity stakes in the seed companies. These stakes became joint ventures and then acquisitions. The acquisitions helped speed new genes to market, capture value for the biotech firm, and deny access to the seed company by other biotech firms. Let us start at the bottom of the chart and work our way up the relationship strength list.

Markets and Contracts. Markets and contracts are standard mechanisms for mediating economic transactions. Figure 7.2 shows that relationships mediated by markets require little coordination and communication between the parties. Indeed, the purchase of commodities from spot markets takes place between buyers and sellers who remain unknown to each other. Markets are used to secure products and services that are standard and freely available.

The contract relationship is somewhat more involved. The buyer and seller communicate and negotiate terms periodically, but there is little subsequent contact unless exceptions arise.

Contracts come to pass when the items being acquired are not standard and are not always available. Some items may need to be customized, and others may be standard but subject to shortages—like shape memory chips for PCs, tablets, and smart phones. A contract guarantees the source of supply for the length of the contract and specifies the customization.

Sourcing and Alliances. Sourcing and alliance relationships require more coordination. Sourcing involves a contract, but it involves a closer and longer-term relationship than the spot contracts discussed in the preceding paragraph. Usually the parties reveal their long-term plans to one another and participate in jointly developing products and services. For example, automobile companies developing engines work with companies developing catalytic converters to remove pollution from the exhaust. Each engine requires a new chemistry, which is unique to that engine. In order to develop this new chemistry, the companies must exchange information to do the design of the engine and catalytic chemistry. Both companies therefore exchange sensitive information. The converter company customizes its product and may make investments in specific equipment. To justify the effort and investment by the converter company, the auto company gives the catalytic supplier a sole-source contract and large volume.

This kind of sourcing relationship has several characteristics. One is the substantial customizing by the supplier for the unique advantage of the customer. In return, the customer makes the customizer the sole or preferred supplier, which reduces the risk and vulnerability for the supplier and ensures the volume to pay for the effort. Sourcing relationships also involve a great deal of communication about future plans and the coordination of product and service development. The parties become partners, jointly developing the unique product. There is usually a formal product development team with representatives from both parties. As with internal lateral processes, there will be an integrator (a product manager from the vendor), so that the product development team can span both companies. The partners will share the same product development software and design information. After the product is designed, the ordering and supplying will be done electronically as well. Thus, sourcing relationships involve fewer, closer, longer-term relationships. The contract usually contains a nondisclosure agreement and limitations on the vendor's use of the technology for others. These agreements tend to span a couple of years.

Although the terminology is not standard, similar relationships between competitors (as opposed to between suppliers and customers) are usually referred to as alliances (or *teaming*, in aerospace). The parties in an alliance also exchange information and commitments and jointly perform an activity and share the outcome. For example, GM and Honda announced their continuing cooperation on fuel cell development in July 2013 and are cooperating and sharing the risk on this expensive new technology. Other partnerships are Toyota and BMW, and Daimler AG, Ford, and Nissan. These research and development partnerships are common because of the size of the investments and risks. The companies also feel less vulnerable the further from the customer that the cooperation takes place. In each case, development teams are staffed by both partners, with an integrator role (project managers) to coordinate the joint effort and manage the relationship. A great deal of coordination and communication between the partners is essential to the joint activity.

Equity Relationships. The equity relationship is so named because it involves the transfer of equity. There are three main types of arrangements for the transfer of equity. In some cases, the network captain takes a minority shareholding in a supplier. Ford, for example, invested in Cummins Engine for a 20 percent stake. The amounts vary, but the network captain takes a substantial, although minority, position. In other types of equity relationships, each member takes a small stake in the others. Airlines took small equity positions in each other when they formed their alliances, like OneWorld and Star Alliance. Although the Japanese *keiretsu* are unwinding at present, these cross-shareholdings were typical in Japan and some European countries. Such cross-share holdings are used in alliances among equals. The most involved equity relationship is the joint venture. Here, a separate company is created with its own equity, which is usually split more or less equally between the parties.

Thus equity relationships can be joint ventures, cross-share holdings, or minority stakes, each with varying amounts of equity involved. They are alliances with a lot of control and significant investment. There may be as much need for coordination and communication as in an alliance, but one or both partners may be more dependent and vulnerable. The exchange of equity symbolizes both greater commitment and longer-term commitment. An equity relationship is usually more difficult to unwind than an alliance, which may even have a termination date.

One of the most prolific users of joint ventures is Corning Glass, a materials science company that continually invents new types of specialty glass for new uses. However, rather than introduce its inventions and move downstream, it forms joint ventures with other companies that already have the downstream business models and experience to profit from the new invention. Corning invented fiberglass (Owens Corning), silicones (Dow Corning), and optical fibers (Siecor). It invented the glass for liquid crystal displays (LCD) and touch screens (Gorilla Glass) and formed a joint venture with Samsung. Most recently, it has a new invention, called Lotus Glass. Again, it has formed a joint venture with Samsung, which has the OLED (organic light-emitting diode) technology to provide the next generation of displays ranging from small handheld devices to large televisions. In all cases, the joint venture allows Corning to maintain ownership of the technology and capture downstream value from the resulting products.

Ownership. Equity is not a guarantee that the partnership will not fall apart, although it increases the probability of success at a cost. The ultimate control is 100 percent ownership of an activity. If the vulnerability is too great for one partner or the opportunity for profit is too large to share, one of the partners will purchase the other.

The application software unit of Apple is a good example. When the Mac first appeared, little application software was available for it, so Apple started its own software unit, which created MacPaint and MacDraw. Outside software houses later became interested in creating software for the Mac, but they were reluctant to share information because Apple's in-house unit was a competitor. Apple decided to make the unit, called Claris, a separate company while maintaining a minority interest. But just before Apple's public stock offering, it pulled Claris back into the company. The reason? Microsoft had introduced Windows 3.0, and Claris was the software company with the most experience writing programs for the new Windows-type operating systems. With ten times as many Windows-compatible computers as Macs, an independent Claris would have a strong incentive to write primarily for Windows and secondarily for the Mac. But as a wholly owned unit of Apple, Claris would support the Mac first. Apple needed full control of Claris to keep that company's interests aligned with its own. For similar reasons Monsanto acquired DEKALB, a seed company, and DuPont acquired Pioneer. Ownership allows them to capture value and get exclusive rights to the seeds.

• • •

Three factors—coordination, vulnerability, and value capture—drive companies to choose more complex forms of relationship. Alliances and sourcing relationships are adopted to achieve the coordination needed to execute customization and joint development; markets and simple contracts are insufficient by themselves. But working jointly with other companies increases the vulnerability of the firm. Equity exchanges reduce the vulnerability and increase the firm's commitment and control and allow greater value capture. The combination of increased coordination, reduced vulnerability, and value capture drives organization designers to choose the more complex relationships.

Partner Selection

The choice of partner is crucial in alliances and equity relationships. (There is less dependence and vulnerability with market and contract relationships.) Firms that are skilled at alliances and equity ventures continuously and thoroughly evaluate potential partners.

The first priority when selecting a partner is to understand the potential partner's strategic intentions. Ford initially chose TRW to provide its safety equipment like seat belts and airbags. TRW needed to understand Ford's intentions. Ford's intention may be to develop TRW as its safety equipment partner. Another auto manufacturer may use a partnership to learn TRW's technology and create its own internal capability. It may then use its internal capability to supply its own needs or to negotiate lower prices from TRW, having stripped it of its technical edge. Knowing these intentions in advance is the key to partner selection. The Ford-TRW partnership has been an effective one as TRW follows Ford into new countries like China. Other factors include compatibility of goals, values, styles, and time horizons.

The Apple-Samsung partnership has not turned out as well. Apple had outsourced its key processor chips, shape memory chips, and touch screen displays to Samsung. A couple of years later, Samsung became Apple's chief competitor. Both companies accuse the other of stealing each other's patents. While they are fighting it out in court, Apple is searching for new partners. It will not be able to be supplied by TSMC until 2014, because it will take that long to acquire equipment and meet Apple's standards. Apple was either unaware of Samsung's intentions or underestimated Samsung's ability to compete.

Corning, a skilled partner, continuously locates partner candidates and assigns them to the company's officers. The top manager then investigates the candidate, and a consulting firm analyzes the company and its history. Corning has found that it can learn more about a company's values by assessing its behavior in the face of adversity. It investigates what the company did during an event such as a plant closure, a hazardous waste spill, and so on. It then gets to know the candidate's managers, inviting them to speak at meetings or attend the annual officers meeting; it has them bring their spouses and gets to know them informally as well. A small joint project may be next. In this way, people at various working levels get to know one another. Each contact is a test: if a candidate passes all of them, Corning may try an alliance. If that is successful, it may try a larger alliance, evolve toward an equity relationship, and eventually suggest a joint venture. The selection process is continuous and thorough.

The selection process requires a lot of time and effort from management. However, this degree of upfront effort is characteristic of successful partnering. As the old saying goes, "You pay me now, or you pay me later." Issues not discovered in the courtship will arise later in the partnership, when they are more difficult to solve and the relationship more difficult to dissolve.

Today the evaluation of partner candidates is getting easier. More companies now have a partnering history that can be examined. Indeed, in the future, being seen as an attractive partner will be a requirement for competitiveness. Thus, the need to gain a good reputation as a partner actually controls certain temptations to behave opportunistically in alliances. More and more companies are investing in the upfront courtship process to find appropriate partners for longer-term relationships.

Partnership Structure

Alliances and joint ventures are joint activities that need to be structured. There are three types of structures for joint activities (Killing, 1983):

- The *operator model*, when one partner takes the management responsibility for the joint activity
- The *shared model*, where responsibility is divided between the two partners
- *Joint ventures*, which can be autonomous

The basic model for the partnership structure is shown in figure 7.3. The two-partner structures shown in the figure may be any of those already discussed above. The alliance (or venture) itself is probably a functional structure focused on developing and supplying a product, service, or technology. Members from both partners form a board to supervise the activity.

The operator model is used in sourcing arrangements and sometimes in alliances and joint ventures. In the Ford/TRW example, TRW probably serves as the operator and manages the product development effort. Ford contributes some people to work on the product and several managers to serve on the board. But the alliance manager and key functional managers are from TRW.

Oil and gas platforms are typically joint ventures formed by three or four oil companies. The basic motivation is to share the risk of dry holes. When a strike is made, the group shares the

Figure 7.3 Partnership Structure for Sourcing, Alliances, or Joint Ventures

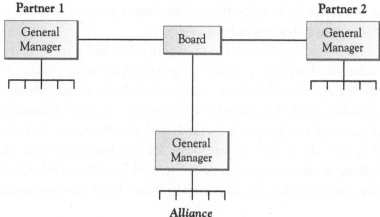

Figure 7.4 The Operator Alliance Model

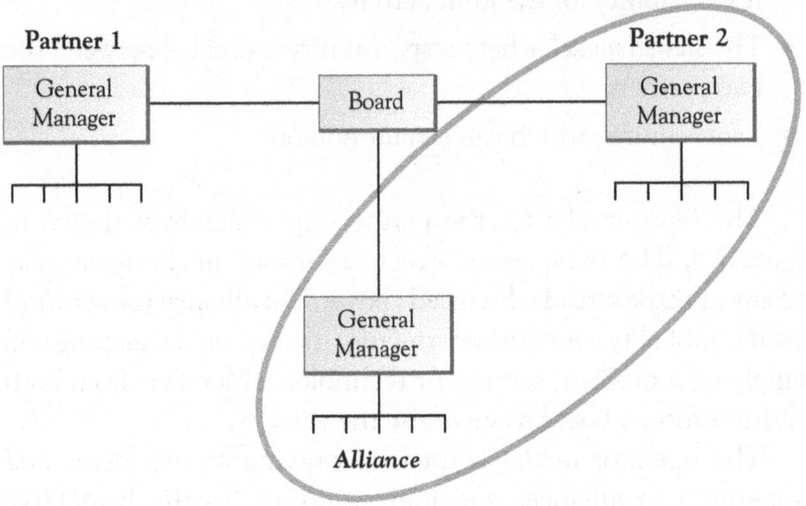

wealth. The platform itself is operated by one of the partners, and the others sit on the board. The decision-making orientation is illustrated by the circled items in figure 7.4. The board acts much like a normal board of directors, reviewing work, approving investments, and agreeing on the selection of key people.

The operator model has been more successful than the shared model. It makes one company responsible, minimizes conflicts, and leads to faster decisions. This model is preferred when one partner has the capabilities to manage the efforts and also works best when the role can be rotated between partners, as in the oil and gas companies example.

The shared model, used in many alliances and joint ventures, is preferred when each partner brings a complementary skill. One of the most successful joint ventures has been Cereal Partners Worldwide (CPW). General Mills brings the product knowledge and provides the heads of research and development and marketing and the CEO. Nestlé provides the manufacturing and distribution into every country in the world except North Korea. It also provides the chief financial officer. Both partners regard

Figure 7.5 The Shared Alliance Model

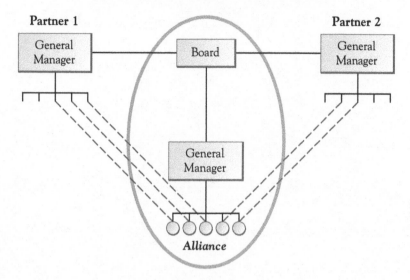

the joint venture, which started in the early 1990s, as a success, and they share board seats equally. The focal point of decision making shifts with this relationship, as illustrated in figure 7.5.

The shared model is characterized by a small and active board, usually consisting of four or five—no more than seven—people. It is staffed with two managers from each partner and the alliance general manager. This general manager comes from one partner, and one of the managers from the other partner chairs the board.

A difficulty of the shared model is the potential for conflict among the partners or indecision. Indecision is likely if managers in the partner organizations interfere instead of using the board as the decision-making focal point. But if the partners are skilled at alliances and joint ventures and if the board is active, the partnership can capitalize on the combination of the complementary skills.

The third type of structure is the autonomous model, shown in figure 7.6. In this model, the decisions are made by the venture itself, which becomes more independent of its parents.

Figure 7.6 The Autonomous Joint Venture Model

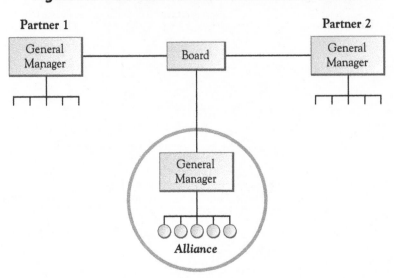

This model is often adopted by many joint ventures. A venture usually begins by using the operator or shared model and evolves into the autonomous model. CPW, the venture between General Mills and Nestlé, has become an autonomous joint venture. All of Corning's joint ventures are intended to become independent companies. As the venture becomes successful and develops its own talent, it becomes less dependent on its parents. The board becomes an ordinary board; the major decisions are made within the venture. The benefit is that the venture can then act more quickly to deal with changing business situations.

Supporting Policies

The design of the network organization is completed with the creation of supporting policies corresponding to the two remaining elements of the Star Model: the selection and development of people and the reward system. Both are enlisted to create behaviors, values, and norms that support the partnering process.

Many of the same skills that facilitate internal lateral processes also facilitate processes between companies. Particularly key are an ability to influence without authority and a facility for working with people from different cultures. Often people can graduate from participation in internal processes to external ones.

Another people issue is the selection and development of people who can deal with the dilemma of partnering. That is, they must reveal information and cooperate with partners but must not reveal certain critical pieces of information. Part of this issue is choosing individuals who can walk this fine line and be comfortable. The other part is training them to understand the aspects of the company's strategy and core competencies that should not be revealed. As more and more people work in direct contact with people from other companies, this training will become crucial.

The reward system needs to be augmented to encourage employees to look for the win-win outcome. Managers at Corning all tell stories of bosses who have reprimanded them for not looking for a benefit for the other partner. Partnering has to be good for both parties. Effective companies promote the seeing of the situation through the partners' eyes.

For example, one company is reevaluating its partnering approach. It has always tried to win in negotiations, and last year it won a very nice royalty agreement from its Japanese partner. But this year, it is not celebrating: the royalty is so favorable that the partner has no incentive to fulfill the partnership agreement. The company is currently renegotiating so that both partners can profit from the relationship. Thus the reward system needs to promote a constant search for the win-win outcome.

Creating and Managing Ecosystems

Software companies have long been known for their ability to create and manage an ecosystem. That is, they cultivate and collaborate with the community of software developers to get these companies to write software applications to run on their platforms. Apple and, particularly, Microsoft have created large communities called ecosystems of software developers that write programs, and now apps, that run on their operating systems, the Mac OS, iOS, and Windows.

Apple was probably the first to use the evangelist role to recruit developers to join its ecosystem. Today, Nike, GE, and the Detroit automakers, among others, are embedding all kinds of semiconductor chips in their products and creating systems software to gather and process all of the data emanating from these chips. These companies are recognizing that they can open these systems and publish the appropriate information (APIs) so that the community of software developers can write apps for their systems or platforms. These companies are fast becoming high-technology software companies. They are creating evangelist roles, recruiting software developers, and creating incubators to support start-ups that will write software for their platforms.

So how do they organize to manage this network of companies that they do not own? Nike was the example we used earlier. It initially created a digital function within its running business. In this function are its own app developers and an evangelist or new business development unit to recruit outside developers to write software apps for Nike+. In order to attract third-party developers, Nike gives them software development tools to make it easy to write software that runs on the Nike+ platform and access to Nike's customer base through the app store. If Nike is successful, it could attract several hundred development companies to its network. At this point, it will need to manage this network just as it had to manage the Nike+ customer community and Asian manufacturing network.

Most high-tech companies manage their networks or ecosystems by segmenting them based on the developer's value to their business. The A players are the largest revenue and value creators. They may also be small but have great potential and receive the most attention. Nike could give them consulting help on running knowledge. It could share its enormous database of running information that is uploaded onto Nike+, along with the consulting. It could include them in the Nike booth at trade shows, engage in joint advertising, and give them advance copies of new Nike+ software. There may be between one and five A players for each evangelist in the unit. The B players receive a little less attention. An evangelist would manage twenty or so B players, and a couple of other evangelists would manage all of the C players over the social network.

Like Toyota and BMW, Nike would do whatever is needed to create value for the network. A developer may experience fast growth and require a new CEO; Nike would help recruit one. A company could experience a problem, and Nike could send in some of its own talent to help. A company may want to sell its business; Nike would find a buyer. It could also play marriage broker and help merge some of its network companies. It may provide a loan to another developer. In general, Nike behaves like the captain of the network. It maintains an overview of the network and takes actions to maintain the network's health.

Nike is also subject to all of the dependencies and vulnerabilities in its relationship that were described above. A lot of competitors are entering the wearable technology business. When Nike shares its running data and expertise with a developer, that developer could use the information to write an app for Google or Amazon. Through contracting and nondisclosures, Nike may be able to limit the developer's ability to write running apps for others. It may be able to fund a separate group at the developer and have exclusivity on its products; it may buy the app; or it may have to invest in equity stakes, create a joint venture with the developer for running apps, or acquire the developer and apps that are critical to Nike.

Equally important is that Nike should not use information from its developers to create its own app ahead of the developer, or it should not share competitive information from one developer with a competitive developer. In part, these networks of independent companies run on trust. It is not authority but trust that holds a network together. The captaincy of a network must be earned and maintained.

In summer 2013, Nike started an incubator to nurture start-ups to write apps for the Nike+ platform. Working with a venture capitalist, it selected start-up candidates for a three-month boot camp. It shares all of its running data with these start-ups if they will write apps for Nike. Then after three months, Nike and the venture capitalist take the start-up hopefuls to San Francisco for a showing before other investors. Nike may also take a stake in them. These start-ups could become independent firms and part of Nike's network, or Nike could acquire all or part of them. Nike is increasingly acting like a high-technology firm.

A Network Organization

The example here is a particularly interesting type of network organization. The company is an engineering and construction firm. The engineering and construction industry operates on a horizontal model with architects, engineers, construction firms of all types and sizes, general contractors, construction materials suppliers, construction equipment providers, and consultants of all types. The industry gets integrated on projects by some large engineering and construction firms like Fluor and Bechtel or by global general contractors like Skanska.

On smaller projects, it would be an architectural firm or a general contractor. The example firm is an engineering and construction firm that specializes in delivering complex factories like pharmaceutical plants and biotechnology plants. It plays the network captain role or project manager from start to volume production at zero defects.

The firm evolved into its specialty over a couple of decades. It became the expert in delivering a complex project fast. When building a pharmaceutical or a biotech plant, speed is the driving factor. The pharma company attains a patent on a new drug, and the clock starts ticking until the patent runs out. So when the company gets approval of a new drug from the Food and Drug Administration, the design and construction of the factory begins immediately. The faster the plant starts producing, the more money the pharma company can make before the patent expires.

As a result, the engineering and construction company has mastered the art of concurrent design. That is, there are decisions made in the design phase that determine the cost and speed of construction. There are design decisions that determine the ease of operation and maintenance of the plant. All of these factors are considered concurrently in the design phase. The design team is staffed with engineers, construction, and operating people from the beginning. When the design is concurrent, the project can proceed more quickly, as well as result in a lower cost of ownership for the plant. In order to implement the current design process, the firm manages the design, construction, certification of the plant, start-up of production, and the transfer of the plant to the owner as one fully integrated project.

The other dimension of concurrent design is the overlap of phases, so that construction begins before the design is complete. The training of operating personnel takes place concurrently with construction. The reason the company can execute concurrent design process is that it has a network organization specifically designed for the implementation of complex, concurrent projects.

The strategy of where to play is to deliver complex factories in the pharma and biotech industries. The company manages all phases from design to volume production. It performs the core design and overall project management and contracts out other activities like construction, plant equipment, plant operation, and specialist expertise. The formula for success—how to win—is delivering a totally integrated plant fast.

Most of the construction industry works on the horizontal model with a sequential approach to projects. At each stage, a separate company does the design, construction, and certification before turning the plant over to the customer. Each company optimizes its phase. Thus, the industry as a whole is underintegrated and suboptimized. The outstanding capability of this particular company is its ability to manage extreme interdependence and optimize the entire design and construction process. Its high-speed concurrent model shifts the normal sequential interdependence of the engineering and construction industry to a reciprocal interdependence model. In addition, the evolving high technology of the biotech industry means a high rate of unpredictable change. The company is always doing something for the first time. Combined, the rate of change and extreme interdependence require a large volume of information and decision-making ability, along with state-of-the-art coordination mechanisms to deliver the concurrent design model.

Several strategic factors reduce the magnitude of the coordination task. First, the company is not diverse; it specializes only in pharma and biotech plants. And second, it stays small. The leaders try to keep the company under one hundred people. The bulk of the population is design engineers, plus some field project management people for construction and start-up, IT specialists, and the normal administrative people in finance and HR. Third, it has state-of-the-art design and project management information systems and technology. The computer-aided design software houses love to work with it because it is always ready to try the next new thing. In addition, it customizes the software for its specialty in order to automate as much of the design process as possible. It also has state-of-the-art databases from its designs, equipment providers, industry analytical tools and data, and biotech knowledge from universities. The idea is to automate as much design interdependence as possible but always use the state of the art. And fourth is its unique approach to talent management.

The firm is highly selective when choosing engineers. Like other firms today, it's looking for people who will work well on project teams. It is also looking for generalists. The engineers could be trained in electrical, mechanical or architectural engineering, but the firm wants them to be able to design all the systems in a factory: heating, ventilation, and air conditioning (HVAC); plumbing; electrical; and structural. All of these systems are interdependent, but most engineering design firms use specialists in each area. Coordination challenges and jurisdictional disputes are then common. The example company wants to avoid these dysfunctions by having uncommon generalist engineers. It calls them Leonardos, after Leonardo da Vinci. (He was supposed to have mastered all of the knowledge of his day in mathematics, mechanics, biology and anatomy, and painting and sculpture.) The concept is that the human brain is the best device for integrating all of the systems in a plant; in other words, intrapersonal coordination beats interpersonal coordination. Using talented generalists reduces the need for interdisciplinary conversations. These engineers are selected based on their past behavior, professed interests, college course work, and in-depth company interviews.

The engineers receive extensive training in the company's design approach, design tools, and culture and then are given a design project. The company engages local fast food restaurants and offers to design its new stores. A fast food restaurant is an easy design task—a straightforward box. But the new engineers have to design the whole restaurant by themselves: the structure, the HVAC, plumbing, and electrical systems to meet the building specifications on a challenging schedule. The engineers have to prove that they can become Leonardos. Depending on the company workload and the engineers' performance, the new engineers may do from one to three of these projects under the supervision of an experienced engineer. This person runs the developmental project unit and deals with the fast food customers. The company breaks even on this business; in fact, it is not intended to make money. It simply gets the customers to pay for the training and development of its new engineers in this way.

Upon completion of the various restaurant projects, the engineer's work is reviewed. The engineer decides whether this generalist approach is appealing, and the company assesses whether the engineer is cut out to be a Leonardo. A mutual decision is made at this point. For engineers who do not stay with the firm, the company helps them find a new position at another firm. The engineers who stay with the company move on to the next factory design project.

After a few assignments, the engineers work on a construction site, where they learn project management. And at this point, another review takes place. The engineer and the company again mutually decide if there is a good fit between the engineer and the company. Engineers who stay decide whether to continue the project management site work or whether to return to design work. This career path creates field project managers who have had design experience and design engineers who have had field project experience. These professionals have a mutual understanding of both sides of the business: they know the languages of both sides and can communicate and coordinate the extreme interdependence of the concurrent model. This generalist model enables the high volume of communication between construction, operations, and design engineering.

The other parts of the organization are its structure, reward system, and exceptional concurrent design project management process. The structure of the organization is simple given its small size. The focus is on projects, with a leader for the two or three active projects and the restaurant unit. People working on the same project are colocated. The building is constructed so that people can move on and off projects easily. The IT and finance people who support a project are located with that project as well, and the others are located in their respective departments.

The company is incorporated but run as a partnership, with the two founding partners actively involved in managing the company. One is a paradigm example of a Leonardo design engineer. The other is a design engineer who prefers to work in the field on construction sites. They chair the partners' committee, which governs the company like a board of directors. There is also an advisory board of prominent members of the biotech community and universities. A talent subcommittee of partners decides on all promotions from associate to director to partner, and the members rotate every year. It is supported by the HR function. A compensation subcommittee decides on how the partnership profits will be allocated each year. The employees receive a competitive salary, a bonus, and a profit-sharing contribution based on company profits. The profit sharing, like most other partnerships, is redeemable on retirement. The subcommittee is supported by HR and finance, and the founders chair all the subcommittees.

The other unusual aspect of the company's organization is the project management process and its network captaincy. The company works on fixed-price incentive contracts, with incentives for early completion. It also strives to work lawyer free by gaining the trust of customers, contractors, and equipment suppliers. It operates with an open reporting system, and when a problem is encountered, it is reported to all parties. Hiding problems is not tolerated. The company's focus is on how to solve the problem, not on who caused it. It attains such openness and visibility through multiple video cameras that are installed all over the construction site. The installation of major equipment and fixtures is recorded along with the daily activity, and the recordings are uploaded to the construction website at the end of each day. The customer, the design engineers at headquarters, and suppliers can all view the site and videos at any time. At the end of the week, the customer receives a summary video and report of progress and problems. The videos have proved to be valuable as part of the permanent record as well. They are used to train the operators and the maintenance crew and are helpful when diagnosing an operating problem because the construction is visible to all.

In addition, the videos have proven useful for site management of the contractors and subcontractors. The company chooses its subcontractors carefully. It wants to agree with the subs on values and work practices, which are the basis for trust in lawyer-free operations. For example, a big complaint of subcontractors is that they are not paid on time, and often the general contractor withholds payment when there is a complaint or dispute. This company instead guarantees to pay contractors and all stakeholders on time and not to withhold payment. In the event of a problem, the company will not pursue blame but will focus on fixing the situation with the sub. The videos are a fast means to diagnosing and fixing problems.

Another practice that the company employs is an end-of-day meeting in comfortable modular space units at the construction site. These meetings are unusual because most contractors do not want to pay overtime. This company invites managers and craftspeople to meet after the day's work and pays them overtime for their participation. During these meetings, the project managers debrief the day for lessons learned and, more important, plan for the next day's work. Specifically, they want to avoid having plumbers work in a space that the electricians were planning to use. The construction industry is notorious for these jurisdictional disputes between plumbers, carpenters, electricians, and others. The company uses this end-of-day meeting to identify and resolve these disputes. There is always some flexibility to rearrange work schedules. At the meeting, the work schedules are adjusted for the next day. Or when a crane, for example, is scheduled by one subcontractor, the meeting tries to find others who can share the crane when it arrives. They constantly see if schedules can be adjusted in real time to match the ebb and flow of construction projects.

These meetings are seen as highly effective. The company brings in facilitators to manage the discussions and make them productive. There have been many adjustments and sharing of cranes and deliveries. The meetings are seen as key to eliminating jurisdictional disputes, attaining speed, and meeting and beating delivery dates. The company believes that the meetings more than pay for themselves.

The company works in a similar manner with its other stakeholders. Since it uses generalist engineers, it employs experts in civil engineering, pollution control, environmental protection, and so on. It keeps track of these experts and keeps them informed so that they can be brought in when needed. It tries to reuse its network of experts, equipment suppliers, and subcontractors on each project and makes them all part of their social network.

In summary, this engineering and construction company demonstrates many of the best practices that network captains use to manage networks. It shows how trust rather than authority can be used to hold networks together. By using transparency of information, all parties can be open and trusting. The result is that a lot of cost and time can be taken out of the project execution. The company has created an approach to fast execution and concurrent design methodologies. Central to integrating all of the engineering specialties and engineering and construction phases is the talent strategy of finding and developing Leonardos. These Leonardos, the trust-based culture, and world-class IT systems combine to form the secret sauce of the company. The combination is the key to delivering biotech plants as quickly as possible.

Summary

This chapter has described the last type of single-business functional organization: the network organization. This type of organization arises when an industry transforms from a vertically integrated model to a horizontal model. A network integrates the industry for the customer rather than a single company. It also arises when firms outsource activities at which other firms are superior. A network typically has a central firm that acts as the captain and keeps the network healthy.

The key organization design issues are the choice of partner, the structure of a partnership, and the type of relationship between the partners. The relationship depends on the amount of coordination, the vulnerability of the partners, and how to capture value. Today when software is everywhere, firms are learning to manage ecosystems and communities as part of their networks.

8

MULTIBUSINESS STRATEGY AND ORGANIZATION

The previous chapters have featured the various strategies and organizations of the single-business model. These next chapters focus on multiprofit center strategies and organizations. Like the single-business functional organization model, the multibusiness model has several various strategies and organizations as well. This chapter describes the standard portfolio strategies and organizations for related diversification and conglomerates and compares these to the single-business functional organization. Chapter 9 then looks at the mixed model, which is growing in popularity. Chapter 10 lays out a key part of the multibusiness portfolio strategy, how to add value to the businesses. Chapter 11 describes how some conglomerates avoid the stock market's "conglomerate discount" by adding value.

This chapter discusses the four types of strategy-organization models: single business, related diversification, mixed model, and conglomerate.

Portfolio Strategy and Organization

The study of corporate strategy and organization has been evolving for about fifty years. Originally management theorists would list the pros and cons of organizing by function, product lines, or geography. Then they would debate which was the best way to organize. All of that changed after the publication of Alfred P. Chandler's *Strategy and Structure* in 1962. What Chandler did was to observe the empirical evidence. He examined the histories of some sixty American corporations and came to the conclusion that the structure of a company depended on the portfolio strategy that it was executing. When a company followed a strategy of executing a single business, it adopted the functional structure, as BMW has done. When a company diversified into new businesses that were related to the core business, it organized around product lines or product divisions, as Kellogg's has done. And when a company diversified into completely unrelated businesses, it adopted the holding company model, as Berkshire Hathaway has done. The structure that a company adopted therefore depended on the portfolio strategy that it chose. Today we follow the principle that different strategies lead to different organizations.

Chandler's work started a tradition of empirical research into the topic. His historical case studies have been augmented by more quantitative statistical studies (Rumelt, 1974) of American enterprises. These analyses were followed by large-scale research studies of American (Stopford and Wells, 1972) and European (Franko, 1976) corporations as they expanded across borders. All of this work supported Chandler's categories of functional, divisional, and holding companies, as well as the basic idea that different strategies lead to different structures. In addition, the Stopford and Wells and Franko studies expanded strategy and structure into the international domain.

The next step in the evolution was to expand from structure to the more comprehensive concept of organization. Some researchers began to examine career patterns and compensation practices in companies following different diversification strategies. Like Chandler, they found different patterns and practices to be associated with different strategies and structures. For example, managers in a holding company pursuing an unrelated diversification strategy had careers only within their divisions (Pitts, 1976). In comparison, managers in divisionalized companies pursuing related diversification strategies had careers across the whole company. In another example, managers in holding companies received a larger proportion of their compensation as bonuses, and these bonuses were based on their division's performance regardless of the performance of the company (Kerr, 1985). Managers in divisionalized companies received a lower percentage of their pay as bonuses, and their bonuses were usually based on the entire company's performance. Two conclusions emerged as these types of findings began to accumulate.

The first conclusion was that Chandler's finding that different strategies lead to different structures was generalizable to the fact that different strategies lead to different HR practices as well. The other conclusion was that these combinations of strategy, structure, careers, and compensation fit together as predicted by the Star Model. These combinations made sense together. The policies reinforced one another. For example, transferring a manager at Berkshire Hathaway's GEICO insurance subsidiary to the Manville building products subsidiary would make no sense because the businesses in a holding company are simply too different to permit companywide careers, whereas the transfer of a marketing manager from Kellogg's cereal business to its Keebler Snack business makes a lot of sense. It results in cross-pollination and sharing of best practices between the divisions. The manager now sees a much broader set of career opportunities across the whole company, and the relatedness of the businesses allows this interdivisional career path to work.

The same logic applies to compensation. A holding company can easily pay larger bonuses based only on a division's performance. The businesses in a holding company are quite independent and measurable and usually have different names. The company can get a lot of motivational leverage with variable compensation. The same bonus policy in a divisional company with relationships between businesses will be dysfunctional. Bonuses for individual divisional performance will lead to competition rather than the desired cooperation. The policies seemed to fit together in useful combinations. Therefore, the different strategies lead to different combinations of structure, human resource practices, and other policies. And these combinations can lead to high performance when the policies are all aligned (Galbraith and Kazanjian, 1986).

In summary, a good deal of research about corporations has supported the concept that different strategies lead to different structures. More recent research has led to expanding the organization's structure to include its HR practices and, as we will see, its processes as well. Today we focus on the generalization that different strategies lead to different organizations. And finally, organization is conceived as a combination of structure, HR policies, and processes. When all of these organizational policies are in alignment with themselves and with strategy, the combination leads to high performance. These conclusions follow the Star Model.

The purpose of this chapter is to identify the types of portfolio strategies that companies pursue and then connect these strategies with the appropriate alignment of structures, HR policies, and processes that facilitate the execution of these strategies. In the following sections, we trace the alignment of the policies shown in the Star Model to the different portfolio strategies.

Diversification Strategy

The strategy at the top of the Star Model is the corporation's portfolio strategy. This portfolio can vary from a single-business, single-profit center to a conglomerate with multiple profit centers in many different kinds of businesses. This variation is usually conceived as a continuum running from low (single business) to high (conglomerate) diversity. Several scholars have attempted to create scales for measuring the diversity of a portfolio (Rumelt, 1974), but we usually wind up making judgment calls.

One attempt to measure diversity used the Standard Industry Classification (SIC) codes from the Department of Commerce. However these codes do not quite capture the diversity that is significant for structuring organizations. More mathematical measures (entropy index and concentric index) that have been tested by others have not succeeded either (Robins and Wiersema, 2003).

The basic unit of analysis is a business unit. There is a consensus on this point. A business was defined in the Introduction as a fully functional unit with its own product and markets. It may consist of several product lines, however. For example, BMW is a considered to be a single business, the automotive business, with several product lines running from its 100 Series to the 800 series.

As a company grows, it often expands into other product and service lines, and its portfolio will expand to include multiple business units, each of them a profit center and a functional organization. But again, determining what is a truly diversified business is not always so obvious.

For example, Novartis appears to be a single pharmaceutical business, but it is structured into four business units: Over the Counter (OTC) Pharmaceuticals, Generic Pharmaceuticals, Ethical Pharmaceuticals, and Eye Care Pharmaceuticals and Lenses. Although they are all related to pharmaceuticals, they all use different business models. The OTC business is a consumer products business run by brand managers, ethical pharmaceuticals is all about new blockbuster drugs and is an R&D business, generic pharmaceuticals is a cost and volume business dominated by manufacturing, and eye care pharmaceuticals sells into a completely different distribution channel with a different set of medical professionals. Unlike BMW, Novartis is a diverse company with a portfolio of four different businesses. An opposite example is Procter & Gamble (P&G), which participates in many industries: soap, paper, detergents, cosmetics, pharmaceuticals, and others. It appears to be very diverse, but every product is a consumer product, with repeat purchases at low prices, sold through mass merchants, and managed through a system of brand management. All of the business units use roughly the same business model for each product line.

Novartis and P&G illustrate the judgment call around portfolio diversity. P&G appears to be the more diverse: it is in more industries and has more business units (about fifteen), but the businesses are all related: consumer products that go to the same consumers through the same channels. They are all influenced by advertising. People, ideas, and even technology move freely across the businesses. As a result, P&G's businesses are not very autonomous, and P&G is quite centralized. Novartis is in fewer businesses, but the businesses are very different, and there is little movement of people, ideas, and technology across the businesses. As a result, the businesses are autonomous, and Novartis is decentralized. In my opinion, Novartis has a more diverse portfolio.

Diversity therefore has two dimensions, but one dimension is more important than the other. The first dimension is simply the number of businesses in the portfolio. BMW has one business, Novartis has four, Nestlé has ten, and P&G has fifteen. But the more important dimension is how different the businesses are. When the businesses operate under different business models, there is less opportunity and less payoff for them to work together. The more diverse the business models are, the less opportunity there is to create synergy or add economic value across the portfolio. P&G and GE have roughly the same number of businesses in their portfolios. But GE is in consumer products, locomotives, and jet engines, which are sold to both the Defense Department and commercial airlines; power generators that are sold to utilities; radiology equipment sold to hospitals; and financial services sold to corporations. P&G is much better able to create value across its portfolio than GE is. (However, as we will see, GE does a good job of finding ways to add value with a conglomerate portfolio.) So it is really the number of different business models that determines the diversity of the portfolio.

Many types of business models exist. One of the most common differences is the B2C (business-to-consumer) and B2B (business-to-business) difference. Even B2C could be split into consumer packaged goods, which are low-priced, repeat-purchase items, and consumer durables, which are postponable, higher-priced items sold on credit. The B2B category could be divided into commodity products and value-added products. B2B businesses can be different depending on where along the value chain they operate. A raw materials company uses a different model than does a component company, a stand-alone product company, or one that delivers systems of products and services. Businesses also tend to be different depending on the customer type. Selling to commercial customers is quite different from doing business with governments and the Department of Defense. So a company following the related diversification model would be like a Kellogg's or P&G whose businesses are all consumer packaged goods. That is, they manage a portfolio of many businesses, but all of the businesses use the same business model. The conglomerate companies also have a portfolio of different businesses, but these businesses use different business models and often come from very different industries and serve very different customer segments.

Corporate Structures

The structure of the corporation follows from its portfolio strategy. It is important to remember that the strategies form a continuum. For purposes of clarity and comparison, however, we will use the three models of single business, related diversification, and unrelated diversification or conglomerate. Table 8.1 indicates how the main characteristics of organizational structures are associated with the three portfolio strategies.

As noted before, the single-business strategy is executed through a functional structure. The structure for BMW, for

Table 8.1 Corporate Strategy and Organization

Portfolio Strategy	Structure	Centralization	Staff	Staff Role
Single business	Functional	High	Small	Policy
Related business	Divisional	Moderate	Large	Policy/review
Unrelated businesses	Holding company	Low	Small	Service

Figure 8.1 BMW Corporate Organization Structure

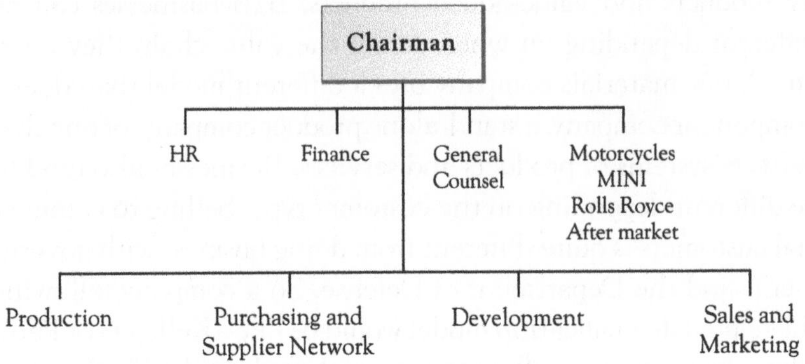

Source: BMW, Annual Report 2012.

example, is shown in figure 8.1. The line operating structure is shown as consisting of the production or manufacturing function, the purchasing function, the development or engineering function, and the sales and marketing functions. The typical staff functions of HR, legal, and finance are shown on the top line. Many of the decisions are cross-functional, centralized in the leadership team. BMW has recently separated out the non-BMW brands and motorcycles, since they account for 5 percent of sales and often get overlooked. Thus, they were separated out for special attention. The rest of BMW is a functional organization. The staffs are few and small; however, they set corporate policy for compensation, accounting rules, and so on.

All single businesses seem to adopt the functional structure regardless of whether they are service businesses (retailers) or manufacturers and regardless of their business model. Figure 8.2 shows the Amgen Corporation organization chart.

Using different labels from the pharmaceuticals industry, Amgen's operating functions are R&D (or product development), operations (or manufacturing), and commercial operations, which is sales and marketing. The staffs are slightly larger, reflecting the regulated nature of the pharmaceuticals business. They have a chief compliance officer reporting to

Figure 8.2 Amgen Corporate Organization Structure

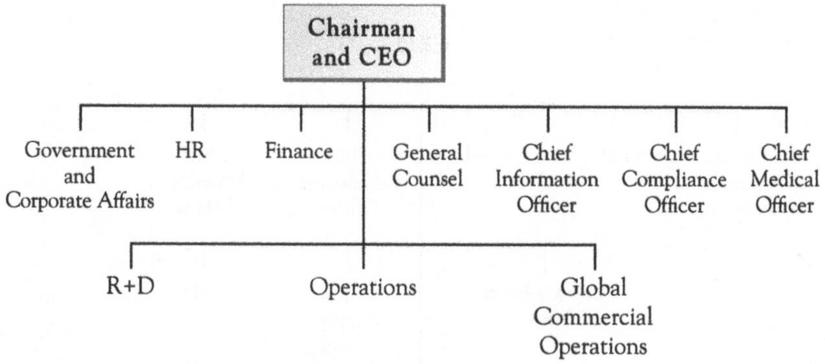

Source: Amgen, Annual Report 2012.

the CEO so that none of its facilities get shut down. The government affairs function also reports to the CEO, showing its authority and importance for dealing with the Food and Drug Administration.

All companies start out as single-business functional organizations. Dell Computer, Google, and Amazon all started as functional organizations. But as they grow and diversify, they evolve into the related business portfolio strategy and the divisional, multiprofit-center model.

Companies adopt the divisional model when they diversify their portfolio and move into businesses adjacent to their core business. An example is Kellogg's, whose structure is shown in figure 8.3. The top structure shows the usual corporate staffs of CFO, HR, chief information officer, and legal. But Kellogg's also features its corporate affairs and nutrition staff because of possible government regulation of food products. The second line shows the distinguishing feature of the related diversification strategy and the divisional structure. The structure shows another group of staffs for marketing, supply chain, and R&D. Some other companies—P&G, for example—also have staffs for strategy and sales, in addition to marketing and R&D. The third line on the chart shows the profit centers. Kellogg's started off in the

Figure 8.3 Kellogg's Corporate Organization Structure

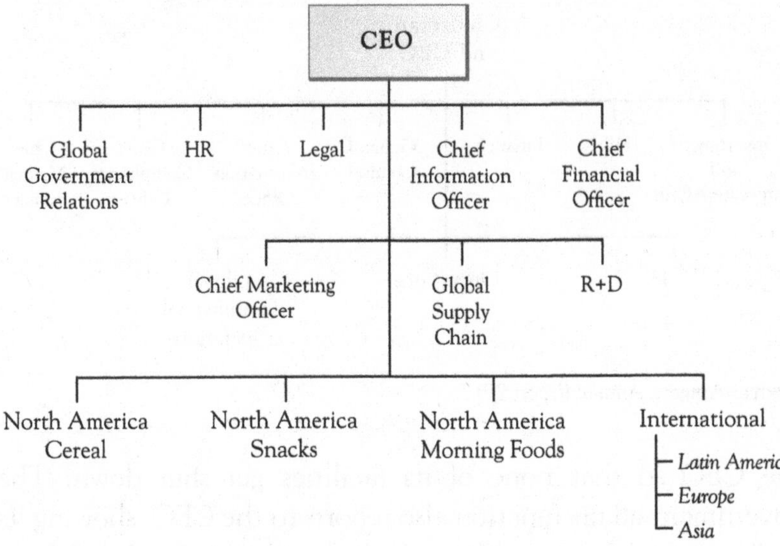

```
                              ┌─────────┐
                              │   CEO   │
                              └─────────┘

 Global        HR      Legal      Chief        Chief
Government                      Information   Financial
Relations                        Officer      Officer

           Chief Marketing      Global      R+D
              Officer           Supply
                                Chain

North America   North America   North America   International
   Cereal          Snacks       Morning Foods    ├ Latin America
                                                  ├ Europe
                                                  └ Asia
```

Source: Kellogg's, *Annual Report 2012.*

cereal business. Then as cereal bars were introduced, it moved into the adjacent snack category. Following that move, Kellogg's acquired Keebler and Pringles, which strengthened its breakfast and snack offerings. Kellogg's now sells Pop Tarts, Eggo waffles, and other products in a profit center referred to as Morning Foods. And finally about a third of Kellogg's sales take place in its International Division, which we will address later.

The divisional structure is more decentralized than the functional structure. Where the cross-functional decisions are made by the top team in the functional structure, they are decentralized to the divisional teams in the divisional structure. Each division is a functional organization. The functions report to the division general manager and their corporate functional counterparts, forming a matrix organization. The divisional structure is only moderately decentralized. The corporate functions actively review plans, develop companywide or division policies, and search for best practices to be shared across the corporation.

The size of the corporate staffs is the subject of many myths and opinions. Wall Street seems to believe that "lean staff" is better than too many staff, regardless of the business portfolio. And corporate staffs are often the butt of many jokes ("How many people work on the corporate staff? About half.")

Nonetheless, several scholars have shed light on the subject (Goold, Pettifer, and Young, 2001). First, the size of the corporate center varies directly with the size of the corporation. However, the rate at which the corporate staff increases tends to slow as the company grows, showing that there are some scale economies. Second, the staffs are larger when they are more influential, as in the divisional structure. The divisional corporate staffs exist for all functions and are active in establishing common practices across the businesses. And finally, when linkages and synergies exist across the businesses, staff size is larger. These linkages or interdependencies are more likely to exist among businesses that are related. Thus, the divisional structure has the largest corporate staffs of the three structural types.

The last strategy structure type is the unrelated diversification strategy, which is executed through a holding company structure. The holding company structure is shown in figure 8.4. Again, it shows the usual staffs like finance, HR, and legal as in the other structures. But there are no other functional staffs like R&D, marketing, or operations. The businesses are simply too different in the holding company to have common practices. The decisions and staffs are all within the businesses. The holding company is very decentralized except for financial decisions. Most of the staff are financial types and monitor the financial performance of the businesses very closely. The staffs provide services for the businesses when asked but exist primarily to support the corporate decision makers.

The functional, divisional, and holding companies are the three pure types of corporate structures. There are also many hybrids that are combinations of these pure types. At one point, Xerox was a large functional organization managing its copier

Figure 8.4 Holding Company

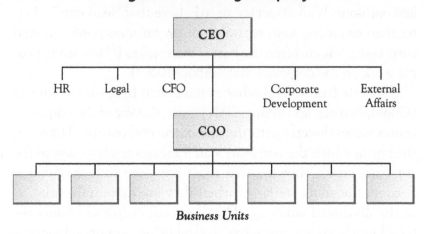

Business Units

business, and 90 percent of the revenues came from copiers. Then it acquired a small printer business and a small disc drive business. These two units were managed like a holding company; they reported separately to the corporation and were kept outside the large functional structure. The same rules as described above apply to both pieces of the structure.

Processes

The principles surrounding the different portfolio strategies also apply to a corporation's processes. We look at the control processes and businesses processes in this section. A summary can be found in table 8.2.

Table 8.2 Corporate Strategy and Organizational Processes

Portfolio Strategy	Control process	Types of Control
Single business	Cost center	Operational Strategic Financial
Related business	Profit center	Strategic Financial
Unrelated businesses	Investment center	Financial

The control process for a single-business functional organization is the cost center process. The corporation itself is the only profit center. Each of the individual functions is a cost center in the budgeting process. The leadership team in a functional organization exercises all three types of control over the company. Operational control applies to the detailed decisions about scheduling, inventories, and pricing. Strategic control entails the designation of products, markets, technologies, and charters to be pursued by the various organizational units. It restricts the domains of units and divisions so that they neither compete nor duplicate activities. Financial control is the straightforward budget allocation, measurement, and accountability to meet the financial targets.

The divisional model uses the profit center control process. Each division is usually a profit center, and it conducts its own system of operational control. The corporation exercises strategic and financial control over the divisions. And finally, the holding company decentralizes both operational and strategic control to the businesses. It measures the businesses as an investment center. The corporate center can get good measures of a complete business to drive its investment decisions. Different strategies therefore lead to different control processes.

The other processes are the generic business processes like the new product development process, the order fulfillment process, the supply chain process, the customer relationship management process, and so on. In the case of these business processes, the functional and divisional structures are the same. Both types strive to implement common processes throughout the organization. The functional organization can pursue common processes because it's a single business. The divisional organization has different businesses, but since they all operate under the same business model, they can also implement common business processes. Having one process across all the divisions is the most efficient policy. In addition, it facilitates the movement of managers across the company, and the managers don't have to learn new processes with each new move.

In both the functional and divisional models, the corporate functions take the responsibility for choosing, implementing, and improving the company's processes. The corporate functions become known as the process owners.

In the holding company, the responsibility for business processes, except for finance, is decentralized to the businesses. With the holding company executing many different business models, it makes little sense to have common business processes, and there is little movement, except for finance, of managers across the company. Thus, we find that business processes and control processes are aligned with the portfolio strategies and the company structures.

Reward Systems

This section discusses only the formal compensation type of rewards. Table 8.3 shows how the different attributes of compensation systems align with the three types of portfolio strategy. The focus of the compensation policies is on the CEO, the leadership team, and the general managers of the businesses. One of the key differences for this group across the three strategies is the degree of interdependence among its members. The functional organization's leadership team is the most interdependent. On the other end of the scale, the leadership group at the top of a holding company is quite independent. Depending on the amount of

Table 8.3 Corporate Strategy and Compensation Practices

Portfolio Strategy	Salary	Bonus	Bases	Measures
Single business	Company	Low	Company	Subjective
Related business	Company	Medium	Division/company	Combination
Unrelated businesses	Industry	High	Division	Objective

synergy in the strategy, the leadership team of the divisional structure has an intermediate level of interdependence. The interdependence factor is the basis for many of the differences in compensation policies at the leadership level.

In the single-business functional organization, the top team must work together. Their compensation policy is mostly companywide and based on competitive practices in the industry. Compensation is mostly salary with some individual bonuses. Highly leveraged individual rewards are generally seen to be dysfunctional. If every manager is concerned only with his or her function's performance, it will detract from total company performance. If bonuses are given, they are based on company performance and are often mixtures of cash and company stock. The measures of individual performance have a substantial subjective component in them. Again it is because of the interdependence of the work. When Cisco went back to a functional structure, it began to assess individuals on their collaborative performance. It continually develops objective ratings from peer reviews. But at the end of the day, the measures have a lot of subjectivity.

The holding companies are exactly the opposite of functional structures: there is no company salary structure. The businesses are all from different industries, so they pay people based on the competitive standards of their industry, not on any common salary structure of the company. At GE, the compensation practices of the financial services industry and the aircraft engine business will be completely different, so compensation policy is decentralized to the businesses, which adopt practices that make them competitive in their industry. They can use a lot of variable pay based on the business unit performance to create motivation for business managers and their teams. The businesses are not dependent on the other business units. They can be measured easily and compared with outside competitors. The rewards are based on objective measures of business performance like return on assets and other typical investment ratios.

The related strategy, divisional structure, is somewhere between the two extremes. There is a single companywide salary structure, which is simple to administer. The company usually follows a single business model in a set of related industries. The single compensation structure facilitates rotational assignments across divisions. The individual bonuses are not as high as at the holding companies, but they tend to be more than in the single-business companies. Bonuses in the related divisional company are usually a combination of 50 percent division performance and 50 percent company performance. Another example is one-third division, one-third company, and one-third personal objectives. The amount of interdependence and the company's desire for collaborative behavior are the main determinants of the choice. The same factors weigh on the choice of subjective and objective measures of performance. The more collaboration there is to support a synergy strategy, the more subjective will be the measures. So once again, different strategies lead to different structures and to different compensation policies.

People

This section covers the People dimension of the Star Model. Human resource policies are some of the most powerful culture builders. These policies are often aligned around building a common company identity and culture. The companies pursuing a single business and a related business strategy are often very focused on using common culture as the glue that holds them together. Holding companies are completely the opposite.

Holding companies place little value on having a common companywide identity or culture. Each business within a holding company can have a strong culture, but there is usually nothing companywide. Holding companies buy and sell businesses and place little value on working across businesses or synergies. There is no rotational policy and usually no companywide management development effort. People identify with their business and its brand. Berkshire Hathaway's fifty-five diverse businesses include Acme Brick Company, Dairy Queen, Benjamin Moore Paints, GEICO Insurance, Clayton Homes, See's Candies, BNSF Railway, and Ben Bridge Jewelers. It is a lot less disruptive to the rest of the organization if holding companies can sell a whole business, brand identity, and culture without affecting morale or disrupting the operations of the divested subsidiary.

The single-business functional organizations and related-business divisional models promote policies that create a unified and, if possible, strong culture. They adopt HR policies like rotational careers. With common processes, compensation systems, and cultures, managers can move easily from one function to another and from one division to another. They have management development programs where managers from across the corporation learn the company way, bond with each other, and create personal networks. Similarly there are events like the annual gathering of the top 150 leaders.

These companies are likely to have a single company brand with which people can identify. Managers identify with IBM, Cisco, or Kellogg's. There are exceptions, like P&G and Unilever with multiple brands; however, people still identify strongly with being part of the mother company. This may be an accident of history. Many consumer goods companies are emphasizing the company brand, as Nestlé and Kellogg's do. They are creating brand architectures like Kellogg's Corn Flakes, Kellogg's Rice Krispies, and Kellogg's Pop Tarts. It is easier for P&G and Unilever to remain a house of brands rather than a branded house.

The differences in culture are clear. The organization designers of the functional and divisional models want to create a unified culture. The use the branding events and HR policies to create a "one company" mind-set in their managers. The holding companies delegate this design to the subsidiaries and make no attempt to create a companywide identity.

Aligned Models

We have looked at each policy area like structure and rewards to compare the differences between the portfolio strategies. The policies are represented as the rows in figure 8.5. These policies are the elements of the Star Model. In this section, I summarize by observing how the policies are aligned among themselves as well as for a type of portfolio strategy. In this case, we focus on the columns in figure 8.5.

Figure 8.5 Portfolio Strategy and Organization

Strategy	Single Business	Related Diversification	Unrelated Diversification
Structure	Functional	Divisional	Holding company
Centralization	High	Moderate	Low
Corporate staff	Small	Large	Small
Control type	Operational Strategic Financial	Strategic Financial	Financial
Business processes	Common	Common	Different
Compensation system	Company	Company	Subsidiary
Bonuses	Company	Company	Subsidiary
Careers	Company	Company	Subsidiary
Subsidiary culture	Companywide	Companywide	Unique to subsidiary
Division name or brand	Company name	Company name	Subsidiary
Example	BMW	Agilent	Berkshire Hathaway

The single-business portfolio strategy is the first and most straightforward: it is a functional structure managing a single business. It is also a centralized structure since most of the cross-functional decisions are concentrated with the top team. This top team is involved in operational, strategic, and financial control decisions. Single-company policies are followed for business processes, HR policies, culture, and brand. In combination, these policies are aligned among themselves and with the portfolio strategy.

The related diversification divisional model shows the same alignment. Since multiple profit centers follow similar business models and are related, they can share resources, people, technologies, and ideas. The sharing means that the divisions are not completely autonomous. A large corporate center moves resources and people across divisions. The central staff ensures enough commonality of policy so that interdivisional transfers take place effectively. Since there is resource sharing and a lack of autonomy, it is difficult to get completely objective measures of divisional performance. These companies use objective, subjective, and multidimensional performance measures. They do not use a lot of variable compensation. When they do use variable pay, it is a combination of corporate and divisional profitability as the basis for bonuses. The HR policies create a common culture and company identity. These policies form a self-reinforcing system. All of the policies are aligned, as predicted by the Star Model, and alignment leads to effectiveness.

Misalignment leads to ineffective performance. If related companies paid large bonuses based on independent and objective measures of divisional performance, the motivation of division managers would increase, but their behavior would be dysfunctional. They would be motivated to be autonomous, look out only for their own divisions, and be reluctant to share resources and adopt common policies. Misalignment leads to frictions among managers; they turn inward and engage in nonproductive arguments.

The unrelated portfolio strategy of holding company is the exact opposite of the divisional model. It is very decentralized with a small corporate center. There is little or no sharing of resources across business profit centers. The center exercises only financial control. All policies are decentralized to the subsidiaries, which adopt practices common in their industries in order to be competitive. The managers identify with their business, not their company. The compensation policy is based on high bonuses and high motivation for autonomous business performance. These policies, listed in figure 8.5, form an aligned set of policies among themselves and with the unrelated portfolio strategy.

At several points, I have said that the portfolio strategies form a continuum. Sometimes we can observe hybrid forms of organization. One hybrid that is becoming more common is a mixed model that has aspects of a related strategy and aspects of unrelated strategy. The next chapter analyzes the Star Model for these hybrid forms.

Summary

This chapter developed the complete organizations for the three basic portfolio strategies: single business, related businesses, and unrelated businesses. Figure 8.5 summarizes the implications of the different strategies along all policy areas in the Star Model. It also shows how the policies in the columns reinforce the desired behaviors of the managers. The policies are therefore consistent with one another and with the portfolio strategy.

9

THE MIXED MODEL

Chapter 8 described three pure types of portfolio strategies and organization for which there is a lot of research evidence. In reality, there is a large variety of hybrids that combine these pure types. Many of them could be positioned between the related diversification strategy and a conglomerate. We call these hybrids the mixed model. They are mixed because they have some attributes of the related model and some attributes of the conglomerate model. The chapter describes how this hybrid came about and what the organization design or Star Model for this portfolio strategy looks like.

Strategy

The strategy for the mixed model came about in two ways. Some companies executing a related diversification model found that a set of common policies no longer worked for all of their businesses, so they needed to differentiate some of their organizational practices in order to be competitive. Hewlett-Packard is an example of this type of company. Other examples can be found in companies that were conglomerates but needed to gain some synergies among their businesses. These companies were under pressure from Wall Street to either show synergies among their businesses or break up the portfolio. AlliedSignal, now Honeywell, is an example of this type of company. In both cases, these companies, from different ends of the spectrum, arrived at the mixed model.

Hewlett-Packard

Hewlett-Packard (HP) is a good example of a related diversifier. From its beginnings in electronic test and measurement, it diversified organically into chemical test and measurement and then medical test and measurement. All of these businesses were executed through a divisional structure where each business had about $100 million in revenue. In essence, each business was a product division that sold a box with sophisticated electronics in it. The products were highly technical, high-margin boxes and were sold to engineers or other technically sophisticated customers. The same processes, culture, compensation practices, funding model, and business model were implemented across the company. This common package of policies became known as the "HP Way."

Then HP entered the computer business. At first, it designed and built minicomputers like Digital Equipment did. The minicomputer product followed the same stand-alone product business model as the other HP businesses. It was a sophisticated product that was sold to manufacturing engineers who wanted their own computers in their factories. But then the computer business began to change from selling stand-alone products to selling systems, or what we today call solutions. The previous model, which was consistent with HP's business model, was to sell minis, workstations, PCs, mainframes, and storage devices. The new model was to sell a computer-aided design (CAD) system that integrated various departments at the customer, who also participated in the new product development process. The sales consisted of a collection of products like computers, storage, printers, and, especially, software that was designed to make all the products work as a system. The business model for systems is different from the one for stand-alone hardware products. In order to be competitive, HP had to differentiate its businesses processes and practices to fit the new systems or solutions business model.

It was a struggle for HP, but it has finally succeeded at creating a thriving solutions business and a mixed-model corporation.

The biggest change was to the culture. Before, each product division general manager pretty much operated independently. Under a solutions model, the products had to be designed to work together at the customer's sites. Before, every division priced its own products. But when the product being sold is a solution, the solution price is usually different from the sum of stand-alone product prices that combine to create a solution.

Pricing always leads to debates about sharing revenues, and there were multiple conflicts until HP finally found a group of general managers who understood the solutions business model. Compensation had to be changed for salespeople. Under the stand-alone product model, each salesperson had a quota of about $1 million a month. Under the solutions model, each product salesperson is a member of a customer sales team. The Boeing team may have just about zero sales one year and then $500 million sales of a companywide CAD system the next. It was a struggle to get the rest of HP to let it change the traditional and successful sales compensation plan. The general managers also had to coordinate the order flow. The order fulfillment process for a solution requires that all products arrive at the customer site together so that the complete system can start as planned. Under the stand-alone product fulfillment process, much less coordination was needed. The solutions model also required the creation of software divisions. The other HP divisions were hardware divisions, and under the hardware model, a division typically spent 8 to 10 percent of sales on R&D. A software business like Microsoft typically spends 15 to 20 percent of sales on R&D. The finance people at HP could not understand why the software divisions had to spend that much money. And so over a number of years, the Computer Systems Group at HP created a solutions subculture, a solutions compensation plan, a solutions new product development process, an order fulfillment process, a software funding model, and so on until they had created a collection of divisions that worked under the solutions business model. Today this group is the Technology Solutions Group. It is a completely separate group within HP.

In summary, the portfolio strategy at HP changed because the business model changed in one of its businesses, the computer business. Originally the business units making up the portfolio did not change. What changed was that one of the businesses in the portfolio no longer fit with the others in the related diversification model. The common processes and policies no longer fit the computer business. The portfolio became a mixture of solution divisions and stand-alone product divisions.

AlliedSignal/Honeywell

AlliedSignal was a classic conglomerate built by Ed Hennessey. Hennessey, like Harry Gray who built United Technologies, was an alumnus of the Litton Industries conglomerate school started by Tex Thornton and Roy Ash. These conglomerates thrived in the 1960s and 1970s. But by the late 1980s and 1990s, they had fallen out of favor. Wall Street analysts were against them, and most of the conglomerates began trading at a discount to the market. This market underperformance became known as the conglomerate discount. They soon came under attack from corporate raiders. As a result most were broken up by raiders or by their own management before a raider could strike. Some sold off some businesses but then searched for synergies in the portfolio of businesses that remained. AlliedSignal was among the latter group.

In the late 1980s, the board of AlliedSignal forced out Hennessey and brought in Larry Bossidy from GE. The new CEO sold some businesses and collected the rest into a chemicals and materials group, an automotive group, and an aerospace group. He then pushed for synergies within the groups. For example, he asked the divisions in the auto group to bundle their products and sell them as packages to the auto original equipment manufacturers. He suggested similar changes for aerospace. At the corporate center, he added a purchasing unit to combine the buying power of the groups. And finally he was early to join the Six Sigma program. An initiative was started and led from the corporate center. AlliedSignal thus abandoned its pure conglomerate strategy; it sold some businesses and collected the others into three groups. Bossidy then pursued synergies both within the groups and between them with initiatives led by the corporate center.

•••

These two examples are typical of companies pursuing a mixed portfolio strategy. Some are former conglomerates pursuing synergies, some are former related businesses pursuing differences, and still others, like Disney and 3M, have always followed the mixed model. The examples also gave a hint about the distinctive structure of the mixed model: the structure is built around groups of divisions.

Structure

The structure of the mixed-portfolio model is based on the collection of similar divisions into a group, a cluster, or a sector. The pure type arises when all divisions in the group follow a single-business model. The structure maximizes the similarity of divisions within a group and the differences between the groups. Each group is a subportfolio of businesses with its own portfolio strategy. The corporation is then a portfolio of groups. Hewlett Packard is an example and is shown in figure 9.1.

The three groups are shown at the bottom of the chart. The first is the Technology Solutions Group (TSG) described above. It is executing the solutions business model and the group is a small version of IBM. It consists of hardware product lines (enterprise servers and storage) and services product lines (consulting, outsourcing), software product lines, and a global sales force that sells the solutions to large accounts and industry segments. The product lines are all profit centers. The business processes, subculture, compensation policies, and other practices are all built around the solutions business model.

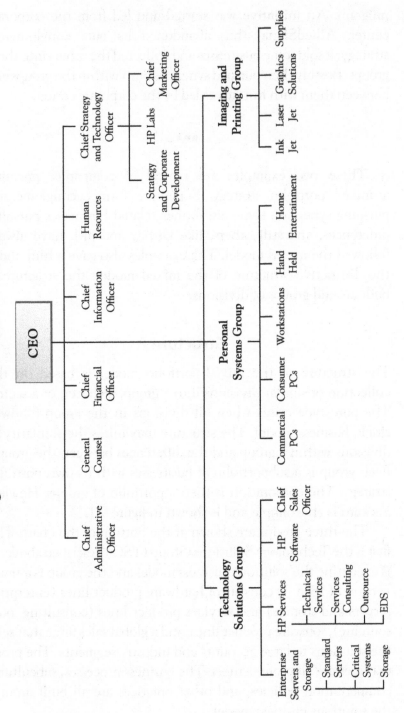

Figure 9.1 The Hewlett-Packard Mixed Model

Another group working under a different business model is the Personal Systems Group (PSG), which is more like the classic HP stand-alone product business. There are five product lines in the group:

- Personal computers are designed and sold through a commercial division and a consumer division.
- High-performance computing needs are met through the Work Station Division.
- Smaller handheld computers and tablets are designed and sold through the Hand Held Division. This is the former Palm Computer business.
- The last division provides products that link PCs with other home entertainment devices like TVs. The products from this group are sold through various types of distributors, retailers, value-added resellers, university bookstores, and so on.

The divisions all operate under similar business models, processes, and policies.

The third group is the Imaging and Printing Group (IPG), an imaging and printing systems provider for consumers and commercial customers. It provides printing hardware, supplies, and scanning devices. The group was another classic HP product-centric group; however, it is moving more and more into printing solutions, running printing services for companies and moving into all types of digital printing equipment, which is replacing older printing presses. The group itself is a mixed-model portfolio strategy: it still has some product sales and divisions, but the Graphic Solutions business is a large-scale solutions provider for large graphic arts customers. The Inkjet division provides inkjet products for consumers and small businesses and publishing solutions for retailers. The LaserJet Division focuses on printing for enterprises. It sells products and supplies as always, but it is expanding into software solutions and managed services. And the Supplies Division is still a product-centric unit for replacing ink cartridges and paper. The group is thus a combination of products and solutions business models. It is becoming more and more like TSG but for printing.

The rest of the mixed model is shown in figure 9.2. We have added a fourth column to the three pure types shown in figure 8.5 in chapter 8. The structure of the mixed model is a group

Figure 9.2 Portfolio Strategy and Organization

Strategy	Single Business	Related Diversification	Mixed	Unrelated Diversification
Structure	Functional	Divisional	Group	Holding company
Centralization	High	Moderate	Low to the cluster Moderate within group	Low
Corporate staff	Small	Large	Low corporate Moderate cluster	Small
Control type	Operational Strategic Financial	Strategic Financial	Strategic Financial	Financial
Business processes	Common	Common	Common within group	Different
Compensation system	Company	Company	Group	Subsidiary
Bonuses	Company	Company	Group	Subsidiary
Careers	Company	Company	Group	Subsidiary
Subsidiary culture	Company-wide	Company-wide	Mix	Unique to subsidiary
Division name or brand	Company name	Company name	Mix	Subsidiary
Example	BMW	Agilent	Hewlett-Packard	Berkshire Hathaway

structure. There may be groups in the divisional and holding company models as well. Any time there are large numbers of divisions, they cannot all report directly to the CEO or COO. Therefore, a group or sector level is added to reduce the spans of the CEO and COO. But the group level in the mixed model will have its own staff to create the processes and policies that are unique to the businesses in the group. And finally, the group itself is a profit center.

In the pure type, the corporate center would be like a holding company with only the usual small staffs for finance, HR, legal, and strategy. The other staffs that are present in the divisional model are decentralized to the group level. However, there are many variations. HP maintains a common brand across the whole company. Therefore, we find a chief marketing officer (CMO) at the corporate level. And since all the groups use digital technologies, there is a central R&D unit, HP Labs. So when there are common and high-priority activities across the company, that activity is represented and led at the corporate center.

Since HP sells to chief information officers at its customers, it wants to showcase its own IT function. Therefore, the CIO reports directly to the CEO.

Processes and Policies

In Figure 9.2, the "Mixed" column represents the pure type. As we have already seen, there are a lot of variations. I next describe the pure type and then give some examples of variations.

Processes

In the pure type, the corporate center is like a holding company and exercises only financial control. The group level exercises financial and strategic control; however, many companies executing the mixed model will selectively add some strategic initiatives. For example, AlliedSignal/Honeywell added a Six

Sigma initiative and hired a quality expert from Xerox to manage it out of the corporate center. HP, with its common brand and technology, has chosen to exercise strategic control over those areas from the corporate center.

The business processes are a distinguishing factor in the mixed model. The pure type would have common processes at the group level to support the group's business model, so the processes would be common within groups and different across groups. This pattern partly exists at HP. The Technology Systems Group follows a solutions business model, and the Personal Systems Group follows a product business model. The TSG sells direct to customers, while PSG sells through resellers. The business processes are quite different between the two groups. The Imaging and Printing Group used to be like PSG. However, it is now moving toward a solutions business model in addition to its product model. The Inkjet Division sells through resellers and can use PSG's processes. The LaserJet Division can use PSG's processes for its product sales and TSG's processes for its solutions business. In this way, IPG can avoid duplicating processes and adopts the company processes that fit its business models.

People and Human Resources Practices

The HR practices of the pure mixed model begin with salary and compensation policies that fit with the competitive practices of the particular group's industry. The first priority is to be competitive in the industry and then to be common across the company. The old AlliedSignal provides a good example. Its groups adopted the compensation practices of the chemical, automotive, and aerospace industries, respectively. In contrast, at HP, there is not much difference in compensation practices among the printing, PC, and computing industries. Thus, the salaries are likely to be common.

The pure-type mixed model often has three types of bonus systems. The corporate center people get a bonus based on corporate performance, group managers get a bonus based on the group's performance, and divisions receive a bonus that is part division performance and part group performance. When divisions are interdependent, the percentage favors the group performance. If the divisions operate more independently, the percentage favors the division performance. These policies are a good approximation of actual practice. However, some companies believe that everyone should have a corporate performance component in the bonus system.

The career system is usually based on the group. Most people move within the group, but there may be some cross-group movement at the leadership level. In order to groom a successor, the mixed companies often need leaders with experience in several groups, so the actual career movement is determined by the level of the manager.

The culture and brand identity vary with the history of the company. HP had its origins in the related diversified model and had a strong culture. With the acquisition of Compaq and the evolution of solutions, the HP Way has been diluted. There are some solutions and product subcultures, and the old HP culture is still strong in the IPG. Disney and 3M are organic growers that have strong company cultures. For companies that arrive at the mixed model, like AlliedSignal/Honeywell and Novartis, the group cultures are stronger. The important issue is usually how interdependent the groups are. At Disney, as we will see, the groups are expected to work together. A common culture and a Disney brand identity help to create the collaborative behaviors that are needed to attain synergies. At Novartis, the groups are not interdependent. There is little payoff from culture building across the groups.

Summary

There are many hybrid portfolio strategies and organizations. One of the most frequently occurring is the mixed model, with some features of the related diversification model and some features of the holding company model. Its distinguishing feature is an organization structure based on a group of divisions. Each group contains some divisions that have a common business model or industry, so processes are common within a group and different between groups. This model has resulted from related businesses becoming more different and holding company businesses becoming more synergistic. A third type merely grew up as a mixture. It fits the model of a continuum based on portfolio variety and types and amounts of value added.

10

ADDING VALUE

The biggest changes in today's portfolio strategies are the explicit attempts by management to add value to their portfolios. No one wants to be accused of running a conglomerate. If you want to provoke the leadership of any company, use the "C" word when referring to their company. The financial markets want specific proof from management. Hence, we are finding the explicit articulation of corporate portfolio strategies.

This emphasis on corporate-level strategy is quite welcome. Until recently, companies were quite good at articulating their business unit strategies and quite poor at articulating the portfolio strategy for creating value with those businesses (Goold, Campbell, and Alexander, 1994). As a result, over the past ten to fifteen years, a number of very creative value-adding strategies have come to light. This chapter discusses the value-adding dimension as the second dimension of portfolio strategy. Then it describes a number of the different ways to add value to a portfolio. In so doing, I use GE as a case study to show how value can be added to a quite diverse portfolio of businesses.

Portfolio Strategy Today

Figure 10.1 displays the two dimensions of portfolio strategy. The first is the diversity of businesses that constitute the portfolio. Diversity is "where to play" with respect to businesses in the portfolio. This dimension was the basis of the discussion in the previous two chapters. Business diversity is still relevant as

Figure 10.1 Portfolio Strategy Today

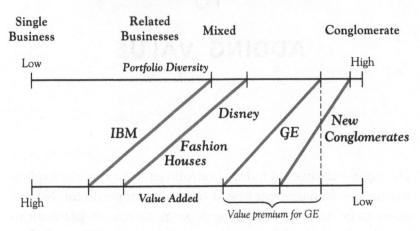

we expand the analysis of portfolio strategy to include value added as a second dimension. By *value*, I mean economic value. It is the "how-to-win" dimension of corporate-level strategy. Strategic focus on value added means that the corporate portfolio generates higher yields, and therefore it trades at a higher economic value.

The diversity dimension runs from low (single business) to high (many unrelated businesses). It runs in the opposite direction too. In a single business, management potentially can create a lot of value by integrating the functions, but as the portfolio gets more diverse, creating value in the portfolio gets more difficult. Indeed, holding companies do not create much value at all, but they do not charge much in the way of overhead either. For example, there are only nineteen people in the corporate center of Berkshire Hathaway. These are all viable forms for managing portfolios.

The lines connecting the two dimensions in the figure show that some companies are taking diverse portfolios and creating a lot of value from them. IBM creates value by combining the products, software, and services from its diverse businesses into integrated solutions for customer segments. Disney and the fashion companies are shown as examples of value creators executing diverse portfolio strategies. They create value by spreading intellectual property among all of their businesses. And GE and other conglomerates create value too. All of these companies are creating more value than would normally be expected given the level of diversity in their portfolios. For GE, the value premium shown in figure 10.1 illustrates that the active management of a diverse portfolio usually yields a low amount of value. However, the companies shown in figure 10.1 have discovered how to create more value. As a result, they trade at a premium to other companies of equal diversity. On this issue, I have a disagreement with Wall Street, which does not believe anyone can add value to a conglomerate. But under Jack Welch, GE traded at a premium. Today, under Jeff Imelt, GE is not trading at a premium. Clearly Welch extracted more money from Wall Street by adding value to the business portfolio. How did he achieve that? Let us dissect the case of GE to illustrate what they did.

Creating Value

There are a number of ways that companies are creating value over and above the individual value of the businesses as stand-alone companies trading on the financial markets:

- Capital and financial acumen
- Talent
- Technology
- Government relations/international
- Leverage (buying, selling, partnering)
- Brand
- Banking capability
- Sharing intangibles, expertise, and knowledge
- Tangible resource sharing
  - Solutions
  - Leveraging intellectual property

As you can see, there are a number of ways that companies have learned to add value. These potential sources of value added are not automatic. The leadership of the company needs to be able to actually make these sources become real.

Capital and Financial Acumen

One hypothesis advanced by economists is that the corporate center can add value by making more effective investments in its businesses than the capital markets can (Williamson, 1975). The idea is that the multibusiness firm is a miniature capital market, and the corporate center is the investor. The hypothesis is that the corporate center will have better information about the businesses and will therefore make smarter resource allocations than the markets. In essence, the corporate center has legal access to insider information.

The hypothesis is a good example of why I call it a "potential" source of value added. It's well known that business units put a positive spin on their reports to headquarters. McKinsey's analyses show that companies have considerable inertia in changing their patterns of resource allocation. But when a company analyzes its strategy and makes changes, it earns 30 to 40 percent more over time (Hall, Lovallo, and Musters, 2012), so the question is whether the internal investors have better information than the external investors. Another McKinsey study shows that companies are slower than capital markets to shift funds to new growth markets and exit declining businesses (Foster and Kaplan, 2001). The corporate center will be a better investor if the relationships with the businesses are characterized by a high level of candor. The corporate center then needs to act on that superior information. It is also known that resource allocations are political decisions as well as economic ones. The largest businesses may use their size to get more than their fair share of the budgets. So the hypothesis that corporate centers add value by making more effective investment decisions can be supported, but only if the center has open communication channels and makes economically justified decisions.

A number of companies have developed significant financial skills. Their finance people know their way around a balance sheet, tax laws, and capital markets. The result is that they can find ways to create profits and add value for their shareholders.

The simplest way to capitalize on a financial advantage is to maintain a AAA credit rating. Then when you buy a company with a lower credit rating, you refinance the other company's debt at your higher rating and immediately drop several million dollars in profit to your bottom line. Having access to cheaper money was one of the sources of profit for GE as it made over two hundred acquisitions during the Welch era. GE, like some other companies, was also a disciplined shopper for acquisitions. It did not overpay. Another financial advantage is to maintain a group of experts who know the tax codes. These people are worth their weight in gold. At GE, the combination of its leasing businesses and industrial businesses meant that GE could take maximum advantage of the depreciation laws. During some years, GE paid almost no taxes. Often, having a variety of businesses creates some unusual legal opportunities for minimizing a company's tax bill. The financially oriented conglomerates are masters of these legal means for profiting from financial and accounting skills.

Talent

The businesses of a company can profit from having access to superior managerial talent. Some companies are highly skilled at recruiting, developing, retaining, and allocating managers. The corporate center with these skills adds value to the business by providing them with talented people. Companies like P&G, PepsiCo, McKinsey, and GE are known for their talent development skills, and other companies often recruit managers from them.

GE's leadership devotes a lot of time, money, and energy to the development of talent. GE always had a tradition of management development, but it was around 1970 that serious attention was given to developing talented managers. GE formed the Executive Manpower Staff (EMS), a dedicated corporate staff unit separate from traditional HR. Its first task was to establish the principle that talented managers were a corporate resource to be employed companywide. Before then, divisions hoarded and kept the best talent to themselves. But in order to use superior talent as a value-adding service from the corporate center, the company needs to have the power to allocate talent to its best opportunity. The second task was to identify and then monitor the development of these talented people. EMS focused on managing the top five hundred people as a corporate resource. Each business also had its own EMS unit.

The business leaders were challenged to identify high potentials in their businesses. These high potentials and the top managers were then tracked to see that they were exposed to a wide range of job experiences. They were followed to ensure that they received the right educational experiences at GE's internal training facility at Crotonville, New York. The decisions about development and allocations were made during talent reviews, called session Cs. The CEO and EMS head would review the talent in a business with the general manager and EMS head from that business. Under Jack Welch, this review was a day-long session. The first part of the day was an in-depth review of the thirty or forty top-talent people in the business. The second part was a discussion about whether the talent was properly allocated against the strategic priorities of the business. The final part was a reception and dinner so that the CEO could meet and talk with all thirty to forty people who were the subjects of the day's discussions.

Over the years, EMS has developed an integrated process for recruiting and selecting people, the sequencing of their assignments, the sequencing of their courses at Crotonville, and identifying talent who would perform at GE (Charan, Drotter, and Noel, 2001). For example, GE does not recruit entry-level MBAs. It has discovered that more humble engineers from midwestern universities (Purdue, University of Cincinnati) and young officers exiting the military thrive at GE. It recruits MBAs after they've had ten to twelve years of experience working for consulting firms like BCG and McKinsey or investment banks like Goldman Sachs. But these seasoned consultants and bankers come to GE as a group of outside hires. GE has arranged some safe landing zones in the strategy function for the outsiders to learn the GE ways before moving into the businesses. The current CEO, Jeff Imelt, is changing the formula. He wants more marketing talent and more non-American recruits. There are always some modifications to the GE talent machine (Bartlett and McClean, 2007).

Today stand-alone businesses can get access to talent through executive recruiters like Heidrick and Struggles or Egon Zender. The businesses in GE's portfolio receive added value only if EMS is skilled at delivering better talent and better at placing that talent. It is always wise to remember that for every activity that takes place at a corporate center, there is an external competitor that can provide that activity as well. Added value takes place only when the corporate center activity is superior to those of the outside vendors. One of the ways that the corporate center can excel in talent is when talent mobility is combined with other sources of value added like technology or specific expertise.

Technology

One of the major sources of value added for a multibusiness company is through access to its proprietary technologies. The business units have access to technologies that cannot be purchased in the open market. One of the best examples has been the 3M Corporation, which has developed a number of unique coating and bonding technologies that have led to many profitable business lines. The 3M policy is that the corporation owns the technologies and the divisions own the markets.

Technical talent and information move freely throughout the corporation. GE has also created value by moving technologies and people across its businesses.

One of the ways that GE Capital has excelled is by drawing on the technologies and technologists in the rest of the organization. It has used all three sources of value added discussed so far—financial acumen, talent, and technology—to create superior businesses. A couple of examples illustrate the point.

GE Capital has a number of equipment leasing businesses in which it has combined its financial skills with its industrial technologies. One example is its railroad car leasing business. GE can provide railroad cars to its customers more cheaply than they can provide their own cars. Moreover, GE has access to cheaper money to finance the cars and can combine the purchases of many customers and get volume discounts. But other financial services competitors can do this too, so GE Capital examined the economics of the business.

The economic profile of the leasing business includes the initial purchase price, the annual depreciation, and the terminal asset value, which for railroad cars is probably scrap. GE saw an opportunity: if it could extend the life of the asset, it would decrease the annual depreciation cost. With lower annual cost, GE could both decrease the lease price to the customer and improve its own margins. Lower lease costs to the customer should increase volumes and thus decrease GE's purchase price of the asset. Now the issue became how to extend the life of the asset. With a little research, it discovered that maintaining the wheels on the cars was the key. If the wheels were not perfectly round or were out of balance, the cars would rattle and shake until they came apart.

GE Capital then went to GE's transportation business, which designs and manufactures electric locomotives, and arranged for a transfer of managers and technicians who had expertise in wheel technologies. It built a maintenance depot in Chicago and began the careful maintenance of all the railroad cars that it owns. Today GE Capital dominates the business with an advantage that its competitors cannot match.

Another example is GE's entry into wind power generation (Magee, 2009). A group of people in GE's energy business had been building competence and an advocacy position for generating power using wind turbines, but they could never get former CEO Jack Welch to fund it. Their time came in 2001 when Imelt took over and Enron failed. As part of the bankruptcy proceedings, Enron's wind energy business was put up for auction. When GE won the auction and got the business at an attractive price, it set about improving the business by bringing in technology and people from its own businesses, like jet engines and gas turbine generators, who understood turbines. Specifically they brought in materials scientists who understand high-strength, low-weight materials. Wind turbines have complicated gearing systems, but so do locomotives, so engineers from transportation were brought in to improve the efficiency of the gears. R&D projects were started in India and China that involved computer simulations of the most effective ways to design and run wind farms. The combination of GE's technology and its relationships with electric utilities has led to a successful start of the business. Revenues are up over 300 percent since the acquisition to more than $6 billion per year. This is an example of where GE was able to add specific value to the business when Enron could not.

General Electric provides some good examples on how to bring the talent and technology of the entire company to bear on individual businesses. It can add value because of its talent mobility and the reduction of barriers among its businesses. Its leaders know it is not a good idea to resist the movement of talent and ideas from one business to another. Organizational attributes like these allow GE to translate potential value added into actual value for shareholders.

Government Relations/International

In some countries and in many emerging market countries, governments are major players on the economic scene. Whether through state-owned enterprises or the funding of infrastructure projects, governments can determine which companies will or will not get the business. Therefore, if the corporate center can build and maintain favorable relationships with governments, the business units in the portfolio can profit from the corporation's relationship.

The experience of Asian conglomerates reveals the advantages and disadvantages of government relationships. The Salim Group in Indonesia and the CP Group in Thailand both profited from favors and contracts from their governments, and their business units were advantaged as a result. But when turmoil hit the Indonesian and Thai governments, these advantages turned to disadvantages, or were neutralized at best. However, in more stable countries and in some key industries, these relationships are essential if a company wants to be a player in that country.

Cisco is an example of a company that is building up its government relations in order to sell its digital networking products. In many emerging market countries, growth means new buildings, new neighborhoods, and even new cities. China estimates that it will need to create forty new cities in the next ten years, and Saudi Arabia is planning four entirely new cities in the desert. Cisco's proposition to these governments is to leapfrog all the old technologies for electrical wiring, telecom, TV, and cable and install state-of-the-art Internet protocol (IP) networks that can carry all this traffic. Cisco calls it "country transformation."

Cisco's plan has several interesting aspects to it. Winning the government is the initial priority. It does this by first focusing on the country's issues, not selling products. In Saudi Arabia, where there is a single industry and high unemployment, Cisco shows how a new city can attract new industry. Sudair City will be close to the oil fields and will have access to electricity for three cents per kilowatt-hour. Cisco proposes wiring the city for broadband with the goal of attracting the data centers that are increasingly being used for cloud computing. Cisco will help the city attract data center customers for whom electric power is the largest cost. They will open networking academies for training the locals for the jobs. The Cisco leadership thus sits with country heads, mayors, ministry heads, and industry heads to discuss how broadband networks could be used for controlling traffic, for education, for medicine, and for smart electrical grids. Cisco has developed the thought leadership to engage the country leadership in useful discussion.

Then Cisco hires a major player to be its country manager. In most emerging markets, the company needs a well-connected country manager who knows the ropes and the key people in government and industry. Cisco also donates a key cutting-edge technology to the heads of state. The Telepresence, a videoconferencing system, has been given to every head of state in the Middle East. It is through relationship-building activities with the countries' leaders that Cisco establishes its presence in a country. It assumes that orders for its various product lines will follow.

General Electric follows a similar practice except that usually its aircraft engine business is the initial entry business. When China buys Boeing jets, GE engines come along with them. Following those engines, GE builds maintenance and engine overhaul facilities. It sends Chinese technicians to the United States for training and airport and airline managers to Crotonville for training and relationship building. In the process, GE becomes aware that China will need forty new airports in the next ten years. It then works with mayors and local party officials to help them develop plans for the whole airport complex, including a dedicated engine repair facility. Next, GE leaders suggest that GE Transportation help with the planning of a rail link between the airport and the city. GE thus tries to become a trusted advisor and consultant to the local government and sell GE products from its infrastructure businesses. Not that all of this is easy; GE is also discovering how difficult it can be to penetrate China. Nonetheless, it is taking this model to South America and Africa as well.

In many countries where connections count, companies build relationships on a leader-to-leader basis, address the country's problems, and provide jobs and training. Once the corporate center has opened the doors, the businesses do the selling and provide the operations. In this way, the corporate center can add value to its portfolio of businesses.

Leverage

Another way of creating value for the businesses is to leverage the scale of the corporation. The principle is to act big when it is good to be big and to act small when it is good to be small. For example, it is almost always good to be big and have scale when buying or selling. Conversely, it is good to be small when launching new products on short cycle times. As a result, companies centralize some buying activities in the corporate center and decentralize product development to the businesses. Clearly the more related the businesses are, the greater the opportunity is for purchasing common items.

General Electric has always searched for ways to use its size in buying and selling. For a while Jack Welch was scheduling summit meetings between himself and his staff and the CEOs and their staffs at other large companies. The idea was to discuss the balance of trade between the two companies and to look for opportunities to increase it. Other than a big contract with General Motors for its Saturn car factory in Tennessee, the talks had only limited success.

The summit meetings have been more successful when the government is the customer. GE uses its reputation, size, and thought leadership concerning infrastructure to get a seat at the table with top government officials. In China, it used its sponsorship of the 2008 Beijing Olympics and its good performance with its exclusive NBC TV broadcasting contract to win a positive reception for its businesses. Today, Jeff Imelt and his team sit with top government ministers to discuss the electrification of the country. On his team are experts from the gas turbine business, oil and gas pipeline business, solar power, wind power, electric locomotive, water, and GE Capital's Energy Finance business. They work with a similar team from the country government and teams from local governments as well. This approach gives great advantage to GE's businesses. A stand-alone wind power company or a solar power company could not begin to have this kind of access to government customers.

GE has taken a similar approach to building infrastructure in the Middle East. This time it formed a joint venture with the government of Abu Dhabi. Specifically, GE Capital and the sovereign wealth fund of Abu Dhabi are the partners. The joint venture, along with the GE businesses mentioned above, works with teams from Middle Eastern governments to electrify their countries. Size matters when dealing with governments, so it seems that GE has found a way to leverage its scale and scope to add value to its businesses.

Another source of leverage from the corporate center is in the delivery of services to the businesses. Transaction services like payroll, billing, accounts payable, and so on are all more efficient if they have scale. Initially companies centralized these activities one by one and placed them in their respective functions at the corporate center. On some occasions, the expected savings did not occur. These companies then outsourced the activity to specialist third-party firms, which can achieve greater scale.

Other companies centralized all of these activities in a shared services unit with a general manager in charge, and they got further improvements. Companies like DuPont and Procter & Gamble have created these global services units and believe that they outperform third-party vendors.

In summary, many companies have found ways to use their scale to deliver benefits to the businesses in their portfolios.

Some have discovered that it takes an organization to deliver these benefits. Merely centralizing an activity does not ensure the benefits of scale. The companies need the right structures, processes, and talent to convert potential value added into real value added.

Brand

One of the most obvious ways to add value to a business is to add the corporation's valued brand to the business's products and services. As a result, companies work hard to manage their brands and reputations. Companies are well aware that a favorable attitude toward the brand lifts the value of their stock. But there are caveats: brands are only a potential value add, and in fact, not all brands add value. There are many mediocre brands out there that add little value. Whether a brand adds value depends on the corporate center's skills at brand building and management.

Banking Capability

A number of corporations have credit subsidiaries. These internal banks make sure that credit is available to qualified customers of the businesses. The subsidiary adds value during difficult financial times or crises. During the Asian financial crisis of 1997, firms like Hewlett-Packard and IBM were able to maintain their sales levels because their credit subsidiaries could provide loans to their customers. These firms had done business with these customers for decades and had a good idea of the credit risk that they were taking. Their customers would have had difficulty getting loans from local banks during the crisis. In addition to making money on the loans, the corporation adds value to its business.

GE Capital started as the credit subsidiary of General Electric. It financed retailers and consumers buying GE appliances. Then, during the financial deregulation of the 1980s, it expanded into leasing, credit cards, and other lending businesses. Some of the value adds of being a bank and an industrial company have already been mentioned. One advantage that has not been noted is the ability of the corporation to manage the numbers that it delivers to Wall Street. Through the use of reserves and buying and selling securities, financial institutions can legally increase and decrease their reported profits. Jack Welch used these means to deliver the numbers that Wall Street liked and drove up GE's stock price and company value as a result. But most of these value-adding techniques are double-edged swords. When the financial markets froze in 2008, Imelt could not manage the numbers and in fact missed the expected number in the first quarter. And GE was not immune to the bad loans that hit all of the other financial institutions. In 2009 its stock was trading like a bank stock. In the process, GE lost its AAA credit rating. It has since sold off some of the GE Capital businesses and now owns mainly the credit subsidiaries and leasing businesses.

Sharing Intangibles, Expertise, and Knowledge

A corporation often develops some unique expertise, competencies, and capabilities. To the degree that the businesses in the portfolio can profit from the expertise, the value of the portfolio is increased. The more the businesses in the portfolio are related, the greater the likelihood is that the expertise can be shared. Sharing best practices is the clearest and most common example of profiting from expertise. The expertise typically resides in the functions at the corporate center, which are responsible for the dissemination of expertise. The functions share the expertise through day-to-day consulting, database, and website maintenance; holding annual conferences; and moving talent around the corporation (Goold et al., 1994). Today companies are deploying social networks companywide and using internal crowd sourcing to tap the collective corporate knowledge.

A good example is Procter & Gamble in the area of consumer and shopper insights. It uses the usual market research techniques of surveys and focus groups. But it also invests in direct observation of consumers while they use P&G's products. The observers often live with consumers to understand the whole context in which the consumer uses their products. This provides P&G with better information about how their products work (or don't) and how they can be improved. But more than any other business, P&G invests in shopper insights. For P&G, the shopper is not always the same person as the consumer or user. Some studies today estimate that 70 percent of a purchase decision takes place inside the store at the moment of purchase. This shopper insight knowledge is managed by a team of fifteen people at the corporate center in Cincinnati. The team coordinates the work of fifty specialists from around the world. By collecting and managing the consumer and shopper insights, it adds value to all of the global businesses in P&Gs portfolio.

Another example is GE Capital's use of the purchasing capabilities of GE's industrial businesses. GE Capital has a business that leases trucks to various installation and repair service people at companies like Verizon, Xerox, and IBM. Because of its size, it can provide, maintain, and lease these trucks at a much lower cost than its customer companies can. The GE purchasing people led this cost-reduction effort. First, they pool the orders of a large number of companies and get volume discounts from the auto companies. Second, they set up certified repair shops in the cities where their customers use the vehicles. In return for the guaranteed business, the repair shops agree to lower costs. Then the purchasing people set up parts suppliers in Taiwan and China to supply the repair parts to the shops. It is the access to cheap money, the procurement skills, and the volumes that allows the leasing business to provide cars and trucks at a much lower cost to customers.

There are many other examples. Most companies have proprietary knowledge and expertise. To the extent that they can share this expertise within their businesses, they can add value to their portfolio. The corporate center is often the hub at the interchange of best practices.

Tangible Resource Sharing

Some firms create value by sharing tangible resources or assets. When these assets have unique value, the businesses receive real value. An example is Intel, which has been able to build cutting-edge factories to manufacture silicon wafers. The profit centers share these facilities and gain advantage over competitors that don't have this access to the newest technologies. Many companies have resources that they share, like test tracks at auto companies and wind tunnels at aerospace companies. These advantages are mostly scale related. But they are an advantage to the businesses only if the shared resources are superior to those of competitors or outside vendors.

Other varieties of sharing are addressed in chapter 12, which focuses on how companies create solutions and leverage intellectual property with their portfolios.

Summary

Companies have been creative in finding ways that the corporate center can add value to the businesses in their portfolios. This chapter listed several methods companies use to add value, and there are probably many other sources of value-adding activities yet to be discovered. The most powerful sources of added value are when the corporate center combines several of these practices and marshals them together. Talent mobility is one of the key techniques, and it brings multiple benefits. By moving people around, companies develop talent, transfer technology and expertise, and build personal relationships and networks.

The value-adding practices examined in this chapter are only potential value-adding activities. In order to convert them to actual practices, the company must successfully understand and execute the potential into the actual. In the next chapter, we examine how some conglomerates have created valuable capabilities.

11

THE VALUE-ADDING CONGLOMERATES

The conglomerate type of organization has been, and remains, quite controversial. It has come in and out of favor at various times. Today the financial analysts begin shouting, "Break up!" at the first indication that a conglomerate is underperforming or misses its numbers. This was clearly the situation in 2008 with General Electric. Even before Jeff Imelt became the new CEO, he was getting advice from journalists on how to succeed a legend like Jack Welch. The advice always contained the suggestion to break up the conglomerate or at least "sell NBC." GE sold 51 percent of NBC-Universal to Comcast in 2009, and in 2013, Comcast bought the remainder of the company.

In this chapter, we look at the evidence about conglomerate performance. Are the breakup fundamentalists correct about conglomerates? Then we look at GE again, along with some other value-adding conglomerates.

Conglomerate Performance

Conglomerates first gained notoriety in the United States in the late 1960s and 1970s. Companies like Textron, Teledyne, Litton Industries, and ITT became well known and were the hot stocks. Their CEOs became celebrities, as Warren Buffett is today. Henry Singleton (Teledyne), Royal Little (Textron), and Harold Geneen (ITT) were all well known.

Then, as usually happens, some financial analysts began to analyze what was going on. One view was that these conglomerates gained a reputation for being a growth story and thus traded at a higher price-to-earnings (P/E) ratio than the market. Under this logic, if a conglomerate that is trading at a twenty-to-one P/E bought firms trading at a ten-to-one P/E, the conglomerate's stock would be driven higher. The conglomerate could get twenty dollars of stock value for each dollar of earnings generated, while the purchased companies could get only ten dollars of stock value. The analysts said, "These guys do not add real value." The celebrity leaders said, "So what! We're still a growth story. Buy the stock." Other conglomerates put together justifications based on the synergies in the portfolios.

In the 1980s, the conglomerates began to be dismantled, as several things happened. First, the founders began to retire, and their successors were unable to continue the growth. As a result, one theory emerged that conglomerates are successful only when they are run by extraordinary individuals. When ordinary managers take over, they are unable to manage all the diversity in the portfolio. Lords Hanson and White believed this theory. So when they retired, they broke up Hanson Trust themselves and put their subordinates in charge of various independent pieces. A second factor was the rise of corporate raiders like Carl Icahn, T. Boone Pickens, and Irwin Jacobs. When a conglomerate's stock price fell below its breakup value, the raiders would move in and take a position in the stock. The company would break itself up, or the raiders would do it for them. Many investors bought the synergy argument and initially supported the raiders.

Another type of conglomerate emerged about this time: the buy-and-sell conglomerate, like Hanson Trust and the British Tyre and Rubber Company (BTR). For a while, they were the top performers on the London Stock Exchange. The buy-and-sell conglomerate leaders believed that ITT made the mistake of holding on to the businesses and could not manage such a diverse portfolio. Instead, they would buy undervalued and overlooked businesses, improve them, and sell them. They typically bought a division from a large company that had used the business for its cash and was thus starved of investment and talent. Hanson Trust or BTR would buy the division, put in investment and talent, and then sell it (Goold, Campbell and Alexander, 1994). In fact, Hanson would sell any business if the price was right, even its original core business. But these conglomerates began to fade as it became more difficult to find undervalued assets. This was a time of the rise of private equity firms that competed for these same assets. So Hanson disbanded as the founders retired. BTR merged with other conglomerates and still exists today as Invensys, a Financial Times Stock Index 100 company.

The conglomerates remain controversial in developed countries. There are calls for breakup any time they underperform. Yet others have survived and continue to exist. These are the conglomerates that have learned to add value.

Quantitative Studies of Performance

Ever since Chandler's historical analysis (Chandler, 1962), strategy professors have been studying the financial performance of the various types of portfolio strategies and structure. Rumelt's (1974) study was one of the first. He found a small positive performance difference for the related diversifiers. There have been many studies since then. When all these studies are reviewed (Grant, Jammine, and Thomas, 1988; Galbraith, 1994a; Palich, Cardinal, and Miller, 2000), two consistent findings stand out. Rumelt initially found that related diversification was more effective than other portfolio strategies. But if one takes a time period during the Hanson Trust and BTR heydays, the unrelated diversifiers outperform the others, so there is no consensus around the relationship between diversification and firm performance. This lack of consensus holds with every review of the research literature (Nippa, Pidun, and Rubner, 2011). However, a second point that emerges is that an optimum amount of diversity may exist somewhere between the related and unrelated types. Remember that portfolio diversity is a continuum, and when the data are tested using a curvilinear model, there is some support for an optimal amount of diversity (Palich et al., 2000). That is, diversification adds to economic performance up to an optimum amount. Thereafter, performance declines because too much diversity causes diseconomies and is difficult to manage. Grant et al. (1988) and Dundas and Richardson (1982) suggest that the optimum is somewhere around three to four industries or business model types. The evidence is not overwhelming, but it may be the beginning of a consensus.

The research of economists and finance professors has produced a good deal of consensus around the existence of a conglomerate discount. They find that a conglomerate trades at a lower stock price than a matching portfolio of stand-alone companies from the same industries (Whited, 2001; Campa and Kedia, 2002). And the greater the number of businesses or industries that are held by the conglomerate, the greater is the discount. They no longer argue about whether a discount exists, but what causes it and whether it is larger or smaller in various countries. It is this evidence that drives the opinions of many investors and analysts on Wall Street and in the City of London.

The Boston Consulting Group (BCG) is, and has been, the most prominent defender of the conglomerate. It does not dispute the existence of the discount but says it results from the prejudice of analysts and investors against diverse enterprises. And it claims that its own analysis of financial performance indicates no difference in the performance of low or high diversifiers. Every few years, BCG reanalyzes its database of three hundred companies (one hundred each from the United States, Europe, and Asia). Its latest report was issued in December 2006 (Heuskel, Fechtel, and Beckman, 2006). When it plots relative total shareholder returns (RTSR) against the number of businesses in companies' portfolios, it finds no relationship. Their findings are shown in figure 11.1.

Figure 11.1   Financial Performance Versus the Number of Diverse Businesses in the Portfolio

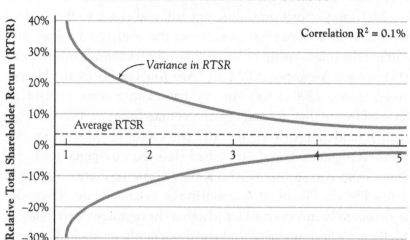

Number of Unrelated Businesses

The correlation shows that diversity explains 1 percent of the variance. It also shows the reduction in variance that diversity brings to the portfolio. So BCG bases its view of prejudice on the lack of real performance differences yet lower stock prices for conglomerates.

The position of Bain and Company, another strategy consulting firm, is exactly the opposite (Zook, 2001). Bain analysts examined the performance of companies versus the number of core businesses that they are executing and find that 78 percent of the high performers have a single core business. Their definition of *core* does not mean single business as I have defined it. They probably would define Kellogg's as having a single core food business or, at most, two. So defining the core is a subjective practice. It is close to the concept of the business model that I introduced earlier. Bain is an advocate of focusing on a business model that could include some related diversification. It advocates exhausting all growth possibilities in the core business and then, and only then, diversifying into other businesses. If a company must diversify, it should enter only businesses that are adjacent to the core business. Bain is a clear proponent of related diversification.

McKinsey's position is different still and closer to Bain's than to BCG's. Its analysts have examined the analyzed database and studied the relationship between diversification and performance (Harper and Viguerie, 2002). In "Are You Too Focused?" Harper and Viguerie (2002) sort the companies into three categories: focused (more than 67 percent of revenues from one business segment), moderately diversified (67 percent of revenues from two business segments), and diversified (less than 67 percent of revenues from two segments). McKinsey chose segments that were defined by the Financial Accounting Standards Board. There did not seem to be any control for whether the segments were related. McKinsey's findings were that the moderately diversified companies were the top performers from 1980 to 2000. They did control for the life cycle of the business and concluded that focus was good in the early stages of the life cycle when growth was fast. But when growth slowed later in the life cycle, moderate diversification led to better performance.

In summary, there has been a great deal of research on the relationship between diversification strategies and economic performance. Many of the studies reach different conclusions and are difficult to compare. They all study different time periods and use different methodologies, databases, measures of diversity, and measures of economic performance. There are time periods when the conglomerates have been the top performers. But if we step back and observe, the bulk of the evidence says that on average, moderate diversifiers and related diversifiers outperform the unrelated diversifiers or conglomerates. The conclusions of these studies are averages or central tendencies discovered in large sample analyses. If we look at the distribution of the performance of conglomerates, we would find that most of them underperform the markets. But we would also find a minority of conglomerates that outperform the market. My interest has always been to study these outliers on a case-by-case basis. How are they able to outperform? How do they do it? In my view, these conglomerates have found a value-adding strategy and have designed an organization to execute it. I agree with the statement from BCG that performance has less to do with diversity and more to do with how the diversity is managed. In the next section, we look at how some of the conglomerates manage diversity.

A Look at Value-Adding Conglomerates

In contrast to many conglomerates that have been derided in the financial press, a few of them stand out for adding value. This section describes four companies that have achieved superior value and outperformed the market's expectations.

Berkshire Hathaway

Before examining the value-adding conglomerates, let us look at the extreme form of conglomerate, Berkshire Hathaway. It has the most diverse portfolio and adds the least amount of value to that portfolio. The subsidiaries are listed in table 11.1. There are fifty-five subsidiaries in all kinds of industries. This portfolio is managed through the simplest of all organizations: all of the businesses report directly to the chairman and vice chairman, Warren Buffett and Charlie Munger, respectively. Buffett describes his management style as being one of abdication. He and Munger are assisted by seventeen others at the corporate headquarters. This group does review the capital investment plans of the businesses and will problem-solve with them when there are questions. When a business underperforms, it will attract attention and review. The corporation will fix the problem by working with an executive recruiter and replace the CEO. But other than reviews and decisions in the capital investment plans and reviews and replacements of CEOs, the businesses are pretty much left alone. It is decentralization in the extreme.

Table 11.1 Berkshire Hathaway Companies

Acme Brick Company	Garan Incorporated	MiTek
Applied Underwriters	Gateway Underwriters Agency	National Indemnity Company
Ben Bridge Jewelers	GEICO Auto Insurance	Nebraska Furniture Mart
Benjamin Moore & Co.	General Re	NetJets
Berkshire Hathaway Homestates Companies	Guard Insurance Group	Omaha World-Herald
Boat U.S.	Helzberg Diamonds	Oriental Trading Company
Borsheims Fine Jewelry	H. H. Brown Shoe Group	The Pampered Chef
Brooks	HomeServices of America, a subsidiary of MidAmerican Energy Holdings Company	Precision Steel Warehouse
Buffalo News, Buffalo, NY	International Dairy Queen	RC Willey Home Furnishings
BNSF	IMC International Metalworking Companies	Richline Group
Business Wire	Johns Manville	Scott Fetzer Companies
Central States Indemnity Company	Jordan's Furniture	See's Candies
Clayton Homes	Justin Brands	Shaw Industries
CORT Business Services	Larson-Juhl	Star Furniture
CTB	Lubrizol Corporation	TTI
Fechheimer Brothers Company	Marmon Holdings, Inc.	United States Liability Insurance Group
FlightSafety	McLane Company	XTRA Corporation
Forest River	Medical Protective	
Fruit of the Loom Companies	MidAmerican Energy Holdings Company	

Berkshire Hathaway's core business is insurance, which generates a lot of investable funds. Buffett and Munger have turned over the insurance businesses to professional managers while they run the investments. They invest like other insurance companies in various financial instruments, but they also buy whole companies when the opportunity arises. They have always invested in undervalued assets. They prefer to buy and hold companies in dull and boring businesses with depressed stocks. The companies usually turn their performance around as the economy or their industries recover. Other than during the dot-com bubble and the financial crisis of 2009, this model has outperformed the markets.

Today Warren Buffett gets opportunities to invest that the rest of the world does not. During the financial crisis that began in September 2008, Goldman Sachs and General Electric both approached him for cash injections. He was only too happy to oblige, and the terms that he got were very attractive. The two financial firms got their cash and an endorsement from one of the world's most successful investors. Berkshire Hathaway's competitive advantage now is the access to investment opportunities that others do not have. Companies seeking capital want both the cash and Buffett's public endorsement.

So in a comparison of conglomerates, Berkshire Hathaway is the extreme. It is strictly a financial vehicle investing in undervalued assets. It provides capital and talent if necessary to these companies, but otherwise leaves them alone. With only nineteen people in the corporate center, it cannot get involved with the businesses. Some of the other conglomerates get more involved in improving the businesses in their portfolios.

General Electric

In chapter 10, I used GE to illustrate many of the types of value added. Despite having a very diverse business portfolio, it has been very creative at using as many means as possible to add value. At the core of its value-added strategy is the creation of talent and its mobility across the company. GE makes superior talent, technology, skills, best practices, and ideas available to all of its businesses. It is able to leverage its size in buying and selling and in size, reputation, and thought leadership to get a seat at the table with country leaders. GE's businesses profit from the corporate focus on infrastructure at a time when emerging market countries are investing in their own infrastructures. The infrastructure businesses are collected in two groups. GE's organization structure is shown in figure 11.2.

GE will need these value adders since it has lost some of its advantage of access to cheap money. But it has another capability that it can use: it has learned how to implement and profit from corporate initiatives.

The corporate initiative process began in 1987 when Jack Welch saw the process as a challenge for the whole company to renew itself strategically. The first initiative was globalization. GE was focused mainly on the US economy in the 1980s, so the

Figure 11.2 GE's Organization Structure

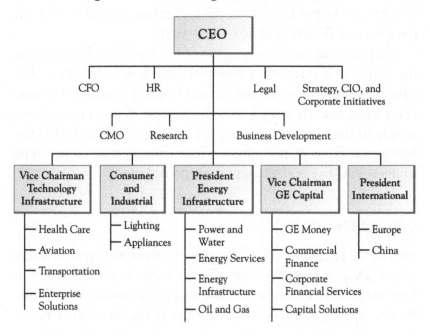

first global initiative was to get global presence and revenues from countries outside the United States. The initiative, which is still being pursued in 2013, has been reoriented several times. From global revenues, it has been changed to global purchasing, global recruiting, and developing products and services to meet local tastes. These initiatives are long-term responses to strategic challenges. During the Welch era, initiatives were added for Growth Through Services (1994), Six Sigma (1996), and e-Business (1999). Each initiative continued year in and year out. Sometimes they were reoriented. At the end of Welch's tenure, only four initiatives remained.

The head of strategy and a corporate initiative unit of twenty people managed the entire process. The process started each January at the Boca Raton meeting of the top six hundred managers. The initiatives are announced and described by the CEO. After the meeting, the initiatives unit sends out the guidelines to the businesses. Each business then chooses a new leader or confirms the existing one. The leader and the business leadership team choose the business initiative team. For each initiative, somewhere around seven people from each business are dedicated full time to the team. These teams participate in a monthly conference call led by the head of strategy, and their leaders meet quarterly, when outside experts present their experiences. Sometimes the meeting is held at a site that the initiative unit thinks is "best in class." The participants exchange experiences and ideas among themselves.

In addition, the initiative process is plugged into events on the corporate calendar. As mentioned, the process is launched at the annual Boca Raton meeting. The initiatives are also discussed at quarterly executive council meetings, an event attended by the top forty leaders. The March meeting in particular is an open discussion of initiatives. If any business has done something noteworthy, the initiative leader and team from that business present their experience and learning to the other businesses. In June, the CEO conducts the annual talent reviews with the businesses and assesses the initiative leaders and team members. The purpose is to see that the initiatives are staffed with high performers. The CEO also gets input from the strategy lead and the initiatives unit. Changes are made if the CEO is not impressed with the staffing.

The initiative team in each business prepares a plan and reviews it with the business leadership team and the initiatives unit. Every fall, a budget is presented as part of the annual budgeting process. The team then commits to a budget, targets, and metrics that will be reported monthly. The CEO usually responds to the monthly numbers by making calls to the high and low performers. The top-performing teams present to the corporate officers' meeting in November and to the annual Boca Raton meeting in January. The strategy head and the initiatives unit orchestrate all of the agendas and presentations.

The initiatives also become part of the executive courses at Crotonville. GE has made hands-on projects a prominent part of the learning process in its executive courses. Most of these projects take place as part of the initiatives. The business initiative teams get several projects conducted in support of their activity. The most outstanding of these projects are presented at the quarterly executive council meetings. In this way, GE maximizes the number of people involved in the initiatives.

There is also a great deal of ongoing contact between the initiative leaders and teams. Any time that one of the businesses discovers something that works, the others are quick to learn what they did and how they did it. The initiative unit is constantly surveying practices at other companies. Leaders from these companies are contacted and invited to attend initiative meetings. Good ideas from inside and outside the company travel fast.

The initiative process has accomplished a number of things at GE. First, the initiatives themselves have been successful at accomplishing strategic changes. Today, GE's businesses all have significant service components to them. They have achieved Growth Through Services. Their revenue from outside the

United States is now over 40 percent of the total. Six Sigma, for example, resulted in significant cost savings and is now embedded in the businesses and no longer requires the special effort of an initiative. Imelt is continuing the initiative process. Globalization and Services continue as before. He has added technical leadership, customer focus, and growth platforms. GE has shown that it can change the whole company and add value with a corporate initiative.

Second, the process has built a learning culture at GE. Instead of a bunch of meetings for the top leaders throughout the year, GE has created an integrated sequence of learning sessions. It is hungry for good ideas from inside and outside the company, and when one is found, the businesses experiment with them. When one is successful, it spreads rapidly across the businesses. The initiative process has thus become a value-adding process for GE. Its portfolio of diverse businesses profit from being part of the process.

In summary, GE has discovered many ways to add value to its portfolio of diverse businesses. It traded at a premium to the market under Jack Welch. Under Imelt, the company faces criticism and trades at a slight conglomerate discount. GE has two challenges: it must show that it adds real value to its businesses and must recover from the financial crisis with a high-performing GE Capital business. GE says it is not a conglomerate. It now has to show how it adds value.

Danaher

The Danaher Corporation has been identified as a conglomerate that "makes everything—especially money" (Hindo, 2007). The Rales brothers started Danaher in the 1980s. They began as a pair of corporate raiders and later converted to private equity. One of their businesses, an auto supplier, adopted the Toyota Production System (TPS). The effects were so dramatic that the brothers took note and commanded all of the manufacturing businesses in the portfolio to convert to the lean manufacturing processes and values of the TPS. The effects were equally dramatic. With that experience, Danaher's value-adding strategy was born. The company would acquire good manufacturing companies, transform them by introducing the TPS, create profitable manufacturing subsidiaries, and continuously improve them.

In the early 1990s, Danaher became an operating company and dropped the private equity strategy. The brothers brought in a CEO from Black and Decker and turned over the day-to-day operations. Over the years, Danaher has perfected its value-adding processes. One is its acquisition process. It is always in the deal pipeline, but it has an exacting and unsentimental process: it will walk away when the price gets too high. Before each deal, it sends in its experts in the TPS to assess how much improvement can be expected from implementing the lean treatment. They buy only companies that can be improved by applying the TPS. Their bid price is then a well-informed one. They also buy only small and medium-sized firms. These companies can be converted to the TPS and their cultures changed to the lean values. They avoid very large companies.

Danaher has created the Danaher Business System (DBS), its own version of the TPS, a complete methodology for running a manufacturing company. It starts with customer satisfaction and completes the treatment with how to manage vendors. The DBS is owned and continuously improved by the DBS office at the corporate center. It is the only unit in the center other than the usual finance, HR, legal, and strategy staffs. Danaher's corporate structure is shown in figure 11.3.

Once a company is acquired, it is rapidly converted to the DBS. A team from both the DBS office and relevant parts of the company descends on the acquisition and begins the transformation. When performance meets expectations, the team disbands, and the new subsidiary begins the never-ending cycle of change and improvement. Danaher repeats this integration process as it makes about one acquisition per month. In 2012, for example, it made fourteen acquisitions. It also has divested

Figure 11.3 Danaher Corporate Organization Structure

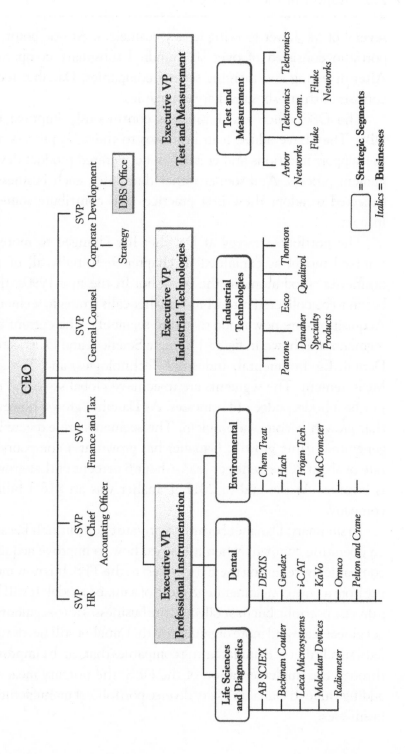

several of its slower-growing legacy businesses. At one point, its portfolio consisted of over six hundred subsidiary companies. After divesting and merging several companies, Danaher today consists of thirty-six subsidiary companies.

The DBS office and businesses continuously improve the DBS. They have added lean processes to the sales process and the support functions and created an accelerated product development process. And sooner rather than later, each business is expected to adopt these best practices and contribute some of its own.

The portfolio strategy at Danaher has changed to more of a mixed model as explained in chapter 9. Initially all of the businesses stood alone in the portfolio. In the mid-1990s, they began to be collected into what Danaher calls strategic segments. Acquisitions are now made to add to segments. The current five segments are shown in figure 11.3: Life Sciences and Diagnostics, Dental, Environmental, Industrial Technologies, and Test and Measurement. The segments are to achieve global scale and not just be a hodgepodge of businesses. As Danaher grows, however, that growth becomes a problem. The segments are expected to generate organic growth. Danaher has grown at a compounded rate of about 20 percent per year. About 6 percent of that growth is organic. At the end of 2012, Danaher was an $18.3 billion company.

In summary, Danaher began as a private equity firm. It became an operating company when it learned how to improve acquired companies by requiring them to convert to the TPS. It is now moving from a pure conglomerate to more of a mixed model. It still has a diverse portfolio but has collected the businesses into segments to get global scale and more organic growth. Danaher still needs to be fed a steady diet of manufacturing companies that can be improved through the implementation of the DBS, the primary means of adding value to Danaher's very diverse portfolio of manufacturing businesses.

Illinois Tool Works

The Illinois Tool Works (ITW) is another company, like Dana-her, that is known mainly to investors. It also acquires many small manufacturing businesses and improves them. At the end of 2012, ITW had 213 businesses, which were gathered into eight business segments. Over the past two decades, ITW has grown at a 16 percent compound annual growth rate to become a $17.9 billion company at the start of 2013. It makes around fifty acquisitions per year to achieve this kind of growth.

ITW's claim to fame is the strict application of the 80/20 rule. Everyone knows that roughly 20 percent of a company's products and customers yield 80 percent of the revenues and profits. ITW is one of the few companies to act on this well-known principle. Its leaders discovered it in one of their businesses that was making frequent changeovers of its assembly lines. They decided to focus the business on just the top 20 percent of products, and the improvement results were so dramatic that they tried the policy on some other business, with the same effect. Since then, they have perfected the process of acquiring a company and applying the 80 percent rule. The sales drop by 20 percent, the margins improve by a factor of two or three, 10 percent of the staff are reduced, and then growth starts. Now all of the managers in the company are schooled in the 80/20 process.

Like most other acquisitive conglomerates, ITC has also perfected its acquisition process. As noted, it searches for small manufacturing companies that can be quickly converted using the 80/20 process. Many of these are family businesses that have no heir to run them. Their pricing rule is that the purchase price should be less than the target company's annual revenue.

ITW, like Danaher, does a thorough job of due diligence. Its experts examine the acquisition candidate to determine how much improvement will result from applying the 80/20 rule. If the target company is already focused, they will walk away. Clearly they have a good idea of what their purchase price should be.

ITW is unique in its approach to acquisitions. It has not created an acquisitions department at the corporate center. Instead, all of its top managers are trained to continuously search for opportunities, negotiate the deal, and close and integrate the acquisition. Like Danaher, ITW needs a steady diet of small manufacturing companies to acquire and improve. It thus encourages its top 250 people to become dealmakers in addition to running their businesses. The managers have all been through a two-day program run by the company's top managers. All of these dealmakers are likely to hear about acquisition opportunities in their locales and industries. They can act before the acquisition candidate hits the radar screens of other acquirers. They can also get help and advice from any of the other 250 managers.

The organization chart for ITW is shown in figure 11.4.

Figure 11.4 shows the normal structure of a conglomerate with its small corporate center. But ITW also has another source of value added: its technology center. Part of the center is to manage the company's 12,000 patents and their use internally and externally. The R&D part of the center works in support of the business units' innovation programs. It is considered an advanced internal consulting service. It builds competencies in areas such as process technologies, prototyping, simulation, and advanced materials that many of the businesses use. The technology center also runs the annual gathering of the technology community to celebrate new patent recipients. In 2011, ITW launched an initiative to scale up the business units from an average of $25 million to $100 million. ITW is also sourcing some commodities centrally. The company feels it is underscaled and underleveraged.

In summary, Illinois Tool Works provides another good example of a value-adding conglomerate. It has consistently outperformed the S&P Index over the past twenty years. It is able to create value for its shareholders by rigorously applying the 80/20 rule to a constant flow of small acquisitions and giving them access to the company's technological prowess. It has a disciplined acquisition process in which all of the top 250 managers participate.

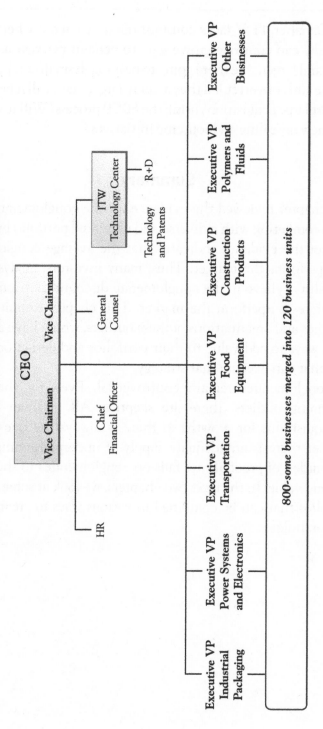

Figure 11.4 Illinois Toolworks Organization Structure

CEO
Vice Chairman   Vice Chairman

HR   Chief Financial Officer   General Counsel   ITW Technology Center
Technology and Patents   R+D

Executive VP Industrial Packaging

Executive VP Power Systems and Electronics

Executive VP Transportation

Executive VP Food Equipment

Executive VP Construction Products

Executive VP Polymers and Fluids

Executive VP Other Businesses

800-some businesses merged into 120 business units

Like Danaher, ITW faces constant questions about whether the company can continue growing at 16 percent per year as it gets larger and larger. Are there going to be enough small companies to acquire and convert? Or if they acquire larger ones, will it be able to convert large acquisitions using the 80/20 process? Will it succeed in its new upscaling and sourcing initiatives?

Summary

This chapter reviewed the evidence for the conglomerate strategy of competing with a diverse and unrelated portfolio business. Most of the evidence indicates that the average conglomerate underperforms the market. Thus, many investors, analysts, and journalists believe in the conglomerate discount. But some conglomerates outperform the market. This chapter examined the strategies and organizations of these outliers, which have all have found ways to add value to their portfolios and design organizations that can execute that strategy.

Conglomerates remain controversial. Even for the high-performing outliers, there are skeptics. All of them depend on acquisitions for growth, so there is always the question of whether there is an adequate supply of underperforming firms. The burden of proof always falls on conglomerates to show that they add value. In the next two chapters, we look at some diverse portfolios that can be combined in various ways to create value for shareholders.

12

SYNERGY PORTFOLIO STRATEGIES

Companies with diverse portfolios (mixed and conglomerate models) historically managed each business as a stand-alone entity. In chapter 11, we looked at the Illinois Tool Works approach to improving an acquired business by applying the 80/20 process to every business. Some conglomerates today, like United Technologies, operate by managing and improving each business unit on a stand-alone basis. However, there are a couple of portfolio models that explicitly pursue synergies among their diverse businesses. One model is the leveraging of intellectual property model, which works by leveraging intellectual property across all the businesses. Disney is the prime example. The other is the solutions model of integrating the products and services of diverse businesses for a customer. IBM is the prime example of this model. Every company pursuing these models has created units whose responsibility is to integrate the other businesses and achieve synergy. But it is not just adding another organizational unit that achieves synergy. It is the design of a complete organization—a complete Star Model—that is the key. In this chapter, I describe the synergy portfolio models and contrast it with the stand-alone model. But first I discuss the concept of synergy and describe how it is implemented.

Synergy

The Wikipedia definition of synergy is that it is the interaction of multiple elements in a system to produce an effect different from or greater than the sum of the individual effects. When initially applied in business, it meant that acquisitions or business units would work together to create more economic value than the sum of the businesses could create on their own. It was then used to justify acquisitions in the conglomerate era of the 1970s and 1980s. Often management overpaid for an acquisition and justified the rich price by the anticipated synergies that would result. When the synergies usually failed to appear, the term lost its meaning. Today it is used in mergers and acquisitions, but it means cost reductions that result from eliminating duplications. In this book, I am referring to its original definition: the creation of economic value that results from two or more business units working together. I am using the term because synergy is actually being created through the collaboration of business units in some of these companies.

The best way to describe the synergy model is to portray it visually. There are three types of pure models of synergy. That is, in addition to the corporate strategy decisions about portfolio diversity and adding value, there are three approaches to adding value through synergy: the stand-alone model, the leveraging of intellectual property model, and the solutions model. The stand-alone model, shown in figure 12.1, adds very little value through synergy. The figure shows the business value chains for

Figure 12.1 Value Chain for United Technologies' Businesses

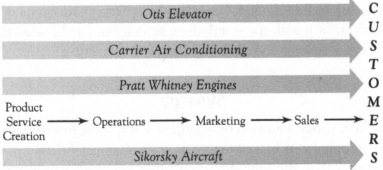

the business units at United Technologies (UT). The value chain shows the interdependent work flow from product and service creation to operations to marketing to sales to the customer. Shown here are some of the UT businesses like Otis Elevator, Carrier Air Conditioning, Pratt & Whitney Aircraft Engines, and Sikorsky Helicopters. UT adds value to each of its businesses on a stand-alone basis. There are always discussions at UT as to whether Carrier and Otis should collaborate when working with common construction customers like Skanska. They always decide not to formalize a collaboration and leave it open to the businesses to decide whether they should work together. The businesses are shown in figure 12.1 as parallel and independent of each other.

The leveraged intellectual property model (IP) is shown in figure 12.2. At Disney, brands (like *High School Musical*) and characters (like Mickey Mouse, Nemo, Buzz Lightyear) are exploited in all of the businesses. In the diagram, Hannah Montana is the example. She started as a TV program on the Disney Channel. When the ratings and fan reactions went through the roof, other Disney businesses picked up the character as well. The collaboration resulted in millions of novelettes through Disney Publishing, millions of albums through Disney Music, a successful theater production through Disney Theatrical Productions, a movie through Disney Films, an attraction at Disney Resorts and Parks, and a source of multiple licenses through Disney Consumer Products. Hannah Montana was the largest-selling product line at Macy's during the 2007 Christmas season.

Disney is able to achieve this synergy despite having a diverse set of business. If analysts classified Disney's portfolio, they would call it a conglomerate. In addition to the businesses in figure 12.2, Disney has ESPN, games, websites, Disney stores, a cruise line, a vacation club, ice shows, and more.

The other synergy model is the solutions model as implemented by IBM, shown in figure 12.3. Rather than leveraging intellectual property across separate businesses, as Disney does, IBM combines the products of the businesses for software, services

Figure 12.2 Leveraging Intellectual Property at Disney

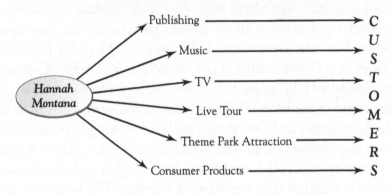

Figure 12.3 Synergy Through Solutions at IBM

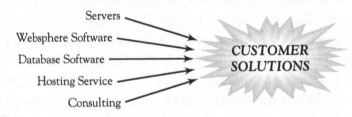

and hardware, into customer solutions. IBM is competitive when it can create value by combining products better than the customer can combine them themselves. Siemens provides another example. The German company can provide 40 percent of the value to build a new hospital: it can provide medical imaging equipment, information technology systems, power generating equipment, building automation equipment, project management, and consulting services. Since it builds many hospitals, it can run the project more effectively than hospitals that build only one or a few new facilities.

Siemens and IBM are also considered to be conglomerates; they have diverse portfolios of different businesses and different business models. IBM has hardware products like servers and mainframes; different types of software products like operating systems, databases, and middleware; semiconductors; financial services; and services like systems integration, outsourcing, consulting, and installation and repair. The next sections describe how these conglomerates can achieve synergy through their organization designs.

Leveraging Intellectual Property

The leveraging conglomerate is not a new type of company. The 3M company, one of the earliest examples, has leveraged its clever chemical engineers who invent innumerable products using 3M's coating and bonding technologies. The company then builds a business around the abrasive products, industrial tapes and adhesives, and consumer products like Scotch Tape and Post-it Notes. Corning is another company that leverages its technologies—specialty glass and ceramics—but no longer builds businesses around the products like CorningWare. Instead, it forms joint ventures and lets the partners do the commercialization. Today Qualcomm is starting to build component businesses off its semiconductors. Some conglomerates in mixed-portfolio companies have leveraged superior technology skills to enter a variety of diverse businesses.

Another type of company that is becoming a leveraging conglomerate is the fashion designer like Armani and Ralph Lauren. They have become, or have partnered, with astute businesspeople. Armani has taken his design expertise into fashion for men and women. His clothing lines originally were sold through fashion retailers like Saks Fifth Avenue. His clothing still sells in the stores, where he now has opened Armani stores within those stores. He also has his own retail stores for men and women in addition to Armani Exchange stores for more moderately priced fashion. Next, he started designing and selling furniture and interior decoration products. Now he has Armani furniture stores in Italy. He then began designing and opening Armani hotels. There were Armani residences under design and construction in Dubai before the financial crisis, which have since been converted to a combination hotel and residences covering eleven floors in the Burj Khalifa. But otherwise, he has been very successful in leveraging his design, talent, and brand across a number of quite diverse businesses.

The champion of leverage is still the Walt Disney Company. Walt Disney himself started the practice with cartoons, toys, and merchandise from the cartoon characters and then Disneyland and theme parks featuring these same characters. Following his death in 1966, the company struggled until 1984. It was then that Michael Eisner and Frank Wells came in as a pair to run the company. They turned the company around and grew it profitably. One of the actions they took was to resurrect the original Disney synergy model. They began with the relaunch of *Snow White and the Seven Dwarfs*, the first of the "event films"; that is, the arrival of the film was a big event in and of itself and generated a lot of free publicity from the media. Disney also partnered with Coca-Cola and McDonald's. Coke issued special cans and had a promotion, and McDonald's gave away Snow White and Dwarf figurines along with its Happy Meals. Inside Disney, all of the businesses participated. (In fact, it was not an option as to whether to participate.) So there would be magazines, books, albums, events at theme parks, an ice show, and so on. The whole company participated in the event. The *Snow White* event was such a success that the process was repeated for the sixtieth anniversary of Mickey Mouse in 1988. With another success, Eisner and Wells began to launch one event film per year.

Eventually these projects were led by a vice president of synergy who reported directly to Eisner and Wells. Each business also had a director of synergy. The vice president and director then formed a cross-business, cross-functional team to coordinate the event, which engaged in some lively debates to arrive at a successful program. The original plan for an event film usually did not benefit every business, so a business would request changes that would help it make money from the project. But the changes might not be good for the storyline or for another business. For example, film soundtracks usually do not make for very popular albums, so the music business always had change requests. Some worked. The soundtrack for *Pocahontas* knocked Michael Jackson off the number one album position. Eisner and Wells used to drop into the synergy group meetings. If there was not enough debate, they would stir the pot and get a debate going. They felt a good film resulted from the creativity that came from heated debates.

Some of these event films were highly successful. *The Lion King* and *Pocahontas* each resulted in a good film and good results for all of the other businesses. *The Hunchback of Notre Dame* was less successful. The power of the event films declined in the 1990s, and many believe that Disney never recovered from the death of Frank Wells in 1994. He and Eisner were a powerful duo, but the magic was no longer there without Frank.

The Disney performance was kept going by sourcing films from Pixar. *Toy Story* in 1995 and *Toy Story 2* in 1998 were big successes. When Bob Iger became CEO in 2005, he acquired Pixar a year later and Marvel in 2009. Both deals came with their creative talent as well as their characters. Then in 2012, he acquired Lucasfilm and the *Star Wars* franchise. Now the leverage or synergy model is back and performing well. The results for *Toy Story 3* in 2012 are as follows: games for Nintendo, Xbox, and PlayStation, $220 million; from books and publishing, $250 million; from DVDs and home entertainment, $650 million; from box office receipts worldwide, $1.1 billion; and from licensing, merchandise, and Disney store sales, $7.6 billion. Total franchise revenue through the first half of 2013 for *Toy Story 3* was $9.8 billion. This does not include results from Toy Story Mania, an attraction opening in all Disney theme parks. So how does Disney organize to get synergy across all of its diverse businesses?

The Disney organization structure is shown in figure 12.4. The list of businesses in the groups show the strategy of *where to play*. They are in all forms of media and entertainment that fit within their family focus. The *how to win* strategy is clearly to produce outstanding films, games, and programs and

Figure 12.4 The Walt Disney Company Structure

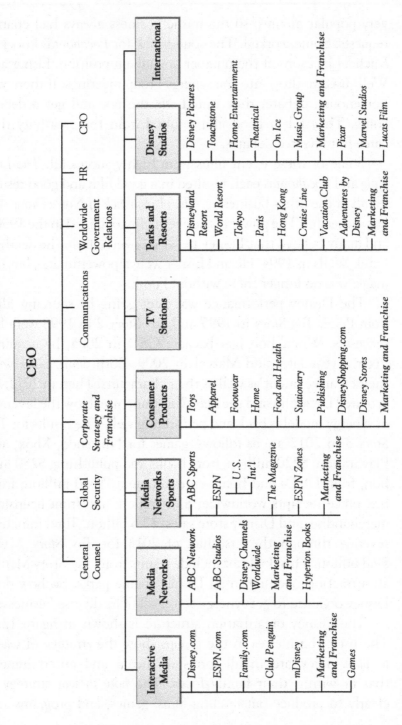

Note: The groups responsible for synergy are in bold type.

then leverage their characters and brands across all of the businesses. At first glance, the structure looks like any mixed model where the businesses, the P&Ls, are clustered into groups of similar businesses within a group and different businesses across the groups. But there are marketing and franchise units in each group and also within some of the large businesses with a lot of synergy work. *Franchise units* are the new name for the synergy groups (they are highlighted in the figure), which disappeared with Eisner in 2005. These are the units that manage the synergy opportunities across the company. The key businesses that generate the franchise opportunities are the Disney Channel (with *High School Musical*), Disney Studios (with Mickey Mouse), Pixar (with Buzz Lightyear), Marvel (with *The Avengers*), and now Lucas (with R2D2). A brand steward from the business generates the franchise and then coordinates the cross-business team for the franchise. The other key group is the Interactive Media Group, which manages all of the digital technologies for the company. For example, the group manages the "Watch" product. "Watch," originally from ESPN, allows a cable customer to watch his or her favorite program on any device. It is sold to the cable operator who sells it in turn to the viewer. So we can subscribe to "Watch" through our cable operator and then watch *Monday Night Football* on our tablet or smart phone. The Interactive Group is the center of digital expertise for all of Disney. They have their own products, like games, but also support the rest of Disney.

The reason that synergy works at Disney is not just because of the franchise units. Disney has designed a complete organization that supports the synergy behavior that is needed. Figure 12.5 shows the complete Star Model for the Disney organization. The figure shows the strategy and structure just described. The processes also support the synergy strategy. As part of the business planning process, each business plans its activities for the next three years, as is normal. But the plans are not just for its business alone. Each business is to identify and prioritize the synergy

Figure 12.5 Star Model for the Disney Organization

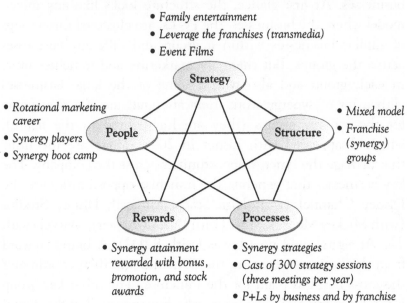

- *Family entertainment*
- *Leverage the franchises (transmedia)*
- *Event Films*

Strategy

- *Rotational marketing career*
- *Synergy players*
- *Synergy boot camp*

People

Structure

- *Mixed model*
- *Franchise (synergy) groups*

Rewards

Processes

- *Synergy attainment rewarded with bonus, promotion, and stock awards*

- *Synergy strategies*
- *Cast of 300 strategy sessions (three meetings per year)*
- *P+Ls by business and by franchise*

opportunities that it would like to pursue. These strategies are presented and discussed three times a year at the Top 300 Manager meetings, called "The Cast of 300." The assumption is that the top three hundred need to know what all of the other businesses are doing. Then the accounting system tracks the revenues and profits of the franchises across the company. It reports them for the originator business and for the implementer business as well. The $250 million in revenue from *Toy Story 3* books, for example, is credited to the publishing business and Pixar Studios.

The HR policies also support the synergy strategies. The leaders are measured against their business goals but are also rewarded for making the franchise system work. People who are promoted are those who are effective at the synergy game. In the business press, there are often reports of people losing their jobs at Disney because they did not work well with their peers. The management development process for future leaders invites people from across the company. They then visit and work in all of the main businesses for two weeks. This program was originally called "The Synergy Boot Camp." People at Disney are selected, developed, and promoted on their synergy skills.

Disney also rotates people among the businesses. This practice is especially used for the marketing and franchise people so they can develop personal networks throughout the whole company. A standard practice has evolved for when a new manager takes a new job, whether the manager comes from inside or outside the company. In all cases, the new manager spends two weeks with an HR manager, who introduces him or her to all of the people at the key interfaces with the other businesses. These are the people the new manager should know in order to work through the franchise system.

In summary, Disney has developed a complete organization and a completely aligned Star Model. All of the policies are aligned with the synergy strategy and all of the other organizational practices. This completely aligned Star Model is an advantage for Disney and hard to duplicate. For every Disney, there is an AOL–Time Warner that tried and failed at the leveraged model. AOL and Time Warner split up not long after the merger, and Time Warner is still splitting itself apart even today.

Synergy Through Solutions

Over the past couple of decades, we have seen a movement to provide solutions, that is, integrated bundles of products and services, instead of, or in addition to, stand-alone products (Galbraith, 2005). IBM led the way in about 1995 when Lou Gerstner committed the company to a strategy of servers, software, services, solutions, and standards. He saw that hardware was commoditizing and the margins were collapsing while software and services were growing.

Once there is a shift to software and standards, all of the customers' IT equipment, telecom equipment, radiology machines, and so on can talk and work together. IBM, Ericsson, GE, and

Siemens all began to integrate their products with software and offer solutions. Since these companies could write software and integrate products better than their customers could, the customers were happy to get added value and outsource the integration to their suppliers. Similarly, the tiering of the value chain in the automotive industry turned tier 1 suppliers into solution providers. Johnson Controls used to provide car seats to the automobile companies. Now it provides a whole interior module that can be dropped into the auto body. There are a number of companies, usually B2B companies, that are becoming solution providers. The challenge for the solution provider is to get all of its business units to work together. If a solution requires that the products and services work together for the customer, the business units that design and produce those products and services must also work together. Getting business units to work together is largely an organization design challenge. In this section, we see how IBM does it.

IBM's portfolio strategy has been evolving since the new era began in 1995. Gertsner first led the change in direction away from the desktop and client server to the Internet in a strategy called network-centric computing. When Sam Palmisano took over in 2002 as CEO, he built on the network-centric strategy by adding the Business On Demand strategy, which took advantage of grid computing and software as a service. Next, IBM embraced the pervasive computing model with its Smart Planet strategy, a campaign to put sensors and microprocessors into everything. In addition, IBM has transformed Business On Demand into cloud computing, added data and analytics, and, more recently, social and mobile computing as new growth initiatives.

Portfolio Strategies

Like many other companies, IBM has been exiting low-growth, low-margin businesses and reinvesting in higher-growth and higher-margin service and software businesses. For example, customers consistently requested Cisco routers rather than

IBM's, so IBM sold its router business to Cisco and, in exchange, received the contract to service Cisco's hardware. Next, it sold its personal computer business and its hard disc drive business. Currently it's rumored to be looking to sell its low-end server business. But IBM invested in software and service businesses like business intelligence, data and analytics, and virtualization software. Between 2000 and 2012, it made more than 140 acquisitions and saw its margins and profits grow from 12 percent and $10.2 billion in 2000 to 22 percent and $17.6 billion in 2012 (IBM, 2012). The profit mix went from 25 percent software, 40 percent service, 10 percent finance, and 24 percent hardware in 2000 to 45 percent software, 41 percent service, and 14 percent for finance and hardware combined in 2012.

Business On Demand

IBM made another transition when Sam Palmisano took over as CEO. Recognizing the next phase of computing, Palmisano and his team launched Business On Demand. Several trends in computing were all coming together to make Business On Demand a reality. First, the Internet had become the world's business infrastructure and an established feature in business. All sorts of commercial transactions and public services were being delivered over the Internet. Second, grid computing or utility computing was also becoming a reality. Higher adoption of open standards and virtualization software made interoperability between computers more feasible. Networks of computers could be linked into a grid and operate as one big computing source. And finally, customers began using software as a service; that is, rather than buying or licensing a product like customer relationship management (CRM) system software from Oracle, customers could use Salesforce.com's CRM system and use it only as much as they needed. Salesforce.com would run the CRM software on their own servers and the customers would receive the CRM result as a service. The convergence of these three developments drove the concept of Business On Demand. Today they are driving the concept of cloud computing.

IBM saw great opportunities in this convergence. First, there was the conversion of the customer's data centers. Many customers had servers from different companies. IBM could consolidate all of these servers with fewer, smaller ones and then add its virtualization software to get them all to function in a unified network. So now if one of the servers is busy, the software automatically farms out the task to other available servers. When all the networks and data centers are linked, the company has one integrated computing grid that its businesses can access for computing and communication wherever and whenever they need to. The convergence gave IBM a lot of opportunities to sell hardware, software, and technical services to convert customers to grid computing and now to cloud computing.

IBM also saw new opportunities in the customer's business processes. Many customers had pulled out their transaction-intensive processes from finance, HR, procurement, and customer service and gathered them into shared services units. These services were processes that were IT intensive, could be improved through redesign to make them enabled by grid computing, and could even be outsourced to IBM or other third parties. IBM chose to focus on these business processes and created a new offering, business process transformation (BPT). But it also needed to build some new capabilities in order to capture these new opportunities. This opportunity was different from outsourcing data centers and help desks.

An early step was the acquisition of the consulting arm of PricewaterhouseCoopers, which brought in thirty thousand consultants with business knowledge to design and run business processes. It also brought in relationships with senior managers at the customers. The purchase decision for BPT was made jointly by the CIO, IBM's traditional customer, and business executives responsible for the business processes. With these new resources and some of their own, IBM went about creating a new business model.

In addition to the joint sale, the new business model was a sequence of steps, and the customer could stop or continue at the completion of each step. First, the consulting business would continue to deliver its usual consulting engagements. IBM would also bring in some of its R&D talent focusing more on service projects. It would use the engagement to access the customer's senior leaders and assess the customer's business processes. Step 2 would be a project to redesign and improve the customer's business processes using its business knowledge and the new grid computing technologies. Third, the customer could choose to run its own processes or outsource them to IBM. And finally, the consultants, researchers, IBM's patent evaluators, and lawyers would search these transformation projects for new products, services, methods, or tools that could be sold, reused on other projects, or patented or licensed to others.

A major effort under way at IBM is to reduce the labor content of services. Rather than sell the expertise an hour at a time, IBM wants to create intellectual property, which is patentable. It wants to create reusable assets that can be sold, licensed, or packaged into software. IBM is a great example of a conglomerate that can combine and recombine its capabilities throughout the company to create value in new business models. Here, it is reapplying its R&D talent and patent methodologies to work with consultants in their services business.

To complete the strategic transition, IBM made several other changes. First, in order to create scale, it placed its own business processes in the business process outsourcing unit. It put its own HR, finance, customer service, and supply chain processes into the new business unit. Second, it put an up-and-coming executive into the CIO role and charged her with converting all of IBM into a Business On Demand company. IBM's leaders want to be the best demonstration to customers on how Business On Demand is done. Today she is continuing that transformation to make IBM itself the best demonstration of cloud computing. And finally, the same vice president who ran the Internet division was made the vice president in charge of Business On Demand. He created a team of twenty-eight agents from each division to formulate the detailed strategy and convert all of IBM's offerings to grid computing and Business On Demand, and now cloud computing.

Over the past several years, IBM has been transforming itself into an on-demand strategy and becoming and on-demand company itself. A good case in point is what IBM did with Dun and Bradstreet. IBM organized D&B's customer information into a useful database on 63 million customers. It then redesigned the business processes connected to the database, creating advanced analytical software to mine the database for insights into customers who might be interested in additional products and services. These insights are then passed along to the tele-hub marketing staff. In the end, D&B outsourced the business processes to IBM and agreed on a seven-year contract worth $180 million. IBM will handle customer service, telemarketing, electronic credit report distribution, and financial reporting for D&B. This example shows the full three-step business model in operation.

Smart Planet

The Smart Planet strategy, the result of yet another new model of computing, began to be implemented in 2008. It merges the digital infrastructure of the world with a physical infrastructure of the world. According to IBM, the new model is

> instrumented. Computational power is being put into things no one would recognize as computers: phones, cameras, cars, appliances, roadways, power lines, clothes and even natural systems such as livestock and rivers. Interconnected. All of this is being connected through the internet which has come of age. Intelligent. We now have the computing power, advanced analytics and

new computing models such as Cloud to make sense of the world's digital knowledge and pulse, and to turn mountains of data into intelligence. (IBM, 2008, p. 12)

This new computing model can be applied to the world's infrastructure, which is buckling under the weight of snarled traffic, wasted energy, insufficient health care, toxic emissions, and so on. IBM sees these problems as a result of dumb networks. What this means is that we do not understand commuter traffic or electricity flow sufficiently well to manage our roads and electricity grids, but with a new computing model we can convert dumb networks into smart ones. As a result, IBM is positioning itself to become a leader in the overhauling of the world's infrastructure.

The strategy had its origins in many places throughout IBM. In the 1990s, there were many projects for embedding micro-processors in devices other than PCs. One project investigated the use of microprocessors in electric meters and thermostats in homes. In 1997, IBM's corporate technology committee recommended that all of these disparate projects be consolidated under an initiative called Pervasive Computing. The leader and small team that were appointed became the Pervasive Computing Division in the software business group and created an extended team consisting of project leaders in all of the other divisions who set about putting a strategy together for the initiative.

In 2000, Pervasive Computing became one of IBM's internal ventures called "emerging business opportunities." A new leader—an accomplished business executive—was appointed. The team continued to refine the strategy and monitor projects. It also created partnerships and worked with account managers to find likely customers who would work to develop applications. Its revenues from products hit $1 billion in 2003. Then the industry groups began to use the products and put them into Smart Planet solutions. The government customer segment developed a traffic management, congestion pricing system for Stockholm. It now has contracts for London, Singapore, and San Francisco.

In another application, IBM was chosen by CenterPoint Energy (CNP), an electric utility serving the Houston area, to build a smart grid. After experiencing power outages and damages from several hurricanes, CNP saw that smart grid technology would be a time and money saver. Working with the utility customer segment and utility consulting practice, researchers from the IBM labs began developing precise outage detection, fault diagnoses, and algorithms for rerouting and reestablishment of service. The result was a self-healing solution for electricity grids. Repair crews are then automatically dispatched to the precise location of the cause of the outage.

There are other aspects to the relationship with CNP. One is a conversion of the entire grid into a single broadband conduit by installing broadband over power lines. Working with partners Corinex and Arteche, IBM created a digital infrastructure for CNP on which multiple applications can run. Another project with CNP involves smart meters. In this project, IBM and CNP have added two business partners: Itron for the meters and eMeter for the software. The network of smart meters allows remote meter reading, connection and disconnection of service without dispatching trucks, peak load and real-time pricing, and the accumulation of data to understanding customer use. The benefit to CNP is cost avoidance and less need for building new power plants.

The meters work on open standards and report usage to anyone the consumer allows. IBM anticipates that iPhone apps will arise for consumers to intelligently manage their own electric power usage.

The CNP project involved many parts of IBM. The meter data management runs on IBM Blade Center servers, which are managed by the IBM Global Services Strategic Outsourcing unit. The project is coordinated by the IBM/CNP account team. At various times, the account team drew on utility specialists from the consulting business acquired from PricewaterhouseCoopers, engineers from IBM research, as well as talent from IBM Global Technical Services and Global Business Services. Licenses were sold for WebSphere, the middleware product line from the software group. The IBM/CNP team is part of the worldwide utility practice. In early 2010, IBM had fifty smart grid projects like this one around the world.

The self-healing solution for utilities is now being readied for patent application and licensing. The solution is to be turned into a product that can be repeatedly sold to utilities around the world. It will be sold like software. The customer obtains a license and services for an installation and maintenance and receives regular upgrades. The new version can be converted to a software service and then sold as cloud computing through the same customer sets. In addition to smart grids, IBM is creating solutions for smart cities, smart stock exchange, smart wind energy, and smart cancer treatment, to name a few.

In addition, IBM has raised the priority for data and analytics. It is to be a $20 billion business by 2015. It has added new software and solutions for converting social networks into social business and mobility services and it continually evolves with the Internet from Business On Demand to cloud computing.

In summary, the IBM integrated solutions strategy has continually evolved, driven by advances in computing technology and opportunities at customers. IBM has transformed its portfolio by exiting hardware businesses and acquiring software and service businesses. If this portfolio were examined as a portfolio of autonomous businesses, IBM would be classed as a conglomerate. But IBM does not operate like a conglomerate. Instead, it integrates the capabilities from all of the businesses into solutions that create value for customers. It combines and recombines these capabilities for different industry groups of customers. It is the task of the IBM organization, and particularly the industry segments, to implement the integrated solutions portfolio strategy.

IBM Organization

The IBM organization structure before Gertsner had a strong geographic orientation: it was based on IBM Americas and IBM World Trade Corporation that served the rest of the world. The key positions outside the United States were the country managers. After encountering difficulty in serving global customers, Gertsner reorganized IBM into global business units and customer-facing global industry groups. The industry groups were matrixed across the countries and regions. There have been many changes to the structure, but it retains its same basic foundation. The current structure is shown in figure 12.6.

Structure

The structure shown here is simplified but captures the essence of IBM's intentions and uses more generic titles like "outsourcing." Figure 12.6 reflects the four-dimensional design of most integrated solutions companies. Reporting to the CEO or Office of Chief Executive are the functions. These are the corporate staff units, most of whose members are working in the product lines, geographies, and industry groups. The back end of the structure consists of product lines for hardware, software, some generic solutions, and services. These groups design, deliver, and sell their products to IBM customers. The global business units in the product groups are the profit centers. The front end of the structure is based on customers collected into industry groups (such as financial services customers) and geography. The industry groups focusing on the largest one thousand global customers replace the countries as a central building block of the sales and distribution structure. In this four-dimensional structure, the product lines are the profit centers. The industry groups are not full profit centers but instead are measured on gross profit, which is revenue and margins. P&Ls are added up for the geographies for tax purposes, but they do not function as the profit centers. The growth markets were broken out as a separate region in about 2008.

Figure 12.6 IBM Structure

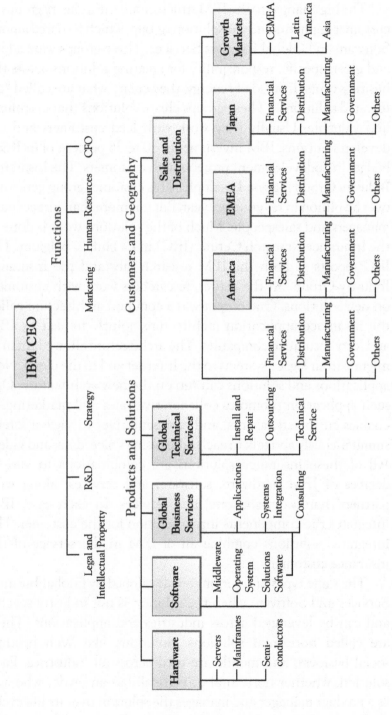

The big changes to the IBM structure are the industry groups or customer segments and the solutions group, which is shared among Software and Global Business Services. These groups were added and given specific responsibility for creating solutions across the business units. Instead of synergy, they create what are called "integrated solutions." These groups create solutions that customers find valuable. Usually they work with lead customers and co-develop solutions. IBM invests about 30 to 35 percent of its R&D budget in codevelopment projects with customers. The Insurance Industry Group is a good example. This customer group generates over $8 billion in revenue per year. But it is more than just account managers and salespeople. Much of the solutions work is done at the Insurance Research Center (IRC) in La Hulpe, Belgium. The IRC reports to both the IBM research labs and the Insurance Industry Group. At the center, researchers work with customers on new solutions. One output was a common architecture called the insurance application architecture, jointly funded by IBM and forty insurance companies. The architecture allowed them to migrate from legacy systems to the Internet and to the cloud. Now applications and solutions can run on the new architecture. One such application promotes collaborative sales and marketing. It enables customers, agents, and representatives to view a screen simultaneously and talk to each other using voice, data, and video. All of these insurance solutions are combinations to various degrees of IBM hardware, software, and services, along with partners' hardware, software, and services. In each case, IBM integrates the components into a solution for the customer. The integrated solutions combine all of IBM in the service of the insurance customer.

The same types of solutions are developed by Global Business Services and Software when the solution is not industry specific and can be leveraged across industries and applications. These are called horizontal solutions. Solutions like Web hosting, social business, and mobile are used across all industries. Each solution, whether horizontal or vertical, has an owner who acts as a product manager and manages the solution over its life cycle.

Usually a potential solution arises from first-of-a-kind project with lead customers. Global Business Services and Software or the industry groups then propose it as a solution to the IBM technical committee. The committee assigns it a priority, a budget, and staffing from participating IBM units. The team then creates a strategy and codevelops the solution. The effort is followed monthly by the committee until it is closed out. The team develops the ecosystem of partners that will be needed. As the launch approaches, sales and field engineers from Global Business Services and Software or the industry group are assigned to the solution team. They are trained and then return to the field, where they join customer teams that believe their customer is a good prospect for the solution. The solution team gets measured on the basis of growth, a gross profit measure, and customer satisfaction. On the basis of customer feedback, the solution is continuously updated and improved. The solution owner also works with patent teams to explore the likelihood of patenting the intellectual property.

So it is the solution's owners in Global Business Services and Software along with the industry groups that create the synergies that make IBM an integrated service provider rather than a conglomerate. The owners and their teams draw on capabilities from across the company. What enables their work are the processes to integrate the company's capabilities.

Processes

The companies that implement the integrated solution strategy are process intense. In addition to normal generic processes like supply chain management, they require process modifications and additions to attain a higher level of coordination. The solutions integration and priority setting require disparate groups across the company to collect, collate, and digest more information, and subsequently they make many more decisions. These additional processes, along with the industry groups and solutions' owners, are the signature characteristics of the integrated solution provider.

IBM integrates all of the businesses and functions into solutions through a companywide infrastructure that is massively horizontal and reconfigurable. It consists of three parts:

1. A stable set of common global business processes
2. A reconfigurable set of teams organized around the ever changing portfolio of opportunities
3. A reconfigurable set of decision forums for resolving conflicts and setting priorities

One of the first things that Gerstner did as CEO after changing the organization structure was to implement thirteen global business processes to hold the structure together. All managers in IBM went through a one-week training program on the use of these horizontal processes. Multidimensional organizations in general and reconfigurable ones in particular are process intense. They have all the processes that one would find in a divisional organization plus several others—for example, a business unit planning process as in a divisional organization, plus a segment and a regional planning process, and a reconciliation process, which works through overlapping memberships and collaboration. A reconfigurable decision-making body resolves any remaining conflicts.

Solutions providers are also process intense. They have a new product development process, plus a new solutions development process and a portfolio management process. The portfolio process is needed because all of the products, hardware, software, and services must work together in an integrated fashion. When IBM launches a new mainframe, for example, it must also launch new compatible software and services to complete the solution. IBM competes not just on a product-by-product basis but also on an integrated portfolio basis.

A key horizontal process is the customer relationship management process. It is in this process that all customer plans, priorities, and opportunities are entered. Each opportunity must be acknowledged and a response entered from all product lines within twenty-four hours. The customer account manager is the opportunity owner and coordinates across all of the businesses through the account team comprising salespeople from all of the businesses. For large opportunities like solutions, the opportunity owner may shift from the account manager to the regional or even global segment manager, so the size of the opportunity is matched with the authority of the process owner.

The other essential business process is the project management process. Almost all work in a reconfigurable organization is performed as a project. A common global project management system is essential as people from around the world move from one project to another. The other essential ingredient is project management talent: every team member must understand how projects work and how to act as a team member and leader.

Thus, a key means of coordination across IBM's multidimensional organization is a large set of robust horizontal business processes. These processes are global and represent a stable component in the reconfigurable organization. They are also automated. IBM tries to put as much complexity as possible into the software that underlies their processes. The reconfigurable portion of the structure is the formation and reformation of teams to address opportunities. Opportunities are of three main types: new product development opportunities coming from businesses, new emerging business opportunities that are managed out of the strategy group, and customer opportunities that can originate with customer account teams in the segments or from emerging market customers. Here, I focus on the segment account teams and how they work.

The segments are first sorted into industries and then into customer accounts. The large accounts, such as P&G and BMW, may do $1 billion or more with IBM each year. These customers have an account manager assigned to them who is a general manager of a billion-dollar business. The account managers have account teams of salespeople from all of the businesses whose products a customer buys. Software and support engineers are assigned to the account, a project management unit manages all the projects that are taking place at the account, and the salespeople report to the account team and their business units. The organization of the account teams is the IBM structure in microcosm.

The segment business plans are built from the account up. The normal orders for products are processed automatically through the business process. When the customer becomes interested in the big solution, only then does IBM configure large teams to first win the business and then implement the project when it is won. That said, the solution opportunity is usually anticipated, so it's put into the customer and segment business plans. From there, the team members see that it is also in all of the business unit plans. The account team members and the project manager educate their counterparts in the businesses about the customer opportunity. These counterparts are the ones who will join the capture team when the customer issues a formal request for a proposal and return to their business units when the proposal is completed. If the proposal is accepted, many of the same people will rejoin the customer account team to form an implementation team that will deliver the solution to the customer. When their work is completed, these people return to their business units.

In this manner, there is a continual assembly and disassembly of solution teams around customer opportunities. There is also a continual setting of priorities in gathering the types and amounts of talent to staff the solution teams. There are three levels of escalation to attain the proper staffing. First, the team members and the project manager line up talent in the business units from which the account team members come. They are guided by company priorities when conflicts arise. Customers are given priorities by the segments. Top-priority customers are the most profitable, have the most potential, or can provide the most information for IBM's learning. There are also solution priorities. If a solution is a first of a kind, it is staffed with R&D people who will help design the solution so that it can be replicated at other customer sites. Many talent allocations can be achieved at this level.

The next level of resolution when two or more account teams need the same resources is the regional or global segment team. If the conflict is within a segment, it can be resolved at the segment level. Conflicts that are cross-segment go to the regional operating committees, which meet once or twice per week to balance opportunities and resources within a region. Failing resolution at the regional level, there is the option of going to the third level, which is the company operating committee or technical committee, depending on whether new technology is required. There are also reconfigurable decision forums.

Opportunities at IBM can come from existing businesses, future businesses, segment customers, and emerging market customers. The opportunities easily exceed the resources of even companies as large and capable as IBM. As a result, priority choices are a challenge to the leadership. When the opportunity set is constantly changing, the priority decision process needs to be fluid as well. Previously at IBM, these decisions went to the management committee, consisting of a few top executives. When Sam Palmisano became CEO, he disbanded the management committee and put in place three decision forums. The technical committee, chaired by the chief technical officer and the head of R&D, managed the new product programs and product portfolio. The chief strategy officer chaired the strategy committee, and the chief financial officer chaired the operations committee. The unique feature of these bodies is their membership. On each decision forum is a core team of seven or eight top managers. The core team is like the old management committee: they are members of all three teams. But the rest of the members come from different levels and parts of the organization. Each committee consists of about twenty-five members. The other members are not core team members, and the composition of the group changes regularly. Different views and knowledge can be brought to bear on issues. The body is reconfigurable and can match the changing set of issues facing IBM. Since most talent is mobile within a region, the regional operating committees are responsible for staffing the solution teams.

Thus, IBM has created an organization that can reconfigure itself to address a changing set of global opportunities. It consists of the stable structure shown in figure 12.6 and a stable set of horizontal processes. The organization reconfigures itself by constantly assembling and disassembling large teams to pursue opportunities. In order to resolve the many priority conflicts, there is a set of decision forums with reconfigurable memberships to address the varying set of issues and the evolving set of agendas.

Reward System

The formal reward system at IBM is based on a three-tier bonus system. For all managers at the top level except in sales, the bonus is based on company performance, unit performance, and the individual's performance. The individual criteria are flexible and reward participation on teams for those who implement Smart Planet solutions. The sales teams are rewarded on the basis of revenue from their customer. However, the revenue is uneven from year to year. Therefore, the metric that determines the bonus is a five-year moving average. In general, the bonus system aligns with the solution strategies.

The other part of the reward system is the promotion process. As usual, promotions are based on performance over longer time frames. The criteria also cover the full range of performance. The managers who work well in teams, focus on the customer, and work well on solutions are the ones who are promoted.

People

Several HR practices support the solutions strategy. Rotational assignments are common among IBM leaders—IBM's acronym is often translated as "I've Been Moved." These transfers generate the personal networks that are so important for collaborating across units and creating solutions. They give managers a complete understanding of the many components that make up the Smart Planet solutions. Managers know about a lot more than just their unit.

•••

In summary, IBM has created an organization that can combine hardware products, software systems, and services of various types to create value for customers. The key parts of this organization are the industry-customer segments that create the Smart Planet solutions. The industry-customer segment leaders are responsible for coordinating all of the units to generate the solutions. The second key aspects to the organization are the common, robust, global processes that hold the organization together, as well as the rapid assembly and disassembly of teams to respond to opportunities. IBM's organization takes a portfolio of what would otherwise be a conglomerate and combines and recombines the components to create value for customers.

Summary

This chapter has described two types of strategies that conglomerates use to create value for customers. Companies following these synergistic strategies use organizations that both create and magnify the synergies between diverse businesses to create value. One type of strategy is to leverage intellectual property across all of the businesses. The intellectual property can be technology, brands, characters, or design expertise, to name a few. Disney is the best example. We see the other type of strategy in integrated solutions providers such as IBM. These companies integrate the products and services of their diverse businesses to create value for customers. In both cases, conglomerates following synergy portfolio strategies are able to create synergies among their diverse businesses, and that is uncommon. For every successful Disney, there is an unsuccessful company that failed, for example, AOL–Time Warner. For every IBM, there is a Sun Microsystems that failed. It takes a completely aligned organization to win at the synergy game.

13

ORGANIZATIONAL DESIGN CHALLENGES AND OPPORTUNITIES RESULTING FROM BIG DATA

The subject of big data has literally burst on the scene in the past few years. Recall our definition earlier that big data refers to the volume, variety, and velocity of data today, combined with analytics to extract insights from those data. Today big data are receiving more than their fair share of media hype. But if we look beyond the hype, we can see some real substance that underlies the phenomenon. Big data have been given some legitimacy by reports from the World Economic Forum, the McKinsey Global Institute, and the Economist Intelligence Unit. In their recent book, *The New Digital Age* (2013), Eric Schmidt and Jared Cohen from Google have given a remarkably balanced discussion of the digital landscape. Nonetheless, the subject has its doubters who warn of the dangers involved (Morozov, 2011). At the end of the day, I believe the dangers and the privacy issues will be resolved and big data, or whatever we eventually call this topic, will be a capability built into all organizations.

Organizations will vary in the speed and difficulty that they encounter in building the capability. As they attempt to build a big data capability, they will encounter some obstacles as well as some opportunities. In this chapter, I discuss two challenges and an opportunity that organization designers must be prepared to meet. The challenges are, first, that there must be a power shift in the organization's structure and, second, there must be an increase in the speed of decision making. The opportunity is that there is potential to build a whole new business around big data that could become a new dimension of organizational structure. But before describing these three design issues, I identify what is new and different about big data.

What Is New About Big Data

We have been using large databases and analytics for the last couple of decades. Transactions have been stored in data warehouses and analyzed with data mining algorithms to extract insights. What is new about big data? There are at least two factors.

First, there are more data and more kinds of data now. These are the volume and variety features. In the past, we stored structured data—data largely from transactions—as rows and columns. Today we store unstructured data from a variety of sources. The data could be photos from a mobile phone, maps from a GPS device, video from a surveillance camera, audio from a call center, e-mails, tweets, and texts. All of these data can be digitized, stored, and analyzed.

Second, these new data are accessible in real time. Before, data in the data warehouse were historical and described outcomes that had already occurred. Now we can receive data about events as they are happening and even influence outcomes before they happen. Historically, credit card companies stored all of their transactions in a database and analyzed them with fraud algorithms. They could detect fraudulent transactions and turn them over to the police to investigate, for example, and distinguish chronic late payers from people who have lost their jobs. Customer service could then take the appropriate actions with these groups. Today a fraudulent transaction can be detected while the fraudster is still at the checkout counter. An algorithm operating in real time can determine that the transaction is a charge on a stolen credit card. The clerk at the checkout counter could be advised to delay the criminal. Store security could be informed to apprehend him or her and confiscate the credit card. Thus, real-time data allow us to influence the outcome and prevent bad outcomes before they happen. This capability is new.

This new capability is possible, however, only if the organization is designed to operate in real time. We need to design a decision process that detects real-time data, analyzes the data to produce real-time insights, processes these insights to arrive at real-time decisions, and then executes them in real time. We need faster-acting companies in order to profit from big data.

Organization Design Challenges

Two design challenges need to be addressed if we're going to profit from big data. The first is to increase the speed of most processes in the company. But before an organization can get data scientists and analytics experts embedded into the decision processes, there must be a shift in power from the experienced and judgmental decision makers to the digital decision makers. We examine the power shift first.

Power Shift

Every organization has an establishment—a current power structure with a vested interest in the status quo. This establishment is currently making investment decisions, setting customer priorities, and deciding on new product features—the same decisions that new insights from big data can improve. But will the current leadership adopt or reject these new insights? In order to be successful, the organization needs to execute a shift in power to the digital experts who generate these new insights from big data. The shift in power is necessary to accomplish the changes that are needed to fully embed the big data capability.

One factor that will determine the magnitude of the power shift is the degree of difficulty or amount of resistance that big data proponents will encounter from the establishment. The amount of that resistance will depend on whether this new capability is competence enhancing or competence destroying (Tushman and Anderson, 1986). For example, when e-commerce came along,

Dell adopted it immediately. Taking orders over the Internet was competence enhancing for Dell because it improved Dell's business model of direct sales to the end user. HP's strength was its relationship with resellers and retailers, so e-commerce was a competence-destroying innovation for it; it would disintermediate HP's resellers. HP was slower to adopt e-commerce and kept its resellers in the distribution chain. Companies need to determine where they are on the enhancing-to-destroying continuum.

Proctor & Gamble is an example of a company for which big data are competence enhancing, and it has embraced big data. It is a highly analytical company that has had an analytics group since 1992, and it will try anything that might increase its understanding of the consumer. As a result, P&G is adapting big data practices ahead of most other companies. The effort is led by the chief information officer, Dan Passerini, and supported by the CEO. They have adapted their hiring practices to bring in more analytically skilled people. For the past five years, P&G and Google have exchanged teams of people annually: Google wants to learn advertising, and P&G wants to learn Google's digital acumen. At P&G, all managers are upgrading their digital skills. Moreover, every manager's digital and analytical performance is assessed in the performance management process. The CIO and the business leaders have identified eighty-eight business processes that are being redesigned and accelerated to operate in real time.

In contrast, a good example of a competence-destroying situation is the arrival of big data in sports. In the movie *Moneyball*, Billy Beane, the general manager of the Oakland Athletics, brings in an analytically skilled assistant, Peter Brand, to advise him on putting together the best team possible on Oakland's very low budget. Peter is twenty-five years old and an economics graduate from Yale who has never played baseball. Of course, they run into the chief scout, Grady, and his scouting team. Grady first tries to keep Peter out of a meeting. "Does Pete really need to be here?" he asks. Then he tries, "You can't put a team together with a computer." The meeting is a clash between Peter's data and Grady's opinions. Billy makes the decisions based on Peter's data, but then they run into the manager, Art Howe, who will not play a data-chosen player. He is insubordinate when Billy commands him to play the player. Billy then makes a trade so that Art has to play Billy's choice. Thus, the arrival of data and analytics at the Oakland Athletics destroyed the experience-based competence of Grady and his team. Today almost all American baseball teams and European soccer teams use big data and analytics to some degree.

These scenes will play out in many companies where an analog establishment is making product and marketing decisions based on years of experience and some data. The digital newcomers will clash with these old pros and lose if they are not supported by the leadership.

Another example is risk management in financial services. Risk management departments were created along with a chief risk officer (CRO) and developed sophisticated quantitative risk models. Just prior to the financial crisis, these risk managers were waving red flags and trying to be heard. The bankers, however, saw them as the "revenue reduction department." When the CEOs backed the bankers, the CROs had little standing. Today nearly all banks have CROs reporting directly to the CEO, and the role is staffed with a talented person. The effectiveness of the CROs and supporting regulation is still being tested. Where the leadership actively considers risk data and recommendations, the CRO and risk experts will be integrated into the decision process. At that point, power will have been shifted.

The question now is whether big data need the equivalent of the CRO. There are quite a few proponents for a chief digital officer (CDO), a role that can take several forms. At P&G, the CIO has played that role. The IT function has always worked with the businesses to introduce new information systems and analytical concepts. Given P&G's analytical orientation, a separate CDO role is probably not needed. The CIO can wear two hats: CIO and CDO.

There are some other examples. Intel is using a partnership between the CIO and the chief marketing officer to take the lead in implementing big data. Intel has a history of two managers in a box, that is, two managers in the CIO role simultaneously. One was a technology type who ran data centers and the other was a manager who was a data user or customer. Starbucks has a full-time CDO who is part of the senior leadership team. IBM has made the biggest addition with an enterprise transformation head who has been in that role for ten years and before that had been the star line manager who ran the server and storage businesses. Her task has been to transform IBM to grid computing and now to the cloud and big data. IBM wants all of its processes to be converted so that they can be a model for customers. The CIO and process design activities all report to this transformation head, and she reports to the CEO. Clearly IBM has put a lot of power and authority behind its equivalent of a CDO.

It seems that the amount of power and authority of a CDO should be matched with the relative amount of difficulty of implementing big data. If big data are a competence-enhancing innovation, a CIO wearing a double hat, as at P&G, could be sufficient. If a company is at the other end of the continuum and big data are competence destroying, more power and authority will be needed for this role. At the destroying end, the role like IBM's enterprise transformation role will be required to adopt big data.

A CDO role of some type is needed even in competence-enhancing companies. A number of corporate-led initiatives are necessary to embed the new capability in the company's decision-making processes. First, companies need a strategy and plan. Where are the best opportunities for investment? Companies also need to link applications with the requisite IT equipment and data architectures and, for the chosen applications, provide the training and tools to the frontline people. The usual strategic choice of where to play presents itself here too: with limited resources, companies cannot do everything at once.

Second, someone has to lead the corporate mind-set that data and information are important company resources. Data are becoming a valuable resource like talent and money. Data and analytics groups are becoming like HR and finance that are matrixed through the company. At a minimum, a corporate leadership group (the head of data and analytics) and several embedded groups (data analysts) in the businesses report to both business heads and the corporate head.

Third, the company must work to integrate and unite the many islands of data and analytics that exist throughout the company. A lot of value comes from combining data from different sources both inside and outside the company. Resistance to sharing and combining data often arises depending on the strength of the organizational silos. Corporate leadership is necessary to create norms and values concerning information sharing, transparency, and trust. Each company tries to arrive at a situation where organizational units have the data that they need to execute their charter, but those data are also available to the rest of the company. In addition, these units should have reciprocal access to company data.

And finally, someone needs to identify and resolve disputes caused by the new capability. People are already charged with making decisions about advertising and new product features. Data and analytics will generate insights that lead to different decisions than current processes do. These differences can lead to *Moneyball*-type clashes and arguments over data versus experience. The desired outcome, of course, is a blend of data *and* experience. A CDO is needed to see that these disputes are settled with the right blend for the company. Other disputes, like issues around channel conflicts, will arise. The digital technology enables disintermediation. For example, the insurance agent was always a sacred cow at insurance companies. Now young people are willing to buy insurance online and circumvent the agent. Inside insurance companies, managers argue about whether and how to go about this new direct-to-consumer sale. The CDO needs to play a mediating role here. In addition, jurisdictional disputes crop up between functions like the CIO, marketing, supply chain, and finance about who owns one digital activity or another. Again, the CDO needs to see that these disputes are discussed and resolved. For these reasons, someone must play the value-adding mediation role in all companies implementing big data.

In summary, companies need a power shift in their structures if they are to capitalize on the big data capability. The data and analytics newcomers need to be supported and integrated into the company decision processes. Otherwise big data and the CDO will be like risk management and the CRO before the financial crisis. Grady and the scouts will not invite Peter to the decision-making meetings, and Art Howe will continue to be insubordinate and not play the right players. But once a successful power shift is under way, the next step is to speed up the decision processes.

Attain Real-Time Decision Making

The second organizational challenge is to increase the speed of decision making, often referred to as increasing the clock speed of the organization. A computer has a clock, which synchronizes the speed of the input unit, output unit, arithmetic unit, and memory unit. Historically computer designers have been increasing the clock speed at which the computer operates. Similarly, organizational designers need to increase their organization's clock speed. All of the units participating in advertising, customer management, new product development, and supply chain management have to synchronize around increasing clock speeds. The ultimate target is real time.

Advertising, I have noted, has been transitioning from a campaign model to a newsroom model. Traditionally advertisers started their ad campaign planning in September for ads to be launched during the Super Bowl in February. They worked up a theme, shot many ads, narrowed them down to a few, bought time from the TV network, submitted their ads, and went to their Super Bowl party to watch them. The media would react to the ads, and audience votes on the ads would be reported on Monday morning following the game. The Nielsen ratings would arrive later that week on Friday.

Coca-Cola and Audi went through the same process for their 2013 Super Bowl ads, but unlike the other advertisers, they gathered in rapid response teams on the day of the Super Bowl. When their first ad was running, they were looking at the Twitter feeds, the Facebook likes, and hits on their websites. Even before the first ad was finished playing, the teams were planning and making modifications to their second ads. Then the infamous power outage occurred: the brand teams gathered in their newsroom and went into action. The Audi team was quick to dig its rival, Mercedes Benz. The reason was that the blackout occurred in the Mercedes Benz U.S.A. Superdome Stadium. They tweeted, "Sending some L.E.D.s to the M.B.U.S.A. Superdome right now." In order to respond in real time, these fast response teams had to be supported by analytics to sift through all of the social media responses and make sense of them. Based on those data, the cross-functional team had to discuss the insights, decide on a response, and post a tweet, an audio, or a video response. The blackout was indeed breaking news, and the newsroom went into action.

Another example of real-time advertising is the Old Spice ad for Red Zone Body Wash. The original ad, shown on traditional TV, depicted a very attractive man wearing only a towel around his waist and applying the body wash. The response on Facebook and Twitter was way above normal, so the advertiser and the agency decided on a social media approach. They gathered a large team of writers, art directors, producers, editors, the actor, and social media specialists. They started with a couple of videos on YouTube and distributed them over Twitter and targeted known influencers. The social media team then scoured the Web for comments on the initial ads. They fed the funny comments or those that came from interesting sources to the creatives, who turned them into humorous videos. The team was able to release several new videos every hour, and the ads became a trending topic on Twitter. Over the two-day promotion, the team created two hundred videos, all in real time in response to topics coming from their viewers. This example shows the cross-functional newsroom in real-time action.

At P&G the supply chain function meets in what they call the control tower. From the control tower, a cross-functional team gathers in special rooms called decision spheres. P&G has forty-two decision spheres throughout the company. These are specially designed rooms with video screens on the walls and access to databases. The rooms are designed to foster real-time, cross-functional decision making. When a paper machine's embedded sensors at the Pampers plant in Wisconsin indicates it requires maintenance, a shutdown is scheduled. If it looks as if the machine will be down for a while, the decision is made to supply Walmart from the Albany, Georgia, plant. The analytics capabilities are tapped to see the best way to reroute trucks and still meet other delivery commitments to customers. This is an example of how big data facilitate real-time decisions in managing supply chains.

In chapter 5, we described how Nike uses big data and social networks to manage its new product development process. Putting sensors in shoes and watches allows Nike to collect enormous amounts of running data and running routes that allow it to create insights for new software applications for the running community. The NikePlus.com community allows Nike to crowdsource ideas from the community for new product ideas. Using the agile software product development process, software product developers are constantly testing new product ideas and apps with users. In return, Nike gets new ideas from the users. The product development team continuously designs products in real time. So once Nike and other manufacturers insert sensors and chips in their products, they are in the software business:

they start to make decisions and act on a timescale that is set by the software business.

In summary, big data allow companies to make decisions in real time. They can involve their customers in dialogues about brands and gather ideas about products. The companies must use cross-functional teams that are in constant contact following a newsroom model or decision sphere to respond to the real time inputs. These companies have increased the clock speed of their decision processes.

Opportunity to Generate Revenue from Big Data

The third organization design feature triggered by big data is actually an opportunity as well as a challenge. The impacts already described were changes that would improve the existing business. Big data will help Nike sell more running shoes because of the added features of NikePlus.com. But the data, analytics, and insights can be revenue producers themselves by creating entirely new businesses for the company.

Companies like Bosch and GE are putting sensors and microprocessors into all of their products and anticipate that the services and software sales from these embedded devices will be a major source of growth in coming years. Bosch has created a central unit, Bosch Software Innovation, to lead a lot of these new initiatives. One project is the design, installation, maintenance, and operation of an electric vehicle charging infrastructure for Singapore. It will provide software and data analysis for the government, retailers, fleet operators, utilities, and parking operators. This infrastructure will generate revenue from a range of services available through Bosch Software Innovation's Internet service platform.

In another example, the large US banks like JP Morgan and Wells Fargo provide reports on consumer trends to clients and other institutions that want to buy them. These banks have vast amounts of data from consumer use of credit and debit cards, checking account and ATM transactions, mortgages, and loans. The banks combine all of these data with publicly available data from governments and apply their new analytical capabilities to develop proprietary insights into consumer trends. In just a few seconds, the banks can generate customized reports that slice the data into smaller and more narrowly defined market segments and geographies according to the specific demands of their clients. This service generates increasing amounts of revenue and profits for the banks.

Citibank, which operates in one hundred countries, can provide these kinds of data and insights on an international basis by taking deposits and making loans in local currency. The next largest bank is HSBC, which operates in around fifty-six countries; no other banks are even close. So Citi has an advantage that cannot be matched when providing a global perspective. It has the consumer data globally that Wells Fargo has nationally. In addition, it is one of the world's two largest foreign exchange providers. It is the largest cash management provider and number two in custody (securities safekeeping). That's in addition to its commercial lending operations around the world. Citibank can detect changes in trade patterns and economic conditions from an analysis of the basic data. It says it can detect the new "silk roads" in emerging markets. It sells its insights to companies like Zara and H&M to help them locate new stores and factories. Banks see future growth coming from data and insights more than from their basic financial transaction businesses.

Nike is still the best example for the organizational design implications from big data. The Nike development history follows the Chandler model that I have been discussing in this book. Nike's recent strategy and structure transition show that big data are not just a new revenue source but perhaps the start of a new digital dimension to organizations. Let us review the stages through which Nike has progressed.

Nike was founded in 1964 and became a fully functional, single-business company designing, manufacturing, marketing, and selling running shoes. Its initial public offering was in 1971. By the 1980s, two things had happened. First, Nike diversified into other types of athletic footwear like basketball, tennis, soccer, and fitness shoes. It retained its functional structure but introduced lateral processes for the new types of footwear. Second, it expanded internationally by establishing sales, local marketing, and distribution subsidiaries. It became a two-dimensional, single business in athletic footwear with functions and regions reporting in to the CEO. In the 1990s it became a three-dimensional organization, diversifying into sports apparel and sports equipment in addition to athletic footwear. It formed profit centers for footwear, apparel, and equipment, plus a separate business for golf. The supply chain, marketing, finance, and HR reported to the CEO in addition to the regions. In 2006, Nike made a big change to focus on customer groups and created five categories: running, men's training, women's fitness, basketball, and soccer. Each category was a profit center and responsible for footwear, apparel, and equipment for its customer set. Nike's leaders were creating integrated solutions for customers who found them valuable. These categories were added to the previous structure, which still retained products, regions, and functions reporting to the leadership. But the categories were not just add-ons. The products were matrixed across categories. Women's fitness was still dependent on the apparel product line, and all categories were dependent on the latest footwear development. This change to categories, or customer segments, made Nike a four-dimensional organization. Then in 2010, Nike created the Nike Digital Sport Division.

The Nike structure is shown in figure 13.1. This division is a profit center and has a number of responsibilities. First, it works with the categories in establishing Nike+ activities like the one in running described in chapter 5. Now Nike has Nike+ Football, Nike+ Basketball, Nike+ Kinect Training within the various categories. Digital Sports supports the categories in creating and managing their communities and with new products like the

Figure 13.1 Nike Organization Structure, July 2013

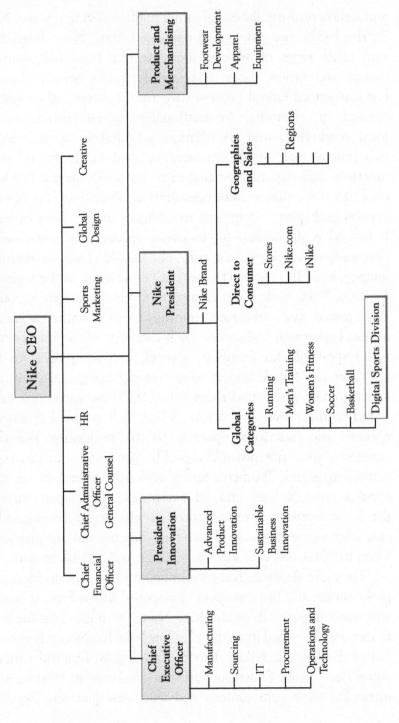

GPS app, an example of another dimension to the Nike matrix. Second, the division is developing its own products and its own sources of revenue. Nike+ FuelBand is the wristband. The product records distance traveled in a day, the number of steps taken, and calories burned. The results can be uploaded at the end of the day and compared with others in the runner's age group. The division has its NikePlus.com website, apps, apparel, and community. It recently introduced a wristwatch with similar features. Now Nike is competing in the wearable medical device market, and more products are on the way. Third, the division takes the lead in building the Nike incubator described earlier. It is responsible for establishing an ecosystem of companies around the devices.

Nike's Digital Division is small, but it may grow into a fifth dimension of strategy and organization. It is not just an added product line; it is responsible for building digital capabilities in the other Nike units as well as generating its own revenue. It is similar to the Disney Interactive Division and the Bosch Software Innovation group. These companies are all following similar models of strategy and organization with respect to the big data capability.

Summary

This chapter reviewed organization design challenges and opportunities brought on by big data. The first challenge is a complete power shift in the decision process to allow the new digital experts to become part of the power structure. If there is no shift in power, a company will make only limited and isolated local progress.

The second challenge is to increase the clock speed of the organization's decision processes. These processes are cross-functional collaborations in real time. It is a shift to a newsroom or control tower type of interaction that takes place in specially designed rooms like P&G's decision spheres. The advertising, customer management, supply chain, and new product development process have the potential to be improved by big data.

The opportunity is that a company's data can be a new source of revenue and growth. In addition to improving existing businesses, big data have the potential to create entirely new businesses as well as a new organizational dimension to our companies. Enterprises like banks and credit bureaus naturally deal with lots of data. When they combine their data from across the company and integrate them with outside data, they can create valuable insights from the analytics. Companies producing products can embed sensors and microchips to collect more data and provide additional services. The analytics and insights from the product sensors present another potential source of revenue.

Both B2B and B2C companies have the ability to harvest data. Nike's evolution is a good example of how successful companies can continue to grow and evolve into five-dimensional organizations.

Bibliography

Barreto, I. "Dynamic Capabilities: A Review of Past Research and an Agenda for the Future." *Journal of Management*, 2010, 36, 256.

Bartlett, C., and McClean, A. GE's *Talent Machine: The Making of a CEO*. Boston: Harvard Business School Press, 2003.

Bartlett, C., and McClean, A. "GE's Jeff Imelt: Voyage from MBA to CEO." *Harvard Business School case 9–307–056*. Boston: Harvard Business School, 2007.

Burns, T., and Stalker, G. *The Management of Innovation*. London: Tavistock, 1961.

Campa, J., and Kedia, S. "Explaining the Diversification Discount." *Journal of Finance*, 2002, 57, 1731–1762.

Chandler, A. *Strategy and Structure*. Cambridge, MA: MIT Press, 1962.

Charan, R., Drotter, S., and Noel, J. *The Leadership Pipeline*. New York: Wiley, 2001.

Cross, R., and Thomas, R. *Driving Results Through Social Networks*. San Francisco: Jossey-Bass, 2009.

D'Aveni, R. *Hypercompetition: Managing the Dynamics of Strategic Maneuvering*. New York: Free Press, 1994.

Dundas, K., and Richardson, P. "Implementing the Unrelated Product Strategy." *Strategic Management Journal*, 1982, 3, 287–301.

Fine, C. *Clock Speed: Winning Industry Control in the Age of Temporary Advantage*. Reading, MA: Perseus Books, 1998.

Foster, R., and Kaplan, S. *Creative Destruction*. New York: Random House, 2001.

Franko, L. *The European Multinationals*. Greenwich, CT: Greylock Press, 1976.

Galbraith, J. R. *Organization Design*. Reading, MA: Addison-Wesley, 1976.

Galbraith, J. R. "The Value Adding Corporation." In J. R. Galbraith and E. Lawler (eds.), *Organizing for the Future*. San Francisco: Jossey-Bass. 1994a.

Galbraith, J. R. *Competing with Flexible Lateral Organizations*. Reading, MA: Addison-Wesley, 1994b.

Galbraith, J. R. "The Reconfigurable Organization." In F. Hesselbein, M. Goldsmith, and R. Beckhard (eds.), *The Organization of the Future*. San Francisco: Jossey-Bass, 1997.

Galbraith, J. R. *Designing the Global Corporation*. San Francisco: Jossey-Bass, 2000.

Galbraith, J. R. *Designing Organizations*. (2nd ed.) San Francisco: Jossey-Bass, 2002.

Galbraith, J. R. *Designing the Customer-Centric Organization*. San Francisco: Jossey-Bass, 2005.

Galbraith, J. R. *Designing Matrix Organizations That Actually Work*. San Francisco: Jossey-Bass, 2009.

Galbraith, J. R., and Kazanjian, R. *Strategy Implementation: The Role of Structure and Process*. (2nd ed.) St. Paul, MN: West Publishing, 1986.

Goold, M., Campbell, A., and Alexander, M. *Corporate Level Strategy*. New York: Wiley, 1994.

Goold, M., Pettifer, D., and Young, D. "Redesigning the Corporate Center." *European Management Journal*, 2001, *19*(1), 83–91.

Grant, R., Jammine, A., and Thomas, H. "Diversity, Diversification and Profitability Among British Manufacturing Companies." *Academy of Management Journal*, 1988, *31*, 771–801.

Greiner, L. "Evolution and Revolution as Organizations Grow." *Harvard Business Review*, May-June 1998, 3–11.

Hall, S., Lovallo, D., and Musters, R. "How to Put Your Money Where Your Strategy Is." *McKinsey Quarterly*, 2012, no. 2.

Harper, N., and Viguerie, S. "Are You Too Focused?" *McKinsey Quarterly*, 2002, no. 2.

Heuskel, D., Fechtel, A., and Beckman, P. "Managing for Value: How the World's Top Diversified Companies Produce Superior Shareholder Returns." Boston: Boston Consulting Group, December 2006.

Hindo, B. "A Dynamo Called Danaher." *Business Week*, February 19, 2007.

IBM. Annual Report, 2008. Armonk, NY: IBM, 2008.

IBM. Annual Report, 2012. Armonk, NY: IBM, 2012.

Kerr, J. "Diversification Strategies and Management Rewards: An Empirical Study." *Academy of Management Journal*, 1985, 28, 155–179.

Killing, P. *Strategies for Venture Success*. New York: Praeger, 1983.

Kiron, D., Palmer, D., Phillips, A., and Berkman, R. "The Executive's Role in Social Business." *Sloan Management Review*, Summer 2013, pp. 83–89.

Lawler, E. *From the Ground Up*. San Francisco: Jossey-Bass, 1994.

Lawrence, P., and Lorsch, J. *Organization and Environment*. Boston: Harvard Business School Press, 1967.

Ledford, G. "Designing Nimble Reward Systems." *Compensation and Benefits Review*, July-August 1995, 46–54.

Lorenzoni, G., and Baden-Fuller, C. "Creating a Strategic Center to Manage a Web of Partners." *California Management Review*, Spring 1995, pp. 146–163.

Magee, D. *Jeff Imelt and the New GE Way*. New York: McGraw-Hill, 2009.

March, J., and Simon, H. *Organizations*. New York: Wiley, 1958.

McKinsey Global Institute. "The Social Economy: Unlocking Value and Productivity through Social Technologies." July 2012.

Miles, R., and Snow, C. "Organizations: New Concepts for New Forms." *California Management Review*, 1986, 28(3), 62–73.

Morozov, E. *The Net Delusion: The Dark Side of Internet Freedom.* London: Penguin, 2011.

Nippa, M., Pidun, V., and Rubner, H. "Corporate Portfolio Management." *Academy of Management Perspectives,* November 2011, pp. 50–66.

Palich, L., Cardinal, L., and Miller, C. "Curvilinearity in the Diversification-Performance Linkage." *Strategic Management Journal,* 2000, *21*(2), 155–174.

Pitts, R. "Diversification Strategies and Organization Policies of Large Diversified Firms." *Journal of Economics and Business,* 1976, *28*, 181–188.

Porter, M. *Competitive Advantage.* New York: McGraw-Hill, 1985.

Ries, E. *The Lean Start Up.* New York: Crown, 2011.

Robins, J., and Wiersema, M. "The Measurement of Corporate Portfolio Strategy: Analysis of the Content Validity of Related Diversification Indexes." *Strategic Management Journal,* 2003, *24*, 39–59.

Rumelt, R. *Strategy, Structure and Economic Performance.* Boston: Harvard Business School Press, 1974.

Schectman, J. "UPS Says New Social Platform Shows Openness of Critiquing Ourselves." *Wall Street Journal,* May 8, 2013.

Schmidt, E., and Cohen, J. *The New Digital Age: Reshaping the Future of People, Nations and Business.* New York: Barnes and Noble, 2013.

Stopford, J., and Wells, L. *Managing the Multinational Enterprise.* London: Longmans, 1972.

Thompson, J. *Organizations in Action.* New York: McGraw-Hill, 1967.

Treacy, M., and Wiersema, F. *The Discipline of Market Leaders.* Reading, MA: Addison-Wesley, 1997.

Trist, E., and Murray, H., eds. *The Social Engagement of Social Science,* Vol. 2: *The Socio-Technical Perspective.* Philadelphia: University of Philadelphia Press, 1993.

Tushman, M., and Anderson, P. "Technological Discontinuities and Organizational Environments." *Administrative Science Quarterly*, 1986, *31*, 439–465.

Whited, T. "Is It Inefficient Investment That Causes the Diversification Discount?" *Journal of Finance*, 2001, *56*, 1667–1691.

Williamson, O. *Markets and Hierarchies*. New York: Free Press, 1975.

Zook, C. *Profit from the Core*. Boston: Harvard Business School Press, 2001.

About the Author

Jay R. Galbraith, an internationally recognized expert on strategy and organization design, is the founder and president of Galbraith Management Consultants, a consulting firm that specializes in solving strategy and organizational design challenges across corporate, business unit, and international levels.

Galbraith is a former business school professor who served on the faculty of the Sloan School of Management at MIT and the Wharton School at the University of Pennsylvania. He is a director of TruePoint, a management consulting firm based in Boston, as well as an affiliated research scientist at the Center for Effective Organizations at the University of Southern California and professor emeritus at the International Institute for Management Development in Lausanne, Switzerland. He also holds a top-secret security clearance in the US government.

With more than forty-five years of research and practical experience, Galbraith's extensive knowledge stems from a background in information processing systems, chemical engineering, and organizational behavior. As the original creator of the widely used Star Model and the front-back organization structure, he transforms organizations across a broad span of industries, including consumer goods, manufacturing, health care, financial services, and telecommunications.

He is the author of dozens of published research papers and books. His most recent book is *Designing Matrix Organizations That Actually Work* (2009). *Designing the Customer-Centric Organization* (2005), *Designing the Global Corporation* (2000), and other publications are the result of hands-on experiences working in companies confronting these design issues. Galbraith's theories on gaining a significant competitive advantage through organization design and customer-centricity have been implemented by top-level executives throughout the world.

As a testament to his ability to combine theory grounded in practical experience, Galbraith was selected by the Academy of Management as the 2011 Outstanding Scholar-Practitioner Award winner.

Galbraith speaks frequently at conferences worldwide and has received acclaim for delivering his extensive knowledge of global organization design in a clear, concise manner that audiences find informative and educational. He earned his doctor of business administration from Indiana University.

Index

Page numbers in italics refer to figures and tables.

structure of, 186, 187, *191*; and value added, *218*. *See also* Divisional model; Mixed model

Relationship continuum, 160–161

Relationship model, 71

Relationship strength, 161

Relationships: complex, factors driving, 161–162, 166, 167; creating, 79, 80, 82, 145; external, types of, design choice governed by, 160–167, 168, 169, 175, 181; government/international, and adding value, 226–228, 228–229, 244. *See also* Partnerships

Relude, 62

Reputation, 135, 168, 228, 230, 236, 244

Requisition-to-settlement process, 120

Resistance, 59–60, 61, 287, 291

Resources: allocation of, 40, 41–42, 43, 90, 133, 142, 143, 148, 220; matching segment opportunities with, 117; tangible, sharing, 232; valuable, including data as, 291

Responsibility, 170

Retail bank structure, 115, *116*, 128–129

Return on skills, 43

Rewards: consistent measurement and, 83; and cost-centric organization, 68; customer-centric strategy and, 69, 129; described, 44–52; impact of, 19; including team performance in, 92, 93, 111, 117, 139; integration of, 103–104; modifying, need for, 15–16, 18; and policies supporting partnerships, 172, 173; portfolio strategy and, 198–200, *202*; product-centric strategy and, 69; purpose of, 44; real-time organizations and, 129; in the reconfigurable organization, 143–144, 146; in the Star Model, 17, *146*, 264; strategy choices guiding decisions about, 20; that support synergy, 264–265, 281; in unique network organization, 182. *See also* Compensation practices

Richardson, P., 238

Ries, E., 11, 58

Risk management, 289

Robins, J., 189

Roddick, A., 51

Rotating leaders, 92

Rotational assignments, 55, 79–80, 92, 101, 142, 200, 201, 265, 282, 283

Rovio, 62–64

Royal Bank of Canada (RBC), 112–119, 128–129, 130

Rubner, H., 237

Rumelt, R., 186, 188, 237

S

Saks Fifth Avenue, 259

Sales organizations, 45, 47, 51

Salesforce.com, 86, 267

Salim Group, 226

Samsung, 165, 167

SAP, 85

Saturn Booster, 32

Saudi Arabia, 226–227

Scale factor, 64, 66, 228–230, 233, 252, 269

Scarcity of resources, 20, 90

Schectman, J., 85

Schmidt, E., 285

Scientific management, 1

Scope factor, 105, 153, 229

See's Candies, 201

Segment managers, 106

Segment teams, *116*, 117, 128, 129, 137–138, 140, 279–280, 281. *See also* Customer teams

Segmentation. *See* Customer segmentation; Market segmentation

Selection, 53, 54, 172, 173, 178–179, 222, 223

Self-managing teams, 37, 92

Self-organizing processes, 38, 39, 128

Semiconductor design companies, 31

Semi-independent units, 123

Sequential interdependence, 9, 178

Service businesses, 28, 29, 30

Shape, 35–37

Shared alliance model, 169, 170–171, 172

SharePoint, 38

Short-term advantages, ability to create, importance of, 133, 147. *See also* Reconfigurable organization

Short-term performance, 46

Siemens, 6, 258, 266

Sikorsky Helicopters, 257

Silicon Valley, 43

Silos, 10, 11, 26–27, 39, 85, 291

Simon, H., 12